High Literacy and Ethnic Identity

High Literacy and Ethnic Identity

Dominican American Schooling in Transition

DULCE MARÍA GRAY

ROWMAN & LITTLEFIELD PUBLISHERS, INC.
Lanham • Boulder • New York • Oxford

ROWMAN & LITTLEFIELD PUBLISHERS, INC.

Published in the United States of America
by Rowman & Littlefield Publishers, Inc.
4720 Boston Way, Lanham, Maryland 20706
www.rowmanlittlefield.com

12 Hid's Copse Road
Cumnor Hill, Oxford OX2 9JJ, England

British Library Cataloguing in Publication Information Available

Library of Congress Cataloging-in-Publication Data

Gray, Dulce María, 1955–
    High literacy and ethnic identity : Dominican American schooling in transition /
Dulce María Gray.
        p. cm.
    Includes bibliographical references and index.
    ISBN 0-7425-0004-7 (alk. paper) — ISBN 0-7425-0005-5 (pbk. : alk. paper)
        1. Children of immigrants—Education—United States. 2. Dominican Americans—
Education. I. Title.

    LC3746 .G73 2001
    371.829'68'7293073—dc21

                                                                    2001019885
Printed in the United States of America

♾™ The paper used in this publication meets the minimum requirements of American
National Standard for Information Sciences—Permanence of Paper for Printed Library
Materials, ANSI/NISO Z39.48-1992.

Para mi padre

Antonio Ferreyra

y mi madre

Teresita Ferreyra

Contents

Preface

I am among those countless academics who use their writing, the process of creating scholarship, to figure out their personal concerns. This book exists because I needed to find answers. I needed to wrestle with, unwrap, confront, and research questions about how, given the odds against ethnic-Latina-immigrant women, I was able to become highly literate—how I was able to complete a doctorate. I needed to know how and why other Dominicans like me had accomplished the task. I was in search of myself. Seeking and formulating answers, I realized subsequently, (re)defined my identity.

Reading and writing have always been the tools I use to make significant meaning. My love of reading and writing are the major reasons why I chose the professorate as my career. My education in literacy studies strengthened that passion; it also taught me that answers to my questions are required if we are to further understand the roles of literacy in the rapidly expanding Dominican community in the United States. (There is a dearth of research on all aspects of the Dominican diaspora; I want this book to contribute to the making of Dominican Studies.) My training in feminist ethnography taught me that at a fundamental level it is impossible to separate personal from professional interests, and that it is dishonest to pretend that the two are not imbricated. Thus, given my epistemological position, it is logical that I use reading and writing to find answers to personally vital questions, and that I pr sent my quest as a revealing autoethnography for public consumption.

Recently I read Edward Said's *Out of Place: A Memoir*. In it he acknowledges that it "was written mostly during periods of illness or treatment." He composed the book while recovering from "three early rounds of chemotherapy for leukemia." Writing, he asserts, was therapeutic. Reconstructing his memories "proved crucial to" his "being able to function at all during periods of debilitating sickness, treatment, and anxiety." Similarly, in *Remembered Rapture*, a current autobiography of her writing life, bell hooks notes that composing was curative in that it allowed her to create a new self-identity:

> To me, telling the story of my growing-up years was intimately connected with the longing to kill the self I was without really having to die. I wanted to kill that self in writing. Once that self was gone—out of my life forever—I could more easily become the me of me . . . it was not just this Gloria I would be rid of, but the past that had a hold on me, that kept me from the present. I wanted not to forget the past but to break its hold. This death in writing was to be liberatory. (80)

Yes! Writing—telling our stories—helps to heal and bring order to our lives. Certainly, that has been the case for me. Researching and composing this book has been more than restorative. It has allowed me to gather the pieces of my Latina-Dominican American identity, to (re)see them and thus (re)build a self that is wiser. It has given me the opportunity to reconstruct my experiences with literacy and thus to (re)configure where I have come from, who I am (and continue to become). Very importantly, writing and researching this book also allowed me to order experiences, so that they reveal insights about the lives of Dominicans in the diaspora.

Those revelations help us see the journey participants in this study traveled in becoming highly literate, especially as we unpacked our Dominican cultural heritage. They help us see how we survive as active agents in this our postmodern times when fissures are the only constant. I believe that the insights in this book are useful particularly to scholars of Dominican and Latino/a studies,

teachers of composition and literacy, and the general reader interested in understanding immigrants' experiences.

This book is an autoethnography, different, I claim, from a
memoir such as Said's or an autobiography such as hooks' in that I
look at one very specific aspect of my life through a scholarly lens,
and in that mine is one of fifteen other voices that describe our
journeys toward high literacy as they are imbricated in Dominican
and United States societies and the spaces in between. The other
participants are some of those few other Dominican immigrants
who have actually managed to complete doctorates and are now
teaching the humanities and social sciences (the same disciplines
that reify our notions of literacy) in U.S. colleges and universities.
My aim is to describe and map our understandings of the relationship between completing the highest level of formal education
available in the United States and symbiotically (re)constructing an
ethnic identity.

I include old pictures of my family (my parents, Antonio and
Teresita Ferreyra; my sister, Homerina; and my brother, Homero)
partly because I want to pay homage and to thank them for their
fortitude, but mostly because I want readers of my work to connect
our stories and theories to the core of a generation of Dominican
immigrants—to see real faces, with real aspirations and struggles. I
would have included pictures of the other participants too, but
early on we agreed that I would protect their privacy.

I define *high literacy* as the enactment of dynamic skills that
extend beyond encoding and decoding the printed word, and which
include the ability to comprehend and manipulate symbols (the
words and concepts) in two or more culturally prescribed ways.
My findings reveal that for this group of Dominican academics becoming and being highly literate shapes us into "Americans," and
that, more importantly, it spurs us to resist complete assimilation.
The process prompts us to seek and live "Dominicanness." My
findings affirm that the definitions, demand for, and enactments of
high literacy are dependent on the specifics of a community, and
that consequently the teaching of literacy (for instance, any level of
college composition) needs to grow out of the particular needs of a
community.

I have organized the chapters following the themes I identified as salient and recurrent while analyzing fifteen hundred pages of our transcribed interviews. In chapter 1, entitled "Talking Theories," I describe the impetus for this study, and the literacy studies and new feminist ethnography theories that inform my methodology for collecting and analyzing the data. In chapter 2, entitled "Internal Geography," I discuss the longings and motivations that we experienced in our hearts and minds, those internally felt factors that, in retrospect, we deem to have propelled us toward acquiring high literacy and questioning our ethnic identity. In chapter 3, entitled "Parents," I map (from both the etic/insider and emic/outsider perspectives) our parents' significant actions and how they influenced our sense of our selves and thus our acquisition of high literacy. In chapter 4, entitled "Professors," I map the significant actions of our teachers and delineate how they facilitated our journey. In chapter 5, entitled "Dominican Cultural Markers," I trace our involvement with two striking aspects of our cultural roots (music and foodways), and I discuss how those (sometimes combative) definitions of internally and externally defined ethnic identity affected our journey. In chapter 6, entitled "Ruminating . . . A Measure of Closure," I discuss the consequences of becoming/being highly literate from personal and pedagogical perspectives.

***

It is my pleasure to thank the many colleagues, friends, and family members who helped in one way or another as I researched and wrote this book. I am particularly grateful to all of the participants who allowed me to interview them and who generously offered their time, ideas, and criticisms. In thanks I have tried diligently to (re)present our stories as true and substantial as they were given to me.

I am indebted to the Rockefeller Foundation Humanities Fellowship Program and the CUNY Dominican Studies Institute. Their grant allowed me to spend three months focused strictly on the manuscript, and to have the support of Silvio Torres-Saillant and Sara Aponte. Silvio, the director of the Institute, has been and continues to be a truly instrumental colleague. Without his effort and prescience, I believe, there would be no Dominican Studies Institute.

At Rowman & Littlefield I want to thank my editor, Christine Gatliffe, for her support and guidance.

At George Mason University I want to especially thank Margaret "Peggy" Yocom and Terry Myers Zawacki. Their critical readings of various revisions of the manuscript were imperative for me. Peggy's wisdom and gracious support of me as her colleague and friend helped to sustain me through difficult moments.

I began researching this book when I was in graduate school at Indiana University-Bloomington, and therefore I want to thank my mentors—Eugene Kintgen, Christine Farris, Jerome Harste, and Bob Arnove—for supporting my scholarly endeavors despite them being considered "foreign" in the department of English.

I want to thank my most significant mentor, Carol Sicherman, whom I met while I was completing undergraduate work at Lehman College. She provided the intellectual stimulation and practical guidance that allowed me to fulfill my yearning for formal education. How different my life would be if Carol had not taken the time to nurture my academic development.

Writing this book was heart wrenching at times, partly because so much of it is personal. I could not have examined all of the material without Lorraine Schooner: she continues to stand by me as I painfully peel away the layers of my being. Her unconditional support and patience have allowed me to finally see the treasures at my core.

As writers know, no matter how much we like the act of composing it is often overwhelming, especially if major events like getting tenure depend on completing the book. I mustered strength to persist because my closest and dearest friends offered me challenging conversations, meticulous readings of my work, savory dinners, and the warmth of their homes. I want to thank these friends in particular for enriching my life beyond what words can describe: Ana Rozada Gardón, Linda Robyn Gray, Mohammed

Hirchi, Yuko Kurahashi, Susan Grace Larkin, Suki Robins, Juan Rodriguez, Theresa and Kevin Terry, and Mary Vogl.

I thank my parents, Antonio and Teresita Ferreyra, dignified survivors of war and emigration. Both taught me to be resilient and to find beauty in the worst of circumstances. My father continually shows me how to be diligent; even in dying my mother showed me how to be courageous.

I thank my sister, Homerina Bond, my brother, Homero Ferreyra, his wife Jennifer, and all of my nieces and nephews—Teresita, David Joshua, Lemuel Antonio, Marina Lynn and Allison—for loving me steadfastly and modeling integrity and generosity.

And I thank my husband, George N. Gray, who has unselfishly invested his heart, intellect, time, and energy in my projects and our life. He continues to add substance, joy, and love to every aspect of my existence. This book is for him too.

1

Talking Theories

Midway through the first semester of my doctoral program, I sat in class with fourteen other students. We were discussing the work of Paulo Freire and E. D. Hirsch and whether literacy has the power to alter socioeconomic status. During a pause, the professor turned to me and said, "What would happen to all those Latinos in the Bronx if they became highly literate? Do you think poverty and crime would be eradicated?"

My thoughts and emotions—my very essence—whirled back to the fifth grade, where I was placed just three months after leaving the Dominican Republic. I still could not understand English clearly, and Sister Mary, an impressively large and assertive woman, marched down the aisle toward my seat, leaned over, and asked something. I do not remember the question. I do remember, as if it were this exact moment, that she grabbed my wrist, forced open my small palm, took the thick wooden ruler from her belt, raised it slowly as high as she could, then smacked it down in the center of my hand. "You don't *ever* speak Spanish in this room; in America we speak English," she said through pursed lips as she tromped back to her desk, and twenty-two all-American giggles rose to near hysterics.

Once again focused on my graduate school classroom, I noticed fourteen white faces turned expectantly in my direction, and just as I began to formulate a response, I realized that the professor was asking yet another question: "Has becoming highly literate changed your life?" Has it, I considered? Me, an immigrant whose functionally illiterate parents came home from their second shift at the textile factory insisting that I turn off the television and listen to Mozart and Chopin instead, or that I read Homer and Plato. What kind of literacy did I enact the summer I spent reading Jane Austen's novels on the fire escape? What about those snowy mornings when my mother and I recited rhythmic lines from *Don Quixote* as she polished my Catholic school shoes? Or the time I scrutinized my father's pay stubs and discovered that his boss had been cheating him out of overtime pay? What exactly did my professor mean by "high literacy" changing my life? And why was she asking me, the only "minority," the only Latina in the class?

"Highly literate," I thought for a moment. Highly literate people are "those who read Faulkner and Wittgenstein," people who have acquired more than the mere skills required to encode and decode texts (Venezky 3). Overwhelmingly, they're people who complete formal education beyond four years of college, and while doing so develop or shape (if not acquire) metalinguistic and metacognitive abilities that prompt them to extend themselves out of their immediate space and time to imagine new and unknown worlds and ideas. Literacy theorist Judith Langer adds that highly literate people are those who reflect, reformulate, and communicate consciously and systematically. Sylvia Scribner explains that being highly literate is often defined as "a state of grace" in which

> the power and functionality of literacy is not bounded by political or economic parameters but in a sense transcends them; the literate individual's life derives its meaning and significance from intellectual, aesthetic, and spiritual participation in the accumulated creations and knowledge of humankind, made available through the written word. ("Literacy in Three Metaphors" 77)

At that moment in my graduate classroom, I did not really know how to respond to those fourteen gazes and my professor's questions. I did know for sure that I felt alone, singled out—but not in a celebratory manner—as the only Latina in the room, in the English department graduate student body, 1 of 800 in a university of 35,000, 1 of 2,000 in a town of 75,000. Walking home, I recognized my anger about having to speak for—as if we are a monolith—all Latina/os. And the professor's seeming supposition that acquiring high literacy changes social status appeared to be a simplistic way to think about the connection between literacy, class, and ethnicity. Nonetheless, her questions prompted a query I have pursued and developed into an ethnographic study on Dominican American academics who teach the humanities and social sciences in the United States, those very disciplines that reinforce our notions about what it means to be literate and to be an American. These are the fundamental questions underpinning—driving—this book that have consumed me for over six years:

- How can I disentangle the change produced by becoming highly literate from the change caused by other factors? Is it possible?
- How/are our identities impacted in the process of becoming highly literate; how/are we transformed?
- What do we lose and gain?
- How/does being highly literate constrain and/or free us?
- How/is being highly literate in English a commodity, an index to measure us as civilized and as worthy?
- Does becoming highly literate "equalize" and "unify" us as Americans the way E. D. Hirsch claims cultural literacy does for all immigrants?[1]

---

[1] Hirsch, the ardent defender of the "back to basics" movement in the 1980s, posits that "shared" knowledge, what he calls "cultural literacy," concerning Western culture is the "basic information needed to thrive in the modern world." He claims that knowing the national vocabulary of the United States and "the appropriate background information," attitudes, and conventions is what constitutes our identity as Americans (14). According to Hirsch, such literacy leads to cultural unification and identity, freedom, rationality, modernity, and industrialization; only "highly literate societies can prosper economically" (1), because literacy is inseparable from democracy (since it is the "oxygen of social inter-

- Or is high literacy only a tool, an *enabling* component, as Harvey J. Graff contends?[2]
- What pushes some Dominican immigrants to acquire graduate degrees in the humanities and social sciences in spite of the statistics showing a low rate of success in higher education?
- Why did we become academics, a profession that reinforces all of our American general notions about high literacy?
- What are the consequences, the compensations, and drawbacks of our positions as highly literate academics?
- How do we use high literacy other than to teach?
- What are our lives like?
- What issues do we confront?

---

course") and the only way societies can hope to become "just" (19). A literate/democratic society "excludes nobody"; literacy in general and cultural literacy specifically, Hirsch believes, "cuts across" generations, social groups and classes (21). Therefore, becoming culturally literate in English is the "only available ticket to full citizenship" (22). He reasons that true "enfranchisement depends upon knowledge, knowledge upon literacy, and literacy upon cultural literacy" (12). Cultural literacy is what gives impetus to our civic involvement and therefore to our individual financial success and thus the economic progress of our nation. His concern with this concept is so great that he and his colleagues have published several dictionaries, and compiled lists of terms and information that we should know before daring to call ourselves Americans.

[2] Graff maintains that literacy is only "an important part of the larger parcel of factors that account for the evolution of modern societies and states" (*The Literacy Myth* xxxvii). There are other more important determiners that affect individual and societal progress: namely, gender, national and ethnic origin, race, class, and age. Other literacy theorists echo this belief: Shirley Brice Heath adds that the process of acquiring and the consequences of attaining any level of literacy are determined by context—family structure, religion, values, and access to goods, services, and power (*Ways With Words* 11). Brian Street maintains that literacy—how it is defined, what it does or does not do to individuals and their society, what individuals do with it—hinges on the specifics of a culture, for instance, on what is considered truth and knowledge (*Cultural Meanings* 2).

- And why do we need answers to these and other questions?

Seeking answers to these questions, examining the lives of other Dominican American academics, I now understand, contextualized mine; it prompted me to discover, perhaps (re)create, who I am (always becoming). It has also shown me clearly that although we have been an increasing presence in the United States since the mid-1960s, there is minimal scholarship on any aspect of the Dominican diaspora. We now number well over a million in population, about the same as Cuban Americans, but we are significantly less successful at becoming academics in the humanities and social sciences. In fact, to date there are approximately thirty of us teaching in United States institutions. That alone pressed me to begin a formal scholarly study.

Conducting the research revealed to me, among other things, that answers to my questions are crucial for various audiences, including our own selves and those Dominicans who will follow us to academe. Mapping—inscribing—our experiences, elucidating them, is useful for scholars of the Dominican diaspora and United States Latino/a studies, and, for those of us who are invested in teaching literacy (particularly at the university level) to immigrants and culturally marginalized students. Considering the literate experiences of these Dominican Americans can enhance our understanding of literacy acquisition, the construction of identity, and our teaching practices.

Proceeding with the Study

Admittedly, this study is inextricably rooted in my need to probe my hybrid ethnic identity and to comprehend its relationship to my development as an academic (trained in literary-bound departments of English) in the United States. Initially I was concerned about that. I didn't want my scholarship to be labeled "confessional mishmosh," but in reading works by other culturally marginalized writers (especially those by feminists), I have found camaraderie. I have reseen how the personal is indeed political, how my work resonates of feminism's roots in women's actual experiences and how weaving my subjectivities provides multilayered reflexive depth.

For instance, even given the problematics of his exclusion of women, in *Pedagogy of the Oppressed*, to me the most privately and professionally significant of Paulo Freire's work, rereading it highlighted that his personal experience with literacy, poverty, suffering, and Christianity in Brazil (and other developing countries) shaped his notions about what it means to teach and learn, and about a liberatory pedagogy that aims to show us how to identify, name, critique, and combat forms of oppression. Freire posits that in interrogating their own circumstances, the oppressed can arrive at a deeper understanding of their own powers; knowing that, in turn, can mobilize them into changing their world. A similar dependence on self-analysis can be seen in feminist theories; one only needs to look at women's consciousness-raising groups or more recently, at the work of Gloria Anzaldúa and bell hooks.

Dominican American poet and novelist Julia Alvarez, whose work helped to validate the uniqueness of my experience as a Dominican immigrant (partly because she was the only one writing and publishing about any aspect of the Dominican condition at that time), candidly admits that personal concerns drive her craft, and that "Our lives, after all, are the very matter of our art" (*Something to Declare* 225). Alvarez's poems and first novel are autobiographical; composing them allowed her to comprehend her ethnic identity. She wrote her second novel, *In the Time of the Butterflies*, because she could not forget being confronted at age ten with the murder of the Mirabal sisters. She wrote her most recent novel, *In the Name of Salomé*, in homage to Salomé Ureña, the "muse" of Dominican letters. In *Something to Declare* she wrote that as she plans her next novel she is deliberate about her choice:

> I had been looking for a Midwest subject, one that would plunge me into the landscape of my husband's people, German farmers from Nebraska. My husband had been such a trooper for the last three years while I worked on my second novel. Every vacation had been taken up by trips back to the Dominican Republic so I could do my research. Sometimes, lying in bed at night, my husband would ask after my characters. How was the Patria chapter

going? Had I found out when it was that amapolas bloom? It was high time that I took on a subject that would allow me to immerse myself in his background. (*Something to Declare* 234)

Likewise, in *The Vulnerable Observer* Cuban American ethnographer Ruth Behar admits that her scholarship is rooted in her personal concerns, especially as those concerns relate to her emotions, which, she explains, transform the processes of collecting data, analyzing, and composing texts into "vulnerable" acts. When she began to insert an obvious personal voice in her scholarship, she worried about being accepted by anthropology and the academy, but she persisted because she could no longer dismiss the "sense of urgency" and earnest "desire to embed a diary" of her life "within the accounts of the lives" of her subjects (19). One of the finest illustrations she provides in *The Vulnerable Observer* is that of conducting fieldwork on death and dying in Santa María del Monte, a village in northern Spain, at the same time that her "adored" grandfather was dying of cancer in Miami Beach. Later, she realizes how she "hated" herself "for having cowardly and ambitiously given priority to work over feeling and love" (69). Subsequently, she dedicates the product of that fieldwork, a book entitled *The Presence of the Past in a Spanish Village*, to both her grandparents, and more tellingly, she confesses that in retrospect she realizes that her "quest to understand 'the presence of the past' in Santa María was but another link in the parallel quest to recover" her own history, which had been buried in multiple migrations from Spain to Cuba to the United States (78).

More fascinating to me, probably because of my experience with a former husband who did not understand my cultural selves or my profession (and, more significantly, I see in retrospect, my inability at that time to relate that experience to my ethnic heritage, or to have the courage to make "private" matters the substance of public writing), is Behar's clear illustration of what she means by personal voice and writing "vulnerable" ethnographies:

As David [her husband] and I drive back [from doing fieldwork] to Ann Arbor, I tell him about how Marta [her subject] told me she often feels worthless, that her life isn't amounting to anything. Tears come into David's eyes; he says that's how he often feels.

In our relationship, the usual division of labor and power has been reversed. David has played the role of faculty wife, caring for our son, Gabriel, and doing the kind of secretarial work for me that male professors are always thanking their wives for in the acknowledgement section of their books. Most of the time, I am able to display gratitude for David's help on a more regular basis and to encourage him in his own work, but I have also been spoiled by the bargain prices he offers on his services; like my male counterparts, I've gotten into the habit of depending on certain unpaid labors from him. So, back at home, when I discover that the tape on which I am expecting to base my paper for the women's health conference hasn't come out, a paper that must be ready to present in a week, I break out in a merciless fury. (*Vulnerable Observer* 100)

Behar's honest inclusion of "private" experiences while collecting data is a resonant example of the personal also being political and thus relevant for scholarly discussion. Her assertion that "a personal voice, if creatively used, can lead the reader, not into miniature bubbles of navel-gazing, but into the enormous sea of serious social issues" is both validating and motivating to me (14). Her work shows me time and again that if I am to understand the subject of my research I must also attempt to understand myself, especially as I am embedded in the dynamics involving the people I study. As she writes, all of us ethnographers must seek to know "what aspects of the self are the most important filters through which one perceives the world and, more particularly, the topic being studied" (13). That practice may make us "vulnerable," but it also enriches our subjects, our work, and us.

That practice has certainly "thickened" the work of Chicano anthropologist Renato Rosaldo, whose scholarship, Behar writes, helped to create the "lacerating representations" that "made salient the question of who has the authority to speak for whom." His work helped to highlight "the brutal role of subjectivity in cultural interpretation by pointing to the unreality and, even worse, the humorlessness of accounts written by Anglo anthropologists" (*Vulnerable Observer* 162). Rosaldo, too, readily admits that his scholarly projects emerge not only from his "discipline, but also from a more personal politics of identity and community" (xi). His "Grief and a Headhunter's Rage," an essay that examines how mourning his own wife's accidental death helps him to understand the rage and grief in Ilongot headhunting in the Philippines, is a testament to how honest and open consideration and inclusion of our subjectivities in research help to produce more substantive representations of our subjects. Rosaldo's wife, anthropologist Michelle Zimbalist Rosaldo, dies while they're conducting fieldwork. It is ludicrous to think that his work (his life!) would not be impacted, to think that his way of perceiving the world (and thus doing research) would not shift. It is even more foolish for any of us to pretend that such monumental transformations ought to be left outside of our ethnographies.

Kamala Visweswaran has been equally candid in explaining that her scholarship is shaped by the implicit and explicit messages she receives as an American of Indian descent:

> in school at Berkeley, where some make a fetish of cultural difference, my long and winding South Indian name was eagerly remarked upon, and the insistent but well-meaning questions began: What were the secrets of Indian cooking? How many untouchables lived in India? What did I think about V.S. Naipaul? In desperation I turned to anthropology. "Indianness" was now being constructed for me, and in turn I was forced to construct it for myself. I could no longer argue with my well-meaning interlocutors by insisting that I was as "American" as they were (therefore equally ignorant and unable to answer their questions), than I could with grade school tormentors who called me names for being brown. . . . To this day, I am not sure that I "chose" to work on India . . . part of what led me to India was the necessity of being "Indian," of being already inscribed as "Indian." (108)

These scholars' acknowledgement that their personal concerns generate and affect their scholarship moved me to be courageous and bold enough to say that I too was compelled to conduct research on Dominican American academics primarily because I needed to look at my ethnic identity. Thus, this book is partly phenomenological; it is an autoethnography that "maps," as Behar has attempted to describe such work, "an intermediate space we can't quite define yet, a borderland between passion and intellect, analysis and subjectivity, ethnography and autobiography, art and life" (*Vulnerable Observer* 174).

The Other Participants in My Autoethnography

Since my questions are fundamentally about specific people's experiences, it seemed to me that the answers were to be found predominantly in those very people—meaning that I needed to do more than read about Dominican American academics. Nonetheless, I began my ethnography by familiarizing myself with the scholarship and literature written in English by Dominican American academics, among them sociologists Rosario Espinal and Emelio Betances, literary critics Daisy Cocco de Filippis and Silvio Torres-Saillant, and poet and novelist Julia Alvarez, who was the only Dominican American writer celebrated by a mainstream audience until mid-1996, when Junot Diaz published *Drown*, a collection of short stories. (In 1998 Rhina P. Espaillat published her second book of poems, and in 1999 Loida Maritza Pérez published her first novel, *Geographies of Home*. Both have been well received and are getting much attention.) *How the Garcia Girls Lost Their Accents,* Alvarez's short stories, turned into a novel (composed, she affirms in *Something to Declare*, "with a strong autobiographical base"), captivated me, partly because the four central characters are highly literate Dominican American women who live very fractured lives (110).

All four sisters have "breakdowns" in the process of redefining themselves as highly literate "ethnic" Americans. Sandi, the most literate, believes that she is "becoming a monkey," that she is losing her humanity. She feels every one of her organs turning into those of a monkey's. Only her brain is left. In desperation, she rushes to "read all the great books," hoping that "maybe she'd remember something important from having been human" (54). She reads and reads, crossing the titles off her list as she finishes devouring yet another "big thinker's" ideas.

Sandi's imagined transformation seemed to me a metaphor for the deracination she endures, a forced forging that is both caused and alleviated by literacy. Literacy facilitates her ingestion of the ethos of the United States, and the shedding of her Dominican cultural heritage—her transformation. And the result is a relentless struggle with her identity that robs her of her humanity, a battle that tears her apart and induces a mental breakdown. But becoming and being highly literate also allow her to recognize her situation, as a woman especially, to examine it and then find healing. Sandi—and Alvarez herself, if we consider that in all of her essays, poetry, and fiction she writes about these issues with perspicacity—illustrates an aspect of the double-edgeness that stands at the crux of current literacy theory regarding immigrants—that is, as Kaestle writes, that literacy

> is discriminatory in two ways, with regard to access and with regard to content. Problems of discrimination are not over when access is gained; there is a cultural price-tag to literacy. Thus, the question of whether literacy is liberating or constraining also has to do with whether it is seen as an instrument of conformity or as an instrument of creativity. (116)

But reading about Dominicans was not enough for me to understand the plight of those few of us who have become academics and are teaching the humanities and social sciences (those very disciplines that reinforce our beliefs about what it means to be highly literate) in U.S. colleges and universities. It did not provide substantive answers about our condition. I needed to talk to Dominican American academics, to know them, and so I sought them for this study. I began by writing to six Dominican American academics in the humanities and social sciences whose work I had read or whose names I had seen at conferences. My only requirement was that they had to have completed graduate programs in U.S. institutions, and that they had to have earned degrees in the humanities and social sciences.

Of those twenty-four, three declined because they were very busy. Thus, including myself (since I examine my experiences also), the final sample consists of twenty-two: thirteen women and nine men of various socioeconomic statuses and races. As a result, the comments of only fifteen (eleven women, including myself, and four men) participants are represented in this book. In both the original sample and the final twenty-one I interviewed, there are more women than men.[3] As agreed, I have changed all of their names to protect their privacy.

I visited and interviewed all twenty-one. Prior to our meeting, I sent each a letter listing the areas that I wanted to discuss. I asked them to think about their responses and to add questions and other ideas to the list. Our initial conversations took place at convenient places of their choosing (offices, homes, and restaurants). Most of the time our conversations happened while we ate, so that the process was relaxed, informal, and often interrupted by other personal asides. The interviews averaged two and a half hours and they centered on questions about the attainment, use, and ramifications of becoming and being highly literate. Though the order was not always followed, I began the interviews with basic questions on when and where they were born, or when, where, and why they emigrated, age, languages spoken, reasons for pursuing high literacy/postgraduate education, and family's educational history and occupation. Then I asked open-ended questions regarding nurturing and discouraging experiences in their educational development, major choices and impacts, ways they use high literacy profession-

---

[3] That ratio is at variance with the American Council on Education's statistics on the number of Ph.D.s earned by Latinos. In their figures men outnumber women slightly. Around the time I started this study, Carter and Wilson's *1994 Minorities in Higher Education Status Report* noted that Latinos "experienced an increase of 7.2 percent in the number of doctorates earned for 1993, part of a steady upward trend, with growth of 54.7 percent during the previous 10 years" (24). In 1993 they earned a total of 834: 422 by men, 412 by women (86). Of those 834, 284 doctorates were earned in the social sciences, 200 in the humanities (87). As I complete the study, the *1998 Status Report* notes that Latinos experienced "3.4 percent increase in the number of doctorates earned" in 1996 (Wilds 38). A total of 950 doctorates were awarded: 478 by men, 472 by women. Of that 950, 335 were earned in the social sciences, 251 in the humanities (Wilds 101).

ally and personally, and transformations they believe to be directly correlated with the attainment of high literacy. I answered all of the questions myself: recurrently during the twenty-one interviews, in the process of triangulating, in my journal entries, and additionally as I composed this book.

In order to clarify and elaborate on the information I gathered, I interviewed ten of the twenty-one respondents a second and third time, mostly in person, occasionally by telephone and correspondence. I audiotaped and transcribed all of the interviews. That allowed me to become very intimate with the narratives in those 1,500 pages. As I revised my manuscript I asked three respondents to read and give me their feedback as participants, colleagues, and whatever other role they deemed appropriate. I am still in close contact with six of the participants. I continue a friendship with three. Consequently, the information I present in this text has been gathered longitudinally over six years. Thus, it is a dynamic history of our specific experiences as they are embedded in and resonate with those of others (immigrants and other Latino/as, for example) in American and Dominican societies.

When I first interviewed the participants in this study, the eleven women were in their thirties and forties. Three (Carla, María, and Sandra) were born and raised in the United States, mostly in New York City, though Carla returned to live in Santo Domingo for ten years. Six others emigrated in either their early or late adolescence. Laura immigrated to Puerto Rico when she was ten and lived there until she began graduate school on the West Coast. Marina emigrated in her early twenties when she was awarded a scholarship to do graduate work. Most completed their graduate degrees in universities on the East Coast; some have additional graduate training in European universities. Most, including me, attended large and competitive research universities. Seven had doctorates; two finished their Ph.D. programs after our initial meeting; one decided that her Master of Arts was enough; and the one with the Master of Fine Arts did not pursue a doctorate, because she decided that her priority was writing, not being an academic. Most were married (or remarried) to non-Latinos and have children. Only one is married to a Dominican American. Four are single: one remains divorced, one has never married; one is openly lesbian, the other bisexual and still examining her sexuality. Presently, they are employed in departments of English, history, Spanish, and sociology in colleges and universities located on the East Coast, but a few are in the mid-Atlantic and southern regions; one is on the West Coast, another in the Midwest. Most are untenured assistant professors, though they are at or near the tenuring process; four are tenured associate professors.

When I first interviewed the four men in this study, they were also in their thirties and forties. César was born and raised in New York City. Ramón emigrated at age ten and has since lived in New York City. The other two lived in various places before settling permanently in the United States. Antonio immigrated to Puerto Rico in his late teens and lived there and in Central America until he started a graduate program on the East Coast. Homero emigrated in his early twenties, completed a doctorate on the East Coast, and then lived in Mexico until his late thirties, when he settled in the United States. Three of the four completed doctorates (one did two Master's degrees) in major universities on the East Coast. Three also did post-graduate work in universities in Spain and Mexico. César has an M.A. in Caribbean literature and an M.S. in library science. Three are tenured associate professors in departments of English, Spanish and sociology in colleges and universities located in the East and mid-Atlantic regions. One is divorced; one is privately gay; the others are married to Latinas.

After analyzing all of the transcribed interviews, I noted that even though I did not ask directly, everyone commented on their self-identity; labels they appropriate; community/ies they represent and or participate in; interests and goals they have; what success means to them; what they believe is required to attain high literacy; salient memories of learning in and out of school; relationships with families; and attitudes about language.

Theoretical Grounding for
This Latina's Autoethnography

In this study I aim to identify, historicize, and problematize the achievements of a group of people who struggled to attain high literacy, and who, in various degrees, are still dealing with defining their ethnic identity and with an evolving sense of entitlement. My goal is to inscribe our experiences for the benefit of, primarily, ourselves and those who follow us, scholars of the Dominican diaspora and other Latino/as, and those of us teaching literacy in the university (especially to immigrants). I examine our experiences through two major theoretical lenses—literacy studies and feminist ethnography. I use literacy theory primarily because it helps to clarify, inform, and position these Dominican Americans' experiences in a broader set of references. I use feminist ethnographic methods precisely because they provide the scaffolding for (re)presenting my respondents' and my voice/s intersubjectively—that is, for creating an autoethnography.

Literacy Theories

I use literacy theory as a lens to help identify and clarify our experiences as Dominican American academics. I come to literacy theory informally through my years of translating documents, balancing checkbooks, filing income tax papers, and functioning as my family's public voice, as well as through my own voracious reading, writing, and thinking—a behavior that was reinforced by my parents' love of music, the arts, and life of the mind. I also come to literacy theory formally by way of my training in a doctoral program that examined the connections between literacy, literature, and language.

I locate my study in the third, current, "generation" of scholarship, which considers the relationship of literacy to individual and social development and focuses on enactments of literacy in spe-

cific contexts.[4] Current scholarship on literacy examines the role
of various levels of literacy in the realization of human potential
and the transformation of consciousness. It investigates literacy's
role in the development of cultural unification and identity, freedom, modernity, and industrialization. It questions whether literacy
really "cuts across"—equalizes—social groups and classes, as
Hirsch claims (21), or whether it is only an enabling component,
just "an important part of the larger parcel of factors that account
for the evolution of modern societies and states," as Graff maintains (*Literacy Myth* xxxviii).

The general public in the United States defines "literacy" as the
ability to encode and decode (to read and write) printed texts, but
current scholarship defines it as an evolving state of "becoming
and being," not a static stage that one arrives at. Ferdman writes
that *becoming* literate "means developing mastery not only over
processes, but also over the symbolic media of the culture—the
ways in which values, beliefs, and norms are represented"; *being*
literate, on the other hand, "implies actively maintaining contact
with collective symbols and processes by which they are represented" (188). I define becoming and being *highly* literate as a lot
more than "reading Faulkner and Wittgenstein," as Venezky does.
I define high literacy as the enactment of a set of dynamic skills
that extend beyond performing superficial transactions with the
printed word, and include the ability to comprehend and manipulate symbols—the words and concepts—in two or more culturally
prescribed ways. I define it as the ability to recognize, understand,

---

[4] In the introduction to the second edition of *The Literacy Myth*, Harvey
J. Graff notes that literacy studies as a field of inquiry has evolved over
three "generations." The first generation, marked by Jack Goody's *Literacy in Traditional Societies* (1968), focused on the history of literacy; the
second, marked by the original publication of *The Literacy Myth* in 1979,
emphasized the analysis of signatures and census records, and began to
consider literacy in relation to publishing and literary subjects. Scribner
and Cole's *The Psychology of Literacy* (1981) and Shirley Brice Heath's
Ways with Words (1983) helped to move literacy studies toward the third
generation, and a focus on critical questions about the role and power of
literacy in specific contexts.

and value different kinds of knowledge, practices, rituals, traditions, and other aspects of the communities we belong to, and to question literacy's role in determining access to power and privilege.

In the United States schooling and all levels of literacy are intertwined. We determine people's literate achievements by the sorts of credentials and diplomas they earn. Therefore, I conflate the terms "high literacy" and "formal post graduate education." They are not necessarily synonymous, but highly literate individuals without formal accreditation are not usually considered as such in our society, nor are they hired as academics that teach the humanities and social sciences in colleges and universities. Thus, in conflating the terms high literacy and schooling I am defining high literacy as a set of intellectual and social practices. That definition is particularly pertinent to "ethnic" and "minority" groups like these Dominican American professors in that (at the very least) it entails appropriating practices that may conflict with those of their cultural and epistemological heritage.[5]

There are no studies on the relationship between high literacy and ethnicity, but there are on basic literacy. For instance, Graff's analysis of nineteenth-century Canada and Kaestle's study of nineteenth- and early twentieth-century literacy in the United States

---

[5] Candace Nelson and Marta Tienda explain the difference between being considered an ethnic and a minority: a minority "is a group whose members are subjected to unequal treatment through prejudice and discrimination by a dominant group. Ethnic groups, on the other hand, are a collectivity sharing common cultural norms, values, identities and behaviors and who both recognize themselves, and are recognized by others as being ethnic. The extent to which ethnicity is a matter of individual choice depends on the group's access (or lack thereof) to the reward system of a dominant society" (53). This difference is clearly illustrated by African Americans and Jews. They are both "ethnic" groups, but African Americans are more of a minority (in the stigmatizing sense) than Jews. Similarly, Cuban Americans are rarely identified as a minority group, but Mexicans, Puerto Ricans, and Dominicans usually are. The reason, Nelson and Tienda would say, "has to do with their very different modes of incorporation and socioeconomic integration experiences"(53).

demonstrate that ethnicity is a stronger determining factor than gender in deciding who acquires basic literacy.[6] They reiterate that ethnicity, gender, and class are not mutually exclusive. But historically, ethnicity (and race) has been used more often as the basis for denying literacy to certain groups (for example, African Americans) and for regulating social status, even after becoming literate. In fact, Kaestle affirms that for ethnic minorities problems "of discrimination are not over when access is gained," and that "the benefits to literacy for members of oppressed groups are often more apparent collectively than individually, and in the long run rather than the short run" (116).

Similarly, Ogbu explains that ethnicity and race present additional barriers to acquiring and enacting any level of literacy: "a white lower-class American is only lower class; a black lower-class American is also faced with a job ceiling and other caste barriers" (233).[7] More alarmingly, he writes that the kind of ethnic

---

[6] The work of Shirley Brice Heath demonstrates that gender helps to determine who acquires literacy. In *Ways With Words* she explains that the boys and girls she studied in the Piedmonts are taught to approach literacy in dramatically different ways. For example, in Trackton's African American community "[t]he measure of a man is his mouth," so males are prepared early by public language input and modeling for stage performances. Their female counterparts are not excluded from the scene, and they watch and join in the general mood of participation, but they are rarely given parts to play and almost never full-stage performance opportunities (79).

[7] Ogbu writes that African Americans have been systematically denied literacy/education: "Before the emancipation, blacks received biblical education because their masters believed it would make them more obedient and faithful. After the Civil War, when blacks were relegated to peon-like status as sharecroppers or were limited to 'Negro jobs' in domestic service and unskilled labor, education followed suit. The ruling white elites believed the tenant farming system would break down if black children received the same education as white children. They would, for example, learn to question the high rates of interest and the exploitative accounting methods the planters imposed on illiterate tenants. Thus, black education was starved of funds. . . . Until perhaps the

label appropriated or imposed determines acquisition. According to Ogbu, ethnic and racial minorities in the United States can be categorized into three ethnic stratifications: autonomous minorities (e.g., Jews and Mormons) who manage to retain their separateness but are not totally subaltern; immigrant minorities (e.g., Italians and Irish) who emigrate voluntarily and experience some discrimination, but not to the extent that they are completely subordinated; and castelike minorities (e.g., enslaved African Americans and conquered Chicanos) who are seen as inherently inferior and are incorporated into society involuntarily and then relegated to substandard status. Ogbu writes that ethnic minorities are "assigned to their respective groups at birth or by ascribed criteria such as skin color, and they have few options to escape that designation" (232-233).

Dominican immigrants straddle all three categories. They do manage to maintain a measure of separateness, albeit not necessarily intentionally; one need only look at Washington Heights, the section of upper Manhattan where most Dominicans settle. If the push and pull factors are not examined, it can be said that they emigrate "voluntarily"; unlike Cubans, they have the option to return to the island. Upon arrival in the States, since the majority are dark-skinned, poor, and undereducated, Dominicans are consequently grouped with African Americans and Chicanos, and thus inherit the "castelike" marker.

Understanding these notions helps us clarify the experiences of those few Dominican immigrants who have been able to acquire high literacy, and it helps us to see that "literacy" means different things in different times and places, and that therefore it is productive to focus on the specific context, and, as John F. Szwed affirms, on the everyday lives of people. It's necessary that we look at the local circumstances, mainly so that we don't separate literacy from the conditions that affect it in direct and indirect ways. No level of literacy/formal education is neutral or objective. Literacy/formal education "is an institution which has the goal of changing peo-

---

1960s, American society never seriously intended blacks to achieve social and occupational equality with whites through education" (237).

ple's values, skills, and knowledge bases," as Heath illustrates (*Ways with Words* 368). She reiterates that people who are already socialized to meet the institution's agenda succeed; those who are not, such as Dominican Americans, often fail. In her study of the acquisition of basic literacy in three Carolina Piedmont communities, Heath found that

> some portions of the population, such as the townspeople, bring with them to school linguistic and cultural capital accumulated through hundreds of thousands of occasions for practicing the skills and espousing the values the schools transmit. Long before reaching school, children of the townspeople have made the transition from home to the larger societal institutions, which share the values, skills and knowledge bases of the school. Their eventual positions of power in the school and the workplace are foredestined in the conceptual structures, which they have learned at home and which are reinforced in school and numerous other associations. Long before school, their language and culture at home has structured for them the meanings which will give shape to their experiences in classrooms and beyond. Their families have embedded them in contexts that reflected the systemic relationships between education and production. (*Ways with Words* 368) [8]

[8] Children from the town and Roadville are more successful at acquiring basic literacy/education. Students from Trackton, on the other hand, "fall quickly into a pattern of failure, yet all about them they hear that they can never get ahead without a high school diploma. Some begin their families and their work in the mills while they are in school. But their mood is that of those who have accepted responsibilities in life outside the classroom, and that mood is easily interpreted negatively by school authorities who still measure students' abilities by their scores on standardized tests. Trackton students often drift through the school, hoping to escape with the valued piece of paper which they know will add much to their parents' and grandparents' pride, although little to their paychecks" (349). There is little hope for students like those in Trackton, Heath maintains, unless "the flow of cultural patterns between" the institution and communities is encouraged. Otherwise, "the schools will continue to legitimate and reproduce communities of townspeople who control and limit the potential progress of other communities and who themselves remain untouched by other values and ways of life" (369).

Dominican immigrants arrive with various worldviews and ways of being (shaped by their ethnicity, gender, and socioeconomic standing, to say the least) that are different from what is generally privileged in the United States, among them the belief that they are not necessarily "foredestined" to succeed in the process of acquiring any level of literacy; they know that acquiring high literacy will be a battle against many odds, the least of them being learning a new language. Studying those few Dominican Americans who complete doctorates can reveal much to us about the enabling process of acquiring and using literacy and about the specific needs of Dominican immigrants.

Szwed exhorts us who study literacy to shun needless abstractions and reductionist models, and to remain close to real cases, individual examples, and hence gain the "strength of evidence that comes with being able to examine specific cases in great depth and complexity" (309). Such is my intent in this study: rather than attempt to make generalizations about high literacy and other Latinos, or other groups, I aim to describe the particular experiences Dominican Americans lived in becoming and being highly literate and then going on to teach the humanities and social sciences in colleges and universities throughout the United States. I aim to identify and map their/our stories—the issues that were/are salient to us.

Of course, there is more to their/our stories than what I researched, and in that sense this study is a "slice," a brief and partial view of very complex circumstances. Subsequent studies with different methodologies (i.e., ethnographic participant observations involving members of their families and communities), or with different aims (i.e., comparing Dominican Americans with other Latinos and or other ethnically marginalized people in the United States) would probably reveal complementary, if not contradictory, views.

Theories of Feminist Ethnography

I come to the methods and theories of feminist ethnography informally via reflexive[9] behavior that has allowed me to survive the
fractures caused by becoming a culturally hyphenated woman. In
other words, since the age of ten, when I emigrated, I have been
living as a participant observer of United States culture (i.e., in it
but not totally part of it—a sort of voyeuristic stance), and I have
(increasingly) consciously inhabited multiple borders. Consequently, I have had to negotiate, examine, critique, compare,
evaluate, and synthesize my positions recursively. I also come to
feminist ethnography formally via my training in cultural and literacy studies and my embeddedness in feminisms particularly as
constituted by women of color and Third World theorists. (I realize
that the terms "color" and "Third World" are problematic socio-
political designations, not just racial or ethnic identifications.) I am
particularly drawn to these methods because they allow me to get
close to the people and places I study. They require that I be inclu-
sive and reflexive, and thus engage in a more egalitarian process of
conducting research and a more collaborative final product. That is
a crucial approach for me as a feminist and a Latina, since historically both those subjectivities have been marginalized.

James Clifford defines any ethnography as a process by which
"diverse experiences and facts are selected, gathered, detached
from their original temporal occasions, and given enduring value in
a new arrangement" (231 *On Collecting Art and Culture*). Ruth
Behar explains that "New" ethnography, unlike traditional ethnog-

---

[9] I define "reflexive" as the practice of reflecting on our own positions as
they are confronted with other new and oftentimes conflicting positions.
Reflexivity, a crucial aspect of feminist ethnography, means that as researchers and human beings we commit to the symbiotic and dynamic
process of understanding our own beliefs while also trying to make sense
of others' ways of being. That is a powerful way to perceive and bridge
potentially divisive differences, and thus to avoid hegemony in collecting, analyzing, and presenting data.

raphy, reflects "a more profound self-consciousness of the work-
ings of power and the partialness of all truth, both in the text and in
the world" (*Women Writing Culture* 4). New ethnography marked
its "narrative production against the novel" (Visweswaran 4); it is
"a strange cross between the realist novel, the travel account, the
memoir, and the scientific report" (Behar *Women Writing Culture*
3). Hence, new ethnography requires that readers and writers be
open to crossing many genres and disciplinary boundaries, and to
self-consciously creating meanings in terms of poetics and politics.

Feminist ethnography builds on traditional and new ethnography. It combines textual innovation and a heightened consciousness of the dynamics involved in researching, particularly in its
attempt to further decolonize the power relations (intellectual and
otherwise) inherent in (re)presenting people. That commitment
recognizes that the researcher, the subjects, the process, and the
product are always positioned symbiotically with cultural, social,
and political ramifications. It presupposes that we are all culturally
constructed, and that in examining a specific self we are also ines-
capably studying a general culture. That does not mean that particular lives and stories are the same as a general culture; it means
that when we look at a group of people like these Dominican
American academics we are also looking at the systematic structures, institutions, politics, history, and other factors that shaped
them. A feminist ethnographic stance demands that I (the researcher) be self-reflexive and simultaneously, as Abu-Lughod
terms it, "something of a ventriloquist."[10]

---

[10] Let me clarify further by providing a contrasting example: Barbara
Fischkin composed *Muddy Cup: A Dominican Family Comes of Age in a
New America* (1997) from a journalist's position. She reports to readers
from an outsider's perspective; she quotes people who are insiders. The
book is based on a series of "objective" newspaper articles she'd written
(ten years earlier) in order to understand immigration by looking closely
at a typical extended family. (Her initial intent was not to understand
Dominicans. In fact, she writes that her editor instructed her to "find a
family of immigrants . . . I don't care where they come from, but the
publisher would like them to speak Spanish" [152]; her Spanish teacher
suggested she choose Dominicans. Fischkin admits that before her editor

In gathering data and in shaping this book, I observe, listen, record, question, discover knowledge, interpret, and analyze my and
the participants' experiences. I examine the *emic* (insider) and *etic*
(outsider) perspectives, which for me (being one of the same kind
of people I study) is a more pregnant symbiotic process. I look at
my multiple selves (researcher, respondent, hyphenated Dominican, white woman, etc.), the participants, and the data I gathered
through the lenses of the participants, the many self-reflexive positions I inhabit, and other scholars' work. That kind of multilayered
approach helps me diminish the risk of projecting only my own
assumptions. That intersubjective method prompts me to connect
as many different viewpoints on the same data as possible; and it
directs me to consciously unpack my own worldview and cosmol-
ogy (the way I order the world around me). That approach is part
of what it means to understand, as John Berger notes, that we "only
see what we look at," that looking is "an act of choice" and that
being self-reflexive multiplies that choice (8); being self-reflexive
widens the selection of lenses through which we see.

Accordingly, I write this book as a scholar who has immersed
herself, participated in, and is invested in this topic and group of
people. I do not consider this approach to be a "handicap" or "diary disease," as Clifford Geertz would call it. On the contrary: it is
a crucial aspect—especially when studying ethnically marginalized
groups, since it fosters equality in (re)presentation; it allows the
researcher to become intimate with those being described, and
thereby to decrease the potential to objectify or "other" them.

Feminist ethnography's most salient characteristic is its commitment to activism—an important issue to me. I want my research

---

gave her the assignment, all she knew about the Dominican Republic was
"the name Trujillo" and that it was "Haiti's boring neighbor" [153]). As
a journalist her aim is to be objective: to give the who, what, where,
when, and why of a situation or event for a readership that expects facts
without too much interpretation and no self-reflexivity. (That position is
compromised because she incorporates literary devices such as narrating
omnisciently [for instance, in chapter 16]). In contrast, as a feminist ethnographer I compose a book that combines multiple intersubjective perspectives, along with my continuously self-reflexive reflections.

process and this final product to inscribe and validate the personal experiences of this group of Dominican American academics, accurately, responsibly, and intelligibly, particularly because there is no scholarship on this topic. I make every attempt to be faithful in (re)presenting these Dominican Americans, but since that process can't ever be fully accurate or transparent, it is important to remember that this book is, as Stephen Tyler characterizes postmodern ethnography and the fragments it attempts to represent, a "meditative vehicle," an "evocation" of a "mutual dialogic production" and of "cooperatively evolved texts" (138-40).

Primary Research Method

Though I use fieldnotes, library documents, and cultural artifacts, I chose personal interviewing as the primary approach to gather information because it allows for highlighting individuals' life stories and experiences as they are grounded in society—in this case, primarily society in the United States and Dominican Republic. Interviewing helps us analyze internalized ideological blueprints. It creates occasions to generate, hear, and inscribe voices. Generally, personal interviewing is an egalitarian practice in that it produces more opportunities for the researched to speak for themselves.[11] The process of voicing and inscribing our experiences, if only for our own sake, is empowering, and it can be, as cultural theorist bell hooks affirms, an opportunity to re-create ourselves. hooks notes that

> Moving from silence into speech is for the oppressed, the colonized, the exploited, and those who stand and struggle side by side

---

[11] For a description of researcher-centered oral history methodology see Paul Thompson, *The Voice of the Past: Oral History* (New York: Oxford University Press, 1978) and David K. Dunaway and Willa K. Baum, *Oral History: An Interdisciplinary Anthology* (Nashville, Tenn.: American Association for State and Local History and the Oral History Association, 1984).

a gesture of defiance that heals, that makes new life and new growth possible. It is that act of speech, of "talking back," that is no mere gesture of empty words, that is the expression of our movement from object to subject—the liberated voice. (211)

Personal interviewing typically entails participating and observing, composing, directing, and listening to the questions initiated by subjects, conducting and recording interviews, transcribing and editing them, then creating a final product, usually a written text, though it can also be films like those made by ethnographer Barbara Myerhoff. The interviews can focus on any or a combination of these forms: open-ended life histories, narratives, testimonies, or they can be centered on specific topics like the ones I conducted.

All of my subjects knew in advance how and why I would collect their stories, what I would ultimately do with them. They knew that I would be triangulating, that is, checking and rechecking (my recomposing of their stories) with a group of colleagues. I was deliberate about guiding each interview in an interactive and subjective manner. We engaged in an exchange of ideas (not a question-and-answer session), a reflexive and generative process, and a mutual inquiry, which was initiated and focused—but not limited—by me. This approach allowed us to arrive at new insights, and it minimized the opportunity for me to behave only as an "objective" researcher who makes detached observations and judgments, or who "others" her subjects. This approach validated experiences, subjectivities, and us; it created an occasion for us to interrogate our circumstances. I hope that our interrogation fosters conscientizaçao, as Paulo Freire calls it—a new self-awareness that prompts us to look critically at ourselves in relation to the world. Consequently, Freire writes, we name our condition and therefore we begin to transform it. Freire writes:

To exist, humanly, is to *name* the world, to change it. Once named, the world in its turn reappears to the namers as a problem and requires of them a new *naming*. Men [and women] are not built in silence, but in word, in work, in action-reflection. (*Pedagogy* 76)[12]

Of course, this feminist ethnographic method of collecting information raises various concerns for me, among them questions about validity. I study a small number of people, because there are only a couple of dozen of Dominicans who teach the humanities and social sciences in U.S. institutions. Hence I emphasize that the validity of this study is not in the breadth (the number of respondents) but in its focus and depth. My intent is to describe a particular culture, Dominican American academics' specific experiences with high literacy, not to make generalizations about all Latinos. Yes, the information in this text is only a slice of these academics' substantial stories. And those stories are only small parts of their whole lives. In that sense, I am creating a fiction. But as Clifford Geertz writes, every act of interpretation is a fiction. Stories we tell about ourselves, ethnography itself, is a "partial truth," as James Clifford terms it. (The common use of pseudonyms in ethnographies is an indication of how that fiction is created.) Feminist ethnographer Kamala Visweswaran explains:

> ethnography, like fiction, constructs existing or possible worlds, all the while retaining the idea of an alternate "made" world. Ethnography, like fiction, no matter its pretense to present a self-

---

[12] Also see Paulo Freire's *The Politics of Education: Culture, Power and Liberation* (Trans. Donaldo Macedo. Mass.: Bergin and Garvey Publishers, Inc., 1985), Freire and Donaldo Macedo's *Literacy: Reading the Word and the World* (Westport, Conn.: Bergin & Garvey, 1987), Freire and Ira Shor's *A Pedagogy for Liberation* (London: Macmillan, 1987), Myles Horton and Freire's *We Make the Road by Walking: Conversations on Education and Social Change* (ed. Brenda Bell et al. Philadelphia, Pa.: Temple Univ. Press, 1990). Also see these works by critical theorists who discuss Freire: Ira Shor's *Critical Teaching and Everyday Life* (Chicago: University of Chicago Press, 1987) and Henry A. Giroux's *Schooling and the Struggle for Public Life: Critical Pedagogy in the Modern Age* (Minneapolis: University of Minnesota Press, 1988).

contained narrative or cultural whole, remains incomplete and detached from the realms to which it points. (1)

This methodology also raises questions about authorship. My
process in collecting information, in making meaning, was collaborative, and in this final text I weave my voice among fourteen others to make it polyvocal, but ultimately, I decided what information was included and excluded, and so I've had to question who is
really the author and whose story is actually being told. In composing this final text, I identified and categorized recurrent themes; I
packaged the oral narratives for public consumption; I edited the
transcriptions, made choices about punctuation (which admittedly
may or may not change some meanings), and deleted repetitions,
words, and passages. I intervened. That can be construed as a form
of domination and silencing, which, as Judith Stacey contends, is
at cross-purposes with basic principles of feminist ethnography.
She argues that there can never be a fully feminist ethnography
precisely because we cannot escape those power relations in the
research process and the composing of the final text, and because
in eliciting (perhaps extorting) stories we may very well betray a
subject's right to silence. We may silence her silence, which, for
women and cultural minorities, especially, sometimes is the same
as agency (Stacey 21-27).

This methodology has also led me to consider my own fractured
positions as researcher of "my own" people. I am an insider and
an outsider, a "halfie," as Kirin Narayan calls those of us who
straddle cultures, but there is never a clear demarcation between
the two. Both positions are symbiotic and supportive of each other.
Abu-Lughod notes that bicultural researchers are positioned in (at
least) two communities (which present the Other and ourselves);
we "speak with a complex awareness of and investment in reception" ("Writing against Culture" 142). Trinh T. Minh-ha also
writes about this quandary:

> The moment the insider steps out from the inside, she is no longer
> a mere insider (and vice versa). She necessarily looks in from the
> outside while also looking out from the inside. Like the outside,
> she steps back and records what never occurs to her the insider as

being worth or in need of recording. But unlike the outsider, she also resorts to non-explicative; non-totalizing strategies that suspend meaning and resist closure. . . . She refuses to reduce herself to an Other, and her reflections to a mere outsider's objective reasoning or insider's subjective feeling. (*When the Moon* 74)

Similarly, Abu-Lughod writes that

every situation is particular . . . the outsider self never simply stands outside; he or she always stands in a definite relation with the "other" of the study. . . . What we call the outside, or even the partial outside, is always a position *within* a larger political historical complex. (*Writing Women's Worlds 40*)

That dilemma is one major reason why I have deliberately engaged in self-reflexivity about how my insider/outsider positions change and enfold each other. In this study I am the subject of analysis as well as the analyst. Those subjectivities allow me to step back and scrutinize our narratives from various stances: ours as individuals, mine (particularly when I analyze, when I move from the individuals' accounts to commenting on the general population; when I examine the relationship between our self-concepts and cultural norms), and all of us in relation to one another, in relation to various current theories, and at times in relation to other Latinos and culturally marginalized groups. My insider/outsider positions, then, are like Chinese boxes, the kind that fit into each other and thus look like only one; the largest one conceals the others and what could be inside each. When opened and spread out, all sorts of realities and layers are revealed.

Looking Forward

The crux of this study is the identification and problematization of highly literate Dominican Americans' specific experiences with high literacy and ethnic identity as those issues are embedded in Dominican and U.S. societies. It is always difficult to determine the degree to which ethnographic data based on oral (re)constructions of experiences simply reproduces internalized ideology.

One way to diminish that dilemma is to consider the data from as many standpoints as possible. In this study I have attempted to provide various frames and lenses through which our stories can be understood.

My hope is that our revelations will clarify, in the present and for the future, what this group of Dominican Americans deems significant about the process of becoming and being highly literate and about constructing an ethnic identity. My hope is that this book will expand Street's notion that any level of literacy is "not just a technical skill, neutral and universal across all societies" (*Cultural Meanings* 2). In other words, I want my work to add to our understanding of the social meanings of literacy (not only from the viewpoints of literacy theorists but) from the perspectives of the people who have lived and named those meanings.

In exploring these Dominican Americans' revelations in depth I hope to illuminate the historical continuum from which they emerged. Certainly, how we conceive of and express literacy and ethnicity is rooted in power relations, cultural, political, and many other sorts of specific agendas. No level of literacy is simply just a neutral set of skills. As we begin this more globally linked twenty-first century, it is imperative that we acknowledge that, and that we reconceptualize literacy (formal education) as being reflective of a way of life, as being symbiotic with the customs and beliefs of a culture and more specifically with particular communities. Acknowledging and unpacking that concept reaffirms that the meanings of literacy and identity are fluid, not static; they are related to specific contexts and therefore they can and do change. That is a powerful concept, especially for those of us who teach literacy to immigrants and other culturally marginalized students, since it can change how and why we teach and relate to students who are different from us.

Antonio Ferreyra in the 1950s before marrying Teresita Espaillat and leaving the Dominican Republic.

Teresita Espaillat Des Champs in the 1950s before marrying Antonio Ferreyra and leaving the Dominican Republic.

2

Internal Geography:
Acquiring High Literacy

I am the oldest of three children, and the only one who completed college. My father can barely read and write, in Spanish only. My mother had the equivalent of fifth-grade literacy, also in Spanish only. But like her mother, she often composed poems, especially during her last months of life when writing became her way of praying for relief from physical pain and assurance that she be welcomed in heaven (a more hospitable place, she was convinced, than the United States). My parents were too consumed with surviving to write anything but sporadic and brief letters to relatives back in the Dominican Republic, or to read anything but informational documents, though when we were children they constantly reprimanded us for watching television and continuously demanded that we read or write instead.

Nonetheless, today, it still amazes me that I'm a university professor who teaches writing and literature in English, my second and now dominant language. I try to figure out how it happened, what allowed it, and I look back to graduate school, when I started this study, and when I began to wonder what in my internal geography pushed me to seek such a high level of formal education, and why I felt it was so necessary for me to complete a doctorate, given what then, and even now, seemed like overwhelming odds?[1] What in my mental continent—the way I thought and felt, the epistemological legacies I'd inherited—pushed me? What internal factors compelled the other Dominican American academics? What issues inside our hearts and minds facilitated and impeded all of us?

When I began to solicit—from myself and the participants in my study—answers to those questions, I realized that all responses would be reconstructions of what we *really* may have experienced. I worried that in recomposing our stories we'd only remember the deeply painful issues, the ones implanted in our iconic memories, the ones that still seize us at the slightest trigger. But more important, I also realized that my methodological approach would be as close as I could get to identifying and understanding our experiences.[2]

Once I analyzed all of the interviews I conducted with participants in my study, I found various recurrent answers—factors that we, Dominican American academics, identify as the internal circumstances that facilitated our acquisition of high literacy. In this chapter I want to examine the most prominent two:

---

[1] According to research done by Torres-Saillant and Hernández, "the educational disadvantages that plague the Dominican community emanate not only from the low level of schooling that Dominican immigrants bring . . . [but also from] the precarious services that Dominican children receive" once in the States (86). For example: "community School District Six [in New York City], the area that has the largest concentration of Dominican children in the classrooms, has one of the state's worst records. . . . George Washington High School, the secondary school of Washington Heights which, by virtue of its location, houses the greatest number of Dominican students, has one of the highest dropout rates in the entire United States. In 1996 Schools Chancellor Rudy Crew included George Washington among those that were to close" (87).

[2] Another approach would be to conduct a longitudinal study following a group as they pursue doctorates, and/or comparing them to other professional Dominican Americans who do not have doctorates.

1) Love and curiosity for and about knowledge and the life of the mind motivated us. Consequently, we had many important questions which required serious (as in formal education) exploration and thoughtful consideration of numerous controversies and perspectives. This led us to read and write every day, and to approach literacy as a viable vehicle for obtaining information and finding solutions to any sort of difficulty.

2) A host of emotional factors relating to deprivation and exclusion motivated us. Most of us grew up in homes with limited income; that led us to feel deprived. That feeling was further compounded by having to straddle cultures (ways of being), and dealing with denigrating messages from mainstream U.S. society. Consequently, we felt incomplete—even defective, as if we were inherently missing many things by virtue of being the "Other" in the United States; we felt torn, in dire need of validation from anyone and anything that would remind us of our worth. As a result, we considered high literacy as the means to escape our circumstances (and perhaps fill an emotional void).

Having Important Questions

Both male and female participants in this study repeatedly affirm that one significant factor prompted us to pursue high literacy: wrestling with "important questions" regarding various issues. Each of us had strategies for inquiring. Since arriving in the United States I kept a journal where in addition to examining ideas I logged vocabulary and bits of new information encountered daily. I gathered it all as if they were pieces of the United States I could capture and then scrutinize in the safety of our apartment. That activity (I realize now as an adult) gave me a sense of ownership over my new language and home.

Laura read rapaciously about U.S. history. She copied what amazed her in notebooks that traveled with her constantly, and whenever she had a moment, she "savored" the inventory. Many others talked about their questions with parents, neighbors, teachers, friends—whomever would listen. No matter the strategy, or the degree of awareness about our behavior, in retrospect we see that we were driven by questions about our Dominican cultural, political, and social history, and about American ethos as it conflicted with that of the Dominican Republic (gender roles, for instance).

Antonio said that his questions fomented as a result of leaving the island and seeing Dominican culture from an immigrant's perspective. In particular, he wanted to know how European mythology influenced Dominican culture. Similarly, Homero wanted to know about the relationship between his primary and secondary homes: "I wanted to know why there was an insurrection in 1965 in the Dominican Republic," why the United States intervened in the country, and why the Dominican government had not been able to organize the "society in a way that would provide justice and prosperity. That prompted me to study sociology, and it still sustains my scholarly interests." Homero explained that he "took advantage of American education" in order to find answers to his questions. As he advanced in school and encountered "versions" of history that "simply did not coincide with the experiences" of his childhood and the stories he heard from his family and friends, he developed further questions. For instance, he knew, because he "lived through it," that "the United States' intervention was not strictly altruistic," and that the Dominican Republic was not just a passive agent either. There were so many other things he wanted to understand:

> I am also very interested in knowing why our societies in Latin America are so backwards in the midst of so much abundance. Our country, the Dominican Republic, is very wealthy. We have resources and we have the capacity. And yet the system that we use—the capitalist system—has proven to be ineffective in yielding results or in helping us organize the society. Dominicans are intelligent enough to learn. Then why is it that we remain in such a backward stage when compared to other countries? That is a question that I pose not only for the Dominican Republic but for the rest of Latin America as well.

Posing questions and seeking answers also propelled Carmen toward acquiring a graduate degree. Her questions were specifically about the condition of Dominicans living in New York City: "I am a very political person and I am very committed. There are a million Dominicans here who are in bad shape and who need to make it. That's the only motivation I needed." Carmen wanted to know why such massive numbers of Dominicans had left the island, and why so many live in poverty once in the United States. She wanted to identify ways she could help them "make it." That is what inspired her to seek high literacy. "Besides," she said,

> I love to learn. I loved going to college and graduate school because I learned so much. I was hungry. I went to school in the morning and I used to sneak into other classes just to listen. I wanted to know why my people are so poor. I wanted to use education to become big to be able to help my people. I have no doubt about my motivation for wanting a Ph.D., for wanting to learn and to be successful in this society.

Like a few of the other participants, Carmen believes that her motivation for pursuing a doctoral degree "makes sense": "It has been a tendency within the last twenty-five years in the Dominican Republic that people go to university.[3] I left at a moment when people were going to university," she explained to me; "it's just that emigrating made my desire more intense and it made it financially and emotionally possible." And indeed, as Carmen contends (and UNESCO has shown), even though no university in the country offers doctorates in the humanities and social sciences, Do-

---

[3] The general illiteracy rate in the Dominican Republic has been in consistent decline. Although no consistent and analogous data exist, the following has been noted: in 1950, 57.1 percent of the 15+ age population was illiterate. In 1970, 33 percent (683,637) of the 15+ age population was illiterate: 34.6 percent (361,235) were females; 31.4 percent (322,402) were males (Wilkie 108, 196). In 1981, 31.4 percent of the country's total population was illiterate. Of the 15+ age population there were 1,519,198 illiterates: 30.9 percent (748,440) were females and 31.8 percent (770,758) were males. In 1990, 16.7 percent of the country's total population was illiterate. Of the 15+ age population there were 743,700 illiterates: 18.2 percent (398,100) were females and 15.2 percent (345,600) were males (UNESCO 1-18). (No consistent and analogous data exist.)

minican society has placed increasing emphasis on all levels of formal education.

In fact, one of the reasons many continue to leave the island is that Dominican institutions "now graduate more people than the economy can absorb" (Spalding 59; Pessar "Linkage" 1206). Paradoxically, so many complete college in the Dominican Republic partly because higher education was/is believed to be the key to economic development. As in most Latin American countries, higher education is revered as the tool that provides increased opportunity for individuals, and thereby the growth of the nation—so much so that after Trujillo's death new legislation was created.[4] In 1961 Congress passed Law 5778, which defined universities as "a community of professors and students who were authorized to elaborate their own laws and regulations" (quoted in Escala 40). Subsequently, open admission was established at Universidad Autónoma de Santo Domingo, the first and oldest university in the Americas.[5]

---

[4] The deliberate effort to make higher education more available to the masses had begun in 1928 when the National Association of University Students was formed. NAUS tried to institute a system of governance by professors and students, but their work was crushed when Trujillo took control of the country on 16 August 1930 (Escala 38). During his dictatorship all but two universities were closed: Universidad Autónoma and the Catholic Seminary (which was allowed to grant equivalent degrees). Both were converted into "docile" tools for Trujillo's personal gain (Escala 40). Trujillo also "closed all but two high schools during the early years of his rule. . . . [but] he did increase the total number of elementary schools" (Tancer 227).

[5] On 28 October 1538, Pope Paul III approved the establishment of Universidad Santo Tomás de Aquino, a cloistered university patterned after Universidad de Alcalá de Henares in Spain. Universidad Aquino was administered by the Dominican order. Subsequently, it became Universidad Autónoma in Santo Domingo. Universidad de Santiago de la Paz was established in 1558. Originally known as Colegio de Gorjón, it was chartered by the king of Spain to function as Universidad de Gorjón, a noncloistered university patterned after the University of Salamanca. Jesuits administered Universidad de Gorjón. Initially, women and blacks were excluded from both universities; only the sons of Spaniards and some hand-chosen Indians were allowed to attend (Gimbernard 106).

As a result, between 1962 and 1971 the Dominican Republic had "the largest average annual enrollment growth in higher education of any Latin American country. While the average growth for the region was 9.7%, it was 19.8% for the Dominican Republic" (Escala 41).

Thus, as the research of Patricia Pessar also reveals, Dominicans arrive in the United States with an ingrained belief that attaining a high level of literacy is the "vehicle for individual mobility" ("Linkage" 1197). Women, especially, place overwhelming emphasis on college education, because they see it as the means to achieve self-sufficiency and financial independence from men and patriarchal demands.[6] "You see," Carmen said during our first interview, her eyes locked fiercely into mine, "Dominican culture conditioned me to want a higher education, but emigrating caused me to think about my people and therefore to want more than just college; I also got a Ph.D. because I wanted to show Americans that Dominicans are different from a lot of the other immigrants."

Similarly, Haydee declared that "numerous reasons pushed" her to pursue high literacy. The most significant one was that she "had no choice," if she was to "survive in the United States," but to confront, question, and disprove stereotypes. She was "compelled" to

---

These universities evolved into the two models for modern Latin American universities (Escala 37).

[6] Ironically, that conditioning (thinking of formal education as a commodity) was blatantly reinforced by Trujillo in that he paid lip service to education by establishing a special Bachillerato, a program of Arts and Letters for young women. This degree-granting program required that they complete three years of general education: English, French, Spanish, music, painting, literature, geography, history of culture, social conduct, and artistic gardening (Tancer 217). Trujillo also established a school to train peasant women to be servants, but then he required that the women work as spies for him, so that the school became a training program to uncover antigovernment plots. Fortunately, "the prompt realization of its purpose by the potential employers" led to an "unorganized but effective boycott against its graduates" and the school was closed (Tancer 216).

"show the Americans" *and* many Dominicans that she is not typical, that she could and would earn a doctorate:

> I must be different. That is what I said when I came here. I must be different from the Dominicans and other immigrants who don't excel. We are stereotyped as losers and troublemakers, people who don't behave or respect. To Americans we're just a bunch of people who waste the resources that are offered to us. I'm *not* one of them. I wanted to be respected, be distinguished and applauded for behaving and taking advantage of the opportunities found in the States. I wanted to take advantage of everything in order to succeed in their system so I could prove them wrong.

Other participants in this study, those who emigrated around age ten, myself among them, were partly driven—or, I should say, predisposed to want to study formally—by wanting to know about our new homes. Shortly after our arrival, we became curious about how the United States "got to be so big and powerful"; why its nonwhite people were/are enslaved in one form or another; why an immigrant cannot become president; why, given that prior to 1961 there were less than 10,000 Dominicans in the States, INS welcomed thousands of us all at once. We wanted to know who is an Anglo, and what is an ethos; why streets were not littered with jewels and wealth, who were Washington, Jefferson, Lincoln, and Kennedy and why everybody always talked about them in the D.R. and the United States. Questioning went on and on. Maybe, some of us believed, if we knew the answers we could then feel as if we belonged.

After one interview with Sandra, I noted in my journal: "yes, I was hungry, in more ways than one, and so were Sandra, Carla, Flor, and Laura. We needed validation. Believed our entrance and acceptance in American society would be eased if we knew about the country. We used literacy as a tool, a commodity to pay for what we gained. Yes, feeling disconnected, lonely, rejected, incarcerated, per se, because of our gender, that too pushed us to become highly literate." Carla had echoed that sentiment months before when I interviewed her. Carla, most of all, says that she drew much motivation from struggling against all those feelings. As a child, when she hadn't yet understood the dynamics of her situation (when she *never* felt like "Oh gee I'm a Dominican American, boy am I lucky!" but instead always felt like "Oh gosh, I have to haul this dead body along with me that says Dominican"), she withdrew into an inner life of thinking. She ensconced herself in the worlds she found in reading and writing where she was not rejected. That unsought training prepared her to want more and to succeed in formal education, but it never changed her seeing herself as an outsider:

> Coming to this country and needing to belong—I could be accepted in reading and writing. I think I wouldn't have become a writer unless that emigrating experience had happened to me. It was a total loss of everything by which I made sense of the world. I wasn't welcomed here. I didn't feel like I could step off from the Dominican Republic and become an American. That possibility was not opened, partly because I had an accent. So, I started to be more solitary, more interior, to read a lot more. Emigrating forced me to grapple with an internal world, to find something inside of myself. I needed an internal homeland.

Reading and writing allowed Carla to find a place of her own, to create a world in which she was comfortable and welcomed. The more she "felt left out" of American society, the more she "sought solitude" in the world of books. That circumstance helped to create, she believes, a yearning for knowledge, and that yearning motivated her to pursue formal education, particularly a graduate program where she began to be conscious of her innerworks:

> Somebody came and gave a talk at our college and said that there had never been a writer that had written really good poetry in a language other than the language in which he first said "Mama." And I thought oh my God. That's like hearing you can't be president if you weren't born here. I really felt for a while that because English hadn't been my native tongue that I just couldn't have the deep rhythmic instinctive connection with the tongue that I would have had in Spanish.

Carla says that her important questions did not center on whether or not she should seek high literacy. As an immigrant from a family of economic means, it was almost a given that she'd acquire education beyond college. Both her parents are highly literate, and most of her male relatives back on the island attended Ivy League universities in the United States. Most of the female relatives had also attended university, usually in the States, but also all over Europe. Carla's mother finished two years of college in the States. She wanted to continue studying, but her father (Carla's grandfather) demanded that she return to the Dominican Republic. He believed two years was enough for a female, and that she had to think about marriage. When Carla's parents migrated to the States they transported many of their beliefs, and therefore they expected Carla to attend university, but they insisted that it be an all-female institution. In such a place Carla's womanhood would be protected. Later, when Carla asked her parents to let her transfer to a coed college with a program in the field she wanted to pursue, they allowed it only after much hesitation and the intervention of her teachers. Her parents reasoned that if American teachers sanctioned Carla's request (more importantly, that if American teachers honored the family by noticing Carla), then they had to accommodate. Carla was allowed to transfer, but their ingrained belief about the role of women continued to affect her into adulthood:

> I think being a woman was discouraging. I found that when I was in a [romantic] relationship where I was expected to be more traditional I really didn't feel happy. I think that was a major thing— to feel like, "I should really get busy on a relationship and leave all this nonsense."

Those inherited Dominican issues with gender follow her still. In the "very strongly male" English department where she works, Carla is "always having to second guess" her ideas and to "worry" when she disagrees with anyone: "It's like going back to the D.R. and being a new and different person from the one that they expect. I have to constantly check myself, to try and be true to what was given to me but also claim and express and combine it with who I've become." Having to be so self-conscious makes her feel lonely, which in turn exacerbates her growing need to question gender roles and Dominican ways of thinking about how and why a woman should be educated.

Like Carla, many of us female participants in this study struggled with the attitudes conveyed to us about gender. For several of us, that very clash pushed us into rebelling, into questioning, seeking options and answers and ways out. Again and again, formal education presented itself to us as more than a means to become economically stable. Time and again, those struggles propelled us into formulating "important questions" and finding the answers through academe. While in graduate school, I tried to resolve my own conflict regarding those messages about my gender and becoming highly literate by researching Dominican women's roles and their involvement in formal education on the island. That way, I figured, I could comprehend where my parents' thinking was grounded.

While reading (sources in English and Spanish) I found that historically there were but a few Dominican women who worked in the public sphere. Salomé Ureña, who completed graduate school in the United States, for instance, was among the first to call herself a feminist in public. Ureña's effort as an educator at the turn of the century focused on helping women see themselves as "active workers" in the society, not just "mere objects" of the home. In addition to founding the Instituto de Señoritas, the first secondary school for women in the D.R., Ureña also formed the first "brigade of women," which included Ercilia Pepín, who in 1910 began to assert that women can and should have equal access to education.

At about the same time that Ureña was attempting to impact Dominican society, El Instituto Profesional de Santo Domingo began to accept female students. Encarnación Piñeyro, a pharmacist, was one of the first to graduate; then in 1912 seven other women graduated, among them Andrea Evangelina Rodríguez, the first female doctor in the D.R. She completed a graduate degree in Paris and wrote a thesis entitled "Niños con excitación cerebral" ("Cerebrally Excited Children"). Upon returning to San Pedro de Macorís, she established a clinic for the control of venereal diseases, and began to participate in the public sphere, but she limited her interests to "gender-appropriate" concerns such as children and the family (Peguero 362). The United States' intervention in 1916 helped to politicize these educated women's activities. Ercilia Pepín spoke against the occupation in public and distributed pamphlets. Later, in 1921 when the military government offered her a position as a delegate in the Pan American Congress, she refused it in protest.

In the 1930s Rafael Leonidas Trujillo's dictatorship set the parameters for what women (the mothers of participants in this study who were girls at the time, and in turn those who were born at the end of his reign, or shortly after) learned to accept as proper behavior for our gender. Trujillo was interested in educating women, Shoshana Tancer writes, because he saw their formal education as an opportunity to inculcate his agenda. To him, education meant attendance at the sort of finishing schools for girls that existed in the United States and England (217). He established several of these schools and manipulated them and the nascent feminist movement. Only one "feminist" organization was formally recognized—Acción Feminista Dominicana. Their aim was to teach women to fight for "laws that favor marriage and family stability," and to "prepare" women to "always marry for love and not out of necessity to the first man who can support" them financially (Fernández 11, my translation). As the organization's bylaws state, their goal was to provide the

> intellectual, social, moral and legal betterment of women, as well as to sustain campaigns against alcoholism, prostitution, drugs, etc., to fight for protective laws for mothers, children, adolescents, women workers, the elderly, etc., to lobby for the establishment of a tribunal for children, to instill in women the need for frugality and to persuade them not to spend on immoderate luxuries; to persuade Dominicans not to sell their land to foreigners; to fight for the preservation of traditions and to support all ideas that prompt the progress and welfare of the republic. (Fernández 10, my translation).

Women allowed to join Acción Feminista Dominicana were required to have "good conduct" (and only a few key members of

Acción determined what "good" meant), be over age eighteen, and be considered "ladies" of high socioeconomic standing. The organization deliberately limited membership so that the movement would become "a true feminist union formed by Ladies and Young Women" who aimed to sustain the "moral and material equilibrium of the home," and therefore the "equilibrium of the nation" (Mota 266-7). But they did not have to work hard at gatekeeping, since in the mid-1930s 70 percent of the population was illiterate; therefore, the masses of women were automatically denied participation (Mota 266).

After Trujillo's assassination, the trend toward providing vocational training for women was continued by Joaquin Balaguer. In the 1970s he increased the number of schools for lower-class women, and he established two types of schools that continue to exist today: schools of domestic arts and industrial schools of domestic science. Schools of domestic arts purport to "teach young women the basic necessities of keeping house, that is, cooking, sewing, and baking"; industrial schools of domestic science prepare women for employment as seamstresses and cooks (Tancer 216). Neither type of school has been particularly successful. Tancer notes that the school of domestic arts "failed because it has been limited to the very few urban women of the lower class who may attend school rather than learn these skills at home, while the industrial school has a five-year course preparing women for virtually nonexistent jobs" (Tancer 216). To this day, middle-class women who can afford to attend regular university are still bound by gender stereotypes:

> It is the women in this group who become the schoolteachers, the secretaries, the store clerks, and the marginal white-collar workers. These are also the women who become beauticians to supplement their husbands' salaries, the husbands frequently being government employees. Even more important than the fact that they are paid more than their lower-class sisters, they have achieved the prestige of a semiskilled profession. (Tancer 218)

Generally, though, during Balaguer's presidency there were no "qualitative changes in the situation of women as a whole, or in the

political and economic system that perpetrates their positions"
(Mota 276). [7] In the 1960s and 1970s, when the majority of us in
this study emigrated, Balaguerista (or "Reformist") feminism continued to be an extension of women's traditional role in the home.
That is, women were prompted to see themselves as "supermoth-
ers" and the political arena as a larger home.[8] According to Mota,
official feminism continued to maintain that

> women's contribution to politics consists of a serene personality,
> tact and skill. The woman in politics is the mother who soothes in
> difficult moments, who tranquilizes a tumultuous world, and,
> above all, who serves as "a permanent example of the moral prin-
> ciples which are the basis of our Christian traditions." (272).

Despite this history, during the 1970s more women were attending and completing university degrees than ever before in the history of the D.R., but the majority continued to be tracked into traditionally "feminine" careers. To this day, women on the island
still generally exist encased in domestic life and men in public life.
Politics and economics still render women subordinate to men.
That is one major attitude toward formal education that all of us
(even if not deliberately) often questioned and certainly resisted.

Learning about Dominican women and their struggles with notions about gender helped me comprehend and combat some of the
impediments (emotional turmoil, for one) I faced in attempting to
complete the doctorate. Symbiotically, acquiring high literacy,
completing higher education, taught me how to research and validated my curiosity. Sandra, Haydee, and Flor experienced similar
processes. They each explained that in learning about Dominican

---

[7] For in-depth analyses of post-Trujillo society see the scholarship of
Rosario Espinal, for instance, "Between Authoritarianism and Crisis-
Prone Democracy: The Dominican Republic After Trujillo," a chapter in
C. Clarke, ed. *Politics and Society in the Caribbean*. London: Macmil-
lan, 1991. 145-165.
[8] For an in-depth examination of women and feminism as the "Super-
mother" syndrome, see Elsa Chaney's *Supermadre: Women in Politics in
Latin America*. Austin, Texas: University of Texas Press, 1979.

women's condition, in particular, allowed them to combat established stereotypes about who they were supposed to be. The knowledge fueled their motivation to be different. Flor told me that she struggled toward high literacy partly because she was determined not to be like her mother, whom she considered "too dependent" on her father and other men. And Sandra was memorably candid during our interviews when she discussed "having important questions" (especially regarding Dominicans' precepts about gender) and examining her family and herself as a woman:

> I hated my mother's life, the fact that she could get beat up and totally dominated and had absolutely no control over her life. This happened to me one time: I was sitting in the living room with my grandfather and the family. My uncle who was my age told me to get up because he wanted to lie down on the sofa. And I refused so he went to push me off and I hit him. My grandfather told me I had absolutely no right to ever raise my hand to a man and proceeded to throw me out, and I was not allowed to go back to his apartment. I must have been about sixteen. So I came back to this education thing as a way out.

Late in high school when she began to learn about Dominican women, Sandra realized that she was expected to be "a little wife," a role that was compounded by her family's poverty in that her labor at home was essential because both her parents worked several jobs. She tried to subvert that role by finding part-time employment: "I realized that if I had a job it would be an excuse not to do the household work." The ploy was ineffective, because while it provided an excuse for not completing some of her female "duties," it also caused her physical and mental exhaustion. In addition to cashiering at the local supermarket, Sandra still had to be the little wife. Thus, she had less time and energy for school tasks and for reading, which she loved to do above all else. But she kept her job because it got her out of the house, and it gave her a sense of "independence and authority."

Sandra was determined to "escape" her home life and her parents' "dysfunctional" and "oppressive" ways of treating the girls. She desperately wanted to be different from them, and formal education, she believed, was *the* viable vehicle that would transport her out, that would allow her to escape intellectual, emotional, patriarchal, and economic oppression. Questioning their ways caused Sandra a great deal of pain—for a long time—because she did not find "acceptable answers" until she began graduate studies. That is when Sandra began to question gender roles, when she began to "really believe" (and enact) that "there are other options, that there are other ways of doing things." Reading feminist theory, examining how other Latinas (Chicanas, Puerto Ricans, and Cubans) dealt with similar issues helped her to become politically and socially active. It was then that she was able to look at how and why she acquiesced to her husband, who thought that her master's degree was a diversion while he completed his M.D., and that there was no need for her to pursue a doctorate. Sandra explained:

> I would take my paycheck and hand it over to my husband who would give me ten dollars allowance a week. Even though I had made a conscious decision that I did not want to live the way the women in my family lived, in my marriage I was doing exactly the same thing. But as I went through graduate school and was exposed to all kinds of new ideas I started questioning these things and saying, wait a minute, it doesn't have to be that way. That realization increased my desire to finish graduate school.

Today Sandra is a very successful professor and administrator, but in order to attend university she had to defy her family's (and what she knows as "Dominican") ways of thinking. When Sandra told her parents that she had been awarded a scholarship to a university far away from New York City, where they lived, they gave her an ultimatum: "If you go, you don't come back home at all." They refused, Sandra reasons in retrospect, because they thought it was improper for a young woman to leave home and live alone. I felt sad when Sandra spoke. I remembered arguing with my parents, attempting fiercely, but never really articulating clearly (because I did not really know how or what to label my feelings), that I wanted to go to college out of the Bronx so I could be a real American. It wasn't just my love of books and knowledge that mattered; it was also that I could be like my American peers—I could leave home the way they did. But in our parents' view it was improper for young women to be unsupervised. Our virginity, our roles as "good" women, would be threatened. According to many of our parents, the only acceptable ways for daughters to leave our homes were to become nuns, marry, or die. Any other possibility was criminal. I chose to marry; Sandra forged her mother's signature.

Our parents had other fears, too, that prevented them from allowing us to go away to college or graduate school. Being recent immigrants, having barely escaped the civil war and its hunger and violence, most of them residing in low-income communities where there seemed to be as much fury as in our war-torn island, our parents were anxious about the safety of their children. They were especially compulsive about guarding the girls whom they believe need more protection than boys do. Sandra's parents had yet two other reasons for not letting her leave: it was not a priority to expend energy and funds on a daughter who would marry and probably never "use" formal education; and, more urgently, they needed for Sandra to find employment and help them with living expenses. Sandra said it would have pleased her parents if she had made "an announcement to work at the factory sewing." Perhaps then she would have attended the local community college on a part-time basis and lived with her parents until she married.

On the other hand, some female participants in this study do not prioritize the importance of questioning their roles as women. Flor says that she did not question much, and that she "endured" less of a struggle in pursuing formal education, because at age seventeen, following her marriage to her American boyfriend, her parents returned to the D.R. That gave her a measure of independence in that she had to answer to him alone, and he was supportive of her desire to pursue high literacy. Nonetheless, her Dominican-bound notions about women haunted Flor. "In high school," she said,

> I was one of the few Hispanics, the only Dominican for sure. Half of the teachers didn't know that I also spoke Italian. I was a curiosity at best . . . and I was the recipient of some unpleasantness. I remember being caught between two young men who were arguing, and one of them spit on the other and it fell on my head. He had been eating a cough drop. There was his cough

had been eating a cough drop. There was his cough drop and his spit on my hair. I went home and I couldn't tell my mother. When I finally told her she ran me to the sink. She started to cry. I was crying. I still get sick thinking about it. It was so humiliating—the fact that these people thought nothing of it. Nothing. Nothing. Nothing. I thought it was a very harsh culture. I think that in our country women were treated differently, maybe more protected and maybe second-class citizens, but that would not have happened, I felt, in my culture. Men would not do that—not with a woman between them, and certainly would not just dismiss it as nothing.

Haydee was also "lucky" (not to have to question or struggle with notions about women) because her father returned to the island leaving her and her mother free to make their own decisions. But the experiences of María, Dilia, Carmen, and Laura resemble those of Sandra. They had to defy their families and intrinsic beliefs about women in order to complete degrees. And even after positioning themselves as "professors," some of the female participants still question their choices. Laura, for example, worries "constantly" about the demands of her untenured position and those of her cultural tradition:

Actually, my family would have preferred that instead of pursuing my studies I would have had a couple of children. My husband and my mother would have been happier and I think more proud of me if once I finished my college education I had had a couple of children. A lot of the time I feel guilty. Sometimes I don't know if I'm doing what is really important.

Questioning gender expectations was almost as ominous an issue for the men in this study. All of them grew up in economically deprived homes, and therefore there was an intensified understanding that being "men" mostly meant providing financial sustenance. If anything threatened that role, they were not considered, as Ramón explains, "real" men. Ramón said that all the men in his family are laborers who work viscerally, and they expected him to find a similar job. But as Ramón went through college they began to expect that he would become a medical doctor, engineer, or lawyer—that he would "get a profession" and help them break the cycle of poverty. Ramón's constant reading and writing did not seem to be a viable—or manly—means for making money. Those activities seemed "easy" and therefore effeminate. Ramón's gender role, his sexuality, had been suspect from the moment he began to show an interest in literacy and the arts. Then in graduate school, when he began to "make connections and to think comparatively," his family began to see him as an "intellectual," but notwithstanding as a man who would not be able to earn a "real" living (and therefore perform his manly duty of supporting a wife, children, and home).

César too explained that he was conscious of his family's resistance to his intellectual interests. Through college and graduate school he was often teased and called "mariquita," or "maricón," a derogatory way of accusing him of being homosexual.[9] They worried that he spent too much time reading, writing, and thinking— not the "manly" things he should have been doing. In doing my own research about male gender roles in the Dominican Republic I came to understand that César's parents' concerns were reasonable, since they lived through the Trujillo dictatorship when, as de Moya and García elucidate,

---

[9] There is a long tradition establishing the markings for each gender role. One example is noted by de Moya and García, who write that Dominican men have faced sexual stereotyping since colonial times. In 1535 Gonzalo Fernández de Oviedo, a governor of the island, wrote about the "berdache" (half man/half woman) and other sexual practices: "What I have said of these people is very public on this and neighbouring islands, and even in the continent, where many of these male and female Indians were sodomites. . . . Indeed, this is a very usual, ordinary and common thing among them. . . . And you should know that the man who plays patient or takes the position of being the woman in that beastly and anathematized act is given the role of a woman, and wears *naguas* (skirts) as women do. . . . This abominable *contra natura* sin was very usual among the male Indians of this island" (123). In 1547, Juan de Echegoian, a married judge was publicly shamed for making a sexual proposal to 16-year-old Hernando de Bascones. His is the first publicized and recorded case of harassment against sexually ambiguous men, or "maricones," as they began to be labeled (124).

a homosexual or bisexual orientation or identity was regarded as a family disgrace and shame, which could retroactively implicate family members and ancestors as "carriers" of this weakness of character. Homosexual and bisexual males were frequently subject to blackmail and aggression, ostracized, or even driven to commit suicide. Many were also forced by social pressure to marry women and to father children, as a means of disavowing the imputation of homosexuality. In the early 1950s, Trujillo went so far as to create two concentration camps for middle- and upper-middle-class intellectual and/or political male dissidents suspected of being, or known to be, homosexual or bisexual. . . . The fashionable Latin American machismo of those days represented the homosexual man, mostly those known to be the orally or anally receptive partner in sexual intercourse, as someone who sooner or later would show the symptoms of feminine degeneracy, and who could transmit these properties to other males. (125)

It seems logical that César's parents would fear what appeared to them to be effeminate behavior. César told me that his family understood and respected his desire to become an engineer or lawyer, but being an academic seemed ridiculous to them—and not just because they knew his salary as an academic would be low. They did not want to accept that their son would be in a woman's profession. That attitude, César explained, was com-pounded by their low socioeconomic class and lack of familiarity with the life of an intellectual. Ideas, they often said to him, don't pay for food or allow you to support a wife and children. Even today, his family does not fully understand or appreciate his profession: "My parents would have rather seen me do something else with my life. They really weren't in tune to what I was doing in graduate school. I try to explain it to them now—only because they've said to me, 'you know, people ask me what you do.' But they would have rather seen me do something else with my life."

Most men in this study told me that the graduate school experience helped them to understand the dynamics, the cultural legacy—the internal map—that shapes their parents' and family's resistance to them becoming academics. Antonio clarifies that wanting to be a college professor in the Dominican Republic is not a good economic choice, and not just because jobs are scarce. A career in higher education is not prestigious or secure. There is little potential to grow and advance. Again, those attitudes are partly founded on the reality that there are endless factors that prevent Dominican academics on the island from developing. As in most Latin American countries, Dominican universities are primarily teaching (as opposed to research) institutions. They emphasize "the education of students for a profession . . . not for graduate training"; there is "generally no concept of a liberal education reflected in the curriculum, except as it exists in the required core curricula of individual majors in some universities"; specialization in an area begins early (Sellew 39).

In the Dominican Republic there are a few master's programs, but postgraduate study consists of only two levels: postgraduate training in a chosen field and the maestría. Postgraduate training requires one year of graduate course work. Students don't have to write a thesis or do research. Students with this degree can work, for instance, as elementary school teachers. The maestría requires two years of graduate course work, original research, and a thesis. Students with a master's can teach at the university. Those who teach at universities are drastically underpaid and overworked. In 1987, for example, Universidad Autónoma had 67,122 students and 1,690 faculty, of whom only 439 were employed full time (Sellew 118). Still today, salaries are so low that academics must maintain other jobs. The few professors who have doctorates from universities abroad are paid little more.

Moreover, books are relatively expensive, and there are only sixty-eight public libraries in the entire country. The three major libraries were founded in the late 1960s:[10] the National Library is

---

[10] There have been a few, mostly private, libraries on the island since colonial times. The first known library belonged to Fernando González de Oviedo in 1533. The Universidad Santiago de la Paz had a library in 1540, and so did Colegio de Garfón and the Convento de los Dominicos in 1551. The first public library, La Biblioteca Pública de Santo Domingo, was founded in 1860 but was dissolved in 1876. There were a few others in Santiago de los Caballeros and San Pedro de Macorís in the nineteenth century. In 1908 two libraries were established: the Biblioteca

noncirculating and contains approximately 25,000 volumes; the Lincoln Library, sponsored by the United States Information Service, circulates a limited part of its 58,000 books; the Enrique Apolinar Henriquez Library, which does not circulate its 3,000 volumes, is a private facility "begun in 1978 by the Society of Dominican Bibliophiles, many of them women, who revere the printed word" (Foster 106). There are just a handful of other circulating libraries. In the late 1980s there were only nine librarians with master's degrees in the entire country.

Given this knowledge, it is no wonder Dominican parents considered academe a poor choice of profession for their immigrant children, generally, but more so for their sons, since a profession is so closely linked to economic security and being able to take care of the responsibilities of a family, and since that profession also helps to define masculine identity. Being an academic is not "manly." Thus, it is logical for men to struggle with their gender role as it relates to high literacy, and to feel disconnected, isolated, and sometimes rejected by parents and family. Wanting to disprove that stereotype was one motivation for pursuing high literacy, but there were consequences.

All of the men in this study said that they began to experience shame—about "betraying" their communities, the people and culture from whom they were distancing themselves in becoming highly literate—and then also about their own feelings of being "underdeveloped," inferior, and "not belonging" in graduate school. Becoming highly literate—for both the men and women in this study—was embroiled in shame and much emotional turmoil.

Pública de la Sociedad and the academic library at the Universidad Autónoma (which served as the national library from 1948 to 1971). The National Library was technically founded in 1927 along with the National Museum, but it wasn't until 1971 when a building was erected to house the collection (Freiband et al.).

Emotional Factors

Shame was a recurrent theme in the stories women told me. That shame was deeply imbricated in social class standing. Carmen felt ashamed of her parents and at the same time angry and guilty for feeling that: "There are so many things they still don't understand. When I go to my mother's house all the neighbors come to tell me they have a pain here, a pain there. No matter how many times I explain, they don't get this Ph.D. thing. They never understood why I was in school until my early thirties or why I am not rich after all the formal education I finished." Carmen felt "so bad" and "sorry" for her parents, because they seemed to be "missing out" on the "wonderful world" she knows. The stronger emotion she still wrestles with is feeling "sorry" for herself, for being ashamed of her family and community. Laura echoed those sentiments, and so do I.

I began to analyze my own shame after I'd heard Carmen's and Laura's stories. In high school I often wished I'd been born to a different—more educated, not impoverished immigrant—family. My mother's explicitly emotional ways and my father's servile demeanor in front of Americans embarrassed me. Early in college I simply did not want people to know my parents. The lacerating shame of one event stands in my memory as vividly as if it happened today: A college friend and I were going ice-skating. She was driving and took us right past the textile factory where my father worked. We stopped for the light, and there, right in front of the car, stood my father, apparently enjoying his break and smoking a cigarette. I looked in his eyes; he looked in mine, and we both knew that I was ashamed of him, ashamed enough not to get out of the car and acknowledge him as my father, to introduce him—ashamed that I had loftier interests, that he and my friend's Brooks-Brother-suit-wearing attorney father would have nothing to say to each other. I was ashamed to be ashamed of the father I loved, the father who toiled so I could end up on a leisurely ice-skating stroll while he only took a ten minute respite from the factory's fumes and grime.

Shame and becoming highly literate, questioning and emotional turmoil: they are symbiotic. They feed on each other. They cannot be disentangled. Much of the emotional turmoil that participants in this study discuss was caused by having to straddle cultures and ways of being, plus having to deal with denigrating messages from Dominican and mainstream U.S. society. That turmoil led us to doubt our capacity to succeed academically and otherwise, to feel defective, and to need validation. Questioning and emotional turmoil functioned, all of us believe (as we look back at our experiences), as both an impediment and an impetus (in that we aimed to disprove erroneous beliefs) to complete our college and graduate degrees, and to enter the professorate.

The other most salient source of emotional turmoil, most of us agree, centered on examining (even if we weren't conscious of that process back then) our ethnic identity. As I conducted this study I realized that, as for many of us, my own anguish began at age ten when we left the island, even though my mindful search for answers about my identity began in graduate school, where I couldn't escape being the only Latina in my doctoral program. In the common definition, I'm not mulatta (which, Carmen notes, on entering the U.S. converts to being black and by default "African American" with all of the prejudicial stereotypes embedded in that label). Hence, I was never as pressed to appropriate that identification. Nor am I Nordic-looking, and thus, even if I considered it, I would not be able to pass as the stereotypical American. I am relentlessly asked where I'm from, especially when I lived in the Midwest, where most people's notions of a Latina/Dominican's appearance did not match my looks. That attitude moved me to question ethnic stereotypes in the United States and in the Dominican Republic, and urged me to examine the consequences of appropriating certain labels. My quest lasted five years—a time filled with anger, pain, and ultimately deep gratification for having arrived at a centered understanding about my heritage and ethnic identity in the midst of the culturally scattered positions I inhabit.

My journey divulged that I'd been anguished by my ethnic identity from the moment I was born, not the point at which I arrived in the United States. When I began to examine that realization, memories surged like torrents—of my cousin, for instance, also named Dulce María and born a month after me. "Blanquita" (purely white), the nickname she has used all of her life, had a fair-skinned German immigrant mother from whom she inherited fine golden hair, azure eyes, and a peaches and cream complexion that everyone thought was too delicate to expose to the Caribbean sun. Like Blanquita's father, my mother was second-generation French whose skin color had been island weathered, and though my father is a milky-skinned green-eyed Galician Spaniard, I have fine ebony hair and eyes, and café con leche coloration.

When I was a child, most members of my family constantly reminded me not to get too much sun, since my skin color was already too brown and thus at greater risk of becoming darker. In and out of our family circle, Blanquita was consistently "la preferida, la muñequita, bella" (the preferred, little doll, beautiful), and I was described as "aunque sea tiene pelo bueno" (at least she has good [meaning fine and straight, as opposed to "nappy" or "kinky"] hair).[11] There was never a doubt as to who would draw

---

[11] In the D.R. it is generally believed that there are only two kinds of hair. The labels ascribed to each help to reveal the intersections between identity, gender, and sexuality: pelo bueno is "good" hair, which is straight and silky; pelo malo is "bad" hair, which is tightly curled, coarse and kinky. Pelo bueno is valorized, since it invokes the phenotypes of Europeans, Asians, and Taínos. Pelo malo is denigrated since it signals an African influence. Pelo bueno is also called pelo muerto (dead hair) and pelo lambio (limp hair), which suggests further stereotyping: that is, whiteness may be the social de rigeur, but it implies, particularly for women, repression and restraint—a limpness or deadness that pelo malo does not have. Pelo malo (and by extension black women who have always been considered more sexual) is free and unruly. Even if unacknowledged, all Dominicans struggle with this issue, including after emigrating (e.g., a man with pelo malo improves, that is, whitens, the race by marrying a woman with pelo bueno; in turn, a woman's value increases if she has pelo bueno). That attitude/belief was clarified for me during several walks in Washington Heights, where numerous beauty shops advertise their expertise in doing *doobies* and *derizados dominicanos* for those who have pelo malo. Doing doobies entails dividing the hair into various flat layers, which are then wrapped tight and held by pins for

the most compliments, or who would be awarded victory over tugs of war for various toys. That is one of endless (subtle and obvious) ways of being and making meaning about my ethnic identity that I didn't know I had ingested until I started to regurgitate and examine my legacy as if I were a doctor diagnosing the vomit of an esoterically ill patient.

Then, completing this study, I began to investigate the experiences of others. I won't ever forget the poignancy of Clarisa's comments on her ethnic identity. Denial had not allowed her to see herself as black, even though on the island she was assigned many derogatory labels. Ultimately, on moving to the United States the complex layers of meanings in all those labels forced her out of her sense of self. "Hay dios mío!" she shrieked during our dinner on the Upper West Side of Manhattan, her eyes astounded, chest bent toward me across the table, right hand spread wide across her chest as if to contain her swelling distress:

> When did I become black? In Santo Domingo I didn't think too much about being a black woman. I saw myself as a person. I left Santo Domingo as Clarisa. I came here and people see me as black first. I was a person, then I am black, and then I am Hispanic, Latina, Dominican, and then a woman. So I lost my identity, who I was. As a result, I have gone through changes in my personality.

Carmen too says she was shocked when she realized that the color of her skin was labeled differently in the United States. She was not called "black" in the D.R., and even if she had, she ex-

---

pins for many hours (depending of the degree of coarseness). Once unwrapped, the hair remains straight for a period of time. Derizados are "uncurlings" or "straightenings" of the hair. Usually, doobies are done without chemicals or oils; derizados may include the use of chemicals and or actual ironing of the hair. Derizados are expensive on the island and in the States, and if done properly they last only about a month. Though many women do both processes themselves, generally only wealthier women can afford this attempt at changing their physical identity.

plained to me also in exasperation, the label didn't mean the same thing. It didn't connote slavery, inequity, deprivation, marginalization, and racism as blatantly as in the States. On the island you did not confront your blackness. Even if you have pelo malo you could get a doobie. In the United States Carmen had no choice but to ask questions—which sometimes produced painful answers—about her ethnic identity in the States and on the island. Like most of us in this study, Carmen and I found out that the majority of Dominicans are mulatto (a mixture of European, mainly Spaniards, and African). There may be a few mestizos (a mixture of Spanish and Indian), but that is unlikely given the fact that Taíno Indians did not survive the Spanish conquest. The combination of hard physical labor and new diseases decimated them within thirty years of the Spaniards' arrival.[12] When Columbus "discovered" the island in 1492 there were approximately 400,000 Taínos and by 1508 there were only 60,000 (Moya Pons *Manual de historia* 26).

The truth is that Dominican ethnic identity is shaped by a melange of cultures and races. Just in the past 150 years there has been an active influx of hybrid Cuban, Puerto Rican, German, Italian, Sephardic Jewish, and Arabic immigrants. Cubans and Puerto Ricans contributed to education; Germans traded tobacco; Italians established commerce; Sephardic Jews were involved in financial and commercial activities; and Arabs (Syrians, Lebanese, and Palestinians) contributed to the retail trade (del Castillo and Murphy 55). Chinese immigrants began to set up laundries, restaurants, and cafes in the early 1900s. Most recently, Chinese from Taiwan and Hong Kong have established supermarkets, motels, luxury hotels, and manufacturing enterprises. In fact, second to Haitians, Chinese are the largest growing immigrant group on the island (del Castillo and Murphy 56).

---

[12] Bartolome de las Casas, whose famous debates on the enslavement of indigenous peoples in the Americas is now so often quoted, attempted to stop the demise of the Taíno. He was based in the Dominican Republic and is known there and elsewhere as the "Protector of the Indians." Problematically, no one seems to point out (perhaps because of his skin color) that he owned indigenous slaves himself and that his solution to the Taínos' problem was to import Africans.

But it is Africa that is most prominently woven into the Dominican Republic, the "land," Torres-Saillant claims, "that originated blackness in the Americas" ("Dominican Racial Identity" 140). Blacks from various English, French, and Danish colonies, Africa, and Haiti have been a constant presence since Columbus arrived on the island. Mass mulattoization, though, did not start until the end of the eighteenth century. The discovery (in 1519) of the riches of Mexico and Peru diminished interest in Hispaniola (as the entire island was called then). By 1540 economic decline was widespread, and by 1605 most of the sugar plantations were abandoned. Therefore, there was no need to import slaves. The island became so insignificant that the Spaniards ceded the western third to France in the 1697 Treaty of Ryswick. Subsequently, the French saw the potential for growing coffee, and they began mass importation of African slaves. The boom lasted from 1740 to about 1790, when slave trade reached its highest level. During that time the Spanish, French, Portuguese, and German colonist population in the eastern two-thirds of the island (what eventually became the Dominican Republic) grew from 6,000 to almost 150,000. Since there were virtually no white women, "the plantation owners were obliged to use the most attractive of the female slaves in order to fulfill their natural impulses"; as a result, between 1780 and 1789, for example, the mulatto population increased from 12,000 to 28,000 (Moya Pons *Manual de historia* 164, my translation).

Today 90 percent of the almost eight million population on the island is mulatto. But, as the research of Torres-Saillant affirms, the society continues to enact "aberrant negrophobia" and "antiblack" attitudes that have been promoted in the media, school textbooks, and the speeches of politicians from the beginning of colonialism. Dominican historian Frank Moya Pons notes that during the end of the eighteenth century "Dominicans perceived themselves as a very special breed of tropicalized Spaniards with dark skin, but nevertheless culturally white, Hispanic, and Catholic" ("Dominican National Identity" 14). Torres-Saillant writes that in the nineteenth century "social position" and economic power began to "supersede skin color in the articulation of identity for people of African descent"; Blacks and mulattos who managed to rise in the social strata became "the equivalent of former *blancos*," thus further eliding their blackness ("Dominican Racial Identity" 134). That is when Dominican intellectuals (who had been overwhelmingly educated in Europe, where antipathy toward nonwhites was thriving) and the masses began to call themselves "blanco de la tierra" in order to affirm a difference from slaves. Today, blackness means Haitianness to Dominicans, and logically so, since a violently intimate history binds the two countries.

When the French took over Hispaniola, they imported thousands of African slaves to the western third of the island. Haiti was established in 1803-4 when slaves ousted the French and set up the first black republic and the second independent nation in the Americas. Haitians invaded and controlled the D.R. from 1822 to 1844. That subjugation left a residual fear of Haitians that exists to this day, one that has been ruthlessly exploited by politicians in the form of racism. For example, in the twentieth century Trujillo welcomed immigrants from European countries (among them, Jewish refugees and many Spaniards fleeing their civil war), but slaughtered between 18,000 and 30,000 (or more, the figure is not certain) Haitians (Moya Pons *Manual de historia* 519; del Castillo and Murphy 58). The genocide was carried out with machetes, bayonets, and rifles: "the bodies bloated the river Dajabón; blood and mutilated human body parts layered the border separating the two countries and the Cibao" (Gimbernard 474, my translation).[13]

Trujillo justified the massacre as necessary to "deafricanizing the country and restoring Catholic Values" (Knight 225). He went on to spend "vast public resources" in order to promote "an image of national identity that stressed the Hispanic European roots" (Torres-Saillant "Dominican Racial Identity"134). The Dominican

---

[13] The horrors experienced that night by Haitians who crossed the border in search of a better life is the focus of Edwidge Danticat's 1998 novel entitled *The Farming of Bones* (New York: Soho Press, Inc.). The novel traces the stories of Amabelle, a Haitian woman orphaned at age eight who emigrates to the D.R., where she works as a maid to the young wife of a Dominican army colonel, and of her lover, Sebastien, a field hand and itinerant sugarcane cutter.

people accepted such attitudes, Moya Pons writes, because they had

> consistently believed that they were white and Catholic, and that their blood was mostly Spanish, with little Indian, and very little black content. After more than a century of confrontations with Haiti, Dominicans had always wanted to rid themselves of their black origins, and had come to believe that Trujillo had actually saved them from the "Haitian danger" when he ordered the massacre in 1937." ("Dominican National Identity" 22)

Similarly, Joaquín Balaguer (Trujillo's former vice president who went on to rule the country during a rarely interrupted presidency of seven terms) fought against Haitian migration on the basis that it would "darken" the society. In 1960, census takers were ordered to record the majority of Dominicans as white, which was not too difficult, since most Dominicans, no matter what shade of color, think that only Haitians are black. Shortly after, with the massive waves of migration to the United States, where racial relations was a "civil rights movement," some Dominicans began to question their racial identity. As Moya Pons writes:

> In New York and other American cities, Dominicans discovered what many Puerto Ricans had discovered years before, that is, that it did not matter what they believed they were: objectively speaking they were African descendants, and their race did not differ very much from that of Haitians or from African Americans. . . . Many returned to Santo Domingo and their hometowns transformed both outwardly and inwardly in their thoughts, their clothes, their feelings, their language, and their music. ("Dominican National Identity" 23).

Nonetheless, antiblack sentiment continues to exist in the D.R. As late as the 1980s, President Balaguer wrote and published a book that "overtly proclaimed the inferiority of blacks and urged Dominicans to strengthen their Spanish background," and later in 1996 conservative politicians used negrophobic discourse to help defeat black presidential contender José Francisco Peña Gómez (Torres-Saillant, "Dominican Racial Identity" 143). That attitude is founded in the colonial eliding of the African influence, and the looking to the "Madre Patria," Spain, for our roots. Today the racial taxonomy of colonial times persists in a scarcely changed permutation. In colonial times the Dominican Republic paralleled the "casta" system which originated in colonial Mexico, where there was an obvious attempt to rank the various people born out of interracial and interethnic sexual contact.[14]

The emphasis then was on ancestry; today the emphasis is both on ancestry and phenotypes—physical appearance: for example, the color of skin and eyes, hair texture, shape and size of the nose and lips. Blackness is still denigrated; the two most popular sayings on the island are "y tu abuela donde esta?" (where is your grandmother?) and "tenemos el negro tras de la oreja" (we are black behind the ears). Both are used to remind dark-skinned people that they are only pretending to be white.

Clearly, Dominican history and policies have perpetuated the denial of Africans' influence in our culture. For instance, historically Enriquillo has been a cultural icon for Dominicans, but Lemba has not. Enriquillo was a Taíno cacique in the early sixteenth century who converted to Christianity. He aligned himself with encomiendados and slaveholders who tracked and returned indigenous and African cimarrones (runaway slaves), until his wife was brutally raped by a Spaniard who was not even chastised. Consequently, Enriquillo joined forces against the Spaniards with the same people he had persecuted. But then he was captured and burned at the stake. Dominicans have mythologized his story: a novel by Manuel de Jesús Galván[15] is included in the curriculum; myriad places carry the name Enriquillo. In contrast, Lemba, a six-

---

[14] Categories in the D.R. included: blanco (white European), negro (black African), mulato (mulatto, the child of one white and one black parent), mestizo (the child of one white European and one indigenous parent), terceron (the child of a mulatto and a white person with one-fourth African ancestry), cuarteron (quadroon, the child of a mulatto and a white with one-eighth African ancestry).

[15] Galván was born in Santo Domingo on Jananry 13, 1834; he died in San Juan, Puerto Rico, on December 13, 1910. He was a noted novelist, journalist, diplomat and attorney. *Enriquillo* was published in 1879.

teenth century cimarron, never helped the Spaniards; he waged war against them for twenty years until he too was captured and burned at the stake. It is not simply an assumption to suggest that little is known about Lemba because he was a cimarron.

Today, although there are a myriad of shades representing "an extensive and rich process of contributions and cultural assimilations drawn from an extremely varied gamut of ethnic groups," Dominicans continue to systematically deny our "condition as mulatto" (del Castillo and Murphy 61). As Clarisa and other participants in this study found out, that denial is further problematized when, in the States, we are labeled "black," "other," "people of color," "spics," and endless other terms. Ramón, for example, is labeled "black" in the States, which he resists, because it's usually used, he feels, to designate him as innately deficient, "minority," "pariah." He had always seen himself as an "indio," which seemed perfectly right, he reasoned, since, after all, his skin color is not truly black, but rather a bronzed brown. In the States he could not call himself Indio, because it is not an American category. As Moya Pons explains, by using that word

> Dominicans do not mean that they are direct descendants of the aboriginal tribes . . . but that they have a distinct color which is not black nor white, but which resembles that of the Indians. By calling themselves *indios*, Dominicans have been able to provisionally resolve the profound drama that filled most of their history: that of being a colored nation ruled by a quasi-white elite that did not want to accept the reality of its color and the history of its race. ("Dominican National Identity 20)

Like Ramón, many of us used graduate studies as a vehicle, perhaps a reason, to unpack our ethnic identity, to understand, for instance, the history that aligned the word "indio" with Taínos' patriotic resistance and death, and the history that points directly to Trujillo as the mastermind of our contemporary use of the label. Torres-Saillant clarifies that history:

> Ethnically, the Indians represented a category typified by nonwhiteness as well as nonblackness, which could easily accommo-

date the racial in-betweenness of the Dominican mulatto. Thus, the [Trujillo] regime gave currency to the term *indio* (Indian) to describe the complexion of people of mixed ancestry. The term assumed official status in that the national identification card gave it as a skin-color designation for the three decades of the dictatorship and beyond. While, in the minds of most Dominicans who use it, the term merely describes a color gradation somewhere between the polar extremes of whiteness and blackness much in the same way that the term *mulatto* does, the cultural commissars of the Trujillo regime preferred it primarily because it was devoid of any semantic allusion to the African heritage and would therefore accord with their negrophobic definition of Dominicanness. ("Dominican Racial Identity" 139)

Ramón, Clarisa, and most of us were also motivated to pursue graduate education in order to disprove the denigrating messages encased in the various labels assigned (on the island and in the United States) to our ethnic identity. In turn, we used that education as an occasion to unpack our ethnic identity. However enriching, part of that journey was emotionally perplexing. It made us feel defensive, disconnected, isolated, rejected, and extremely fatigued.

School is where we felt most inadequate, hence being validated there mattered most. For me, getting "highest honor" in my college English program, being awarded several scholarships to earn the master's degree, and then being accepted into a doctoral program that also provided a teaching fellowship was validating (and helpful beyond the financial aid). That authentication confirmed, in my mind, that I had overcome a great obstacle, a huge deficiency that had been plopped on my lap in the process of becoming an American. However, it still did not take away the sense of inadequacy I continue to carry at some deep level.[16]

---

[16] Marina, for example, is now a successfully tenured educator, but she is still haunted by the ongoing chaos inherent in being conscious of her ethnic identity:

A while ago I realized that I've been working against lots of things, and that I have to compensate for lots of things. We think that Anglos don't care. Our brothers and sisters from bigger [Latin American] countries don't care either. In the Latin American con-

Conversely, getting that affirmation also heightened my need to prove that I am capable and that I do own my place in academe. The day I received my Ph.D. diploma I wanted to show it to everyone I'd ever met, including that professor who in my first semester in graduate school singled me out as the spokesperson for impoverished Latinos in the Bronx. Look, I did it! I did it. But I also wanted to hide that diploma, to tuck it away where no would ever know that I'd become highly literate in my second language and cultural home. I feared that people would know the truth, that I fooled them, tricked them into "giving" me (not that I earned it) accreditation. Had I been given that diploma because I was the only and first Latina in the program? Did the department give it to me so *they* wouldn't look like failures? So they could show how supportive of diversity and minorities they are? So I could be placed in some administrator's statistics? Was I, an immigrant who grew up in the Bronx, really worthy of the title "Doctor?" Had I truly mastered American discourse, the "standard" that determines doctorate material? How could I ever live up to such a huge responsibility? How could I get a job without the "Latina Ph.D." vestige? Would my Anglo students respect me? Would I have anything really to teach any students? After all, that first semester in graduate school, when I was also teaching college composition to international students, one Chinese fellow reminded me, right after our first session, that he was dropping my course, because, he said apologetically, he wanted to learn "correct English from a *real* American." How real of an American professor of English literacy and literature could I be? How real was my diploma? However irrational all of those issues may actually be, like other participants, I endured that sort of emotional turmoil. Versions lingered as I worked toward getting tenure.

---

text the Dominican Republic is a very small unimportant country. We don't have powerful intellects to compete with countries like Argentina and Chile and Mexico. My field is male dominated by older men from bigger countries. So I always have to compensate for being an immigrant, woman, being short, being younger, and being from an unimportant country—you name it.

Needing validation, yet another symptom of the emotional turmoil that both helped and hindered us in becoming highly literate,
was a major concern for many of us in this study. Carla was very
blunt about it: "My older sister and I became academic achievers.
That's how we tried to get validation. That's how we made ourselves welcomed in this country that was otherwise not very wel-
coming." For many of us (especially those of us who grew up in
lower socioeconomic conditions), becoming highly literate was the
most clearly sanctioned way of distinguishing ourselves, creating
an approved identity, and feeling valued. For María and myself,
doing well in school from early on, being validated in the public
sphere, in whatever small way, allowed us to feel a "tiny hope, and
a slight possibility" that we could "actually pull it off," that we
could indeed walk away from the university with a piece of paper
that renamed us "doctor" and thus endowed us with a new sense of
self.

María thrived on being "considered smart," partly because she
did not think of herself as being truly intelligent. "So," she explained to me, "when other graduate students used to come to me
and say, 'give me help with this, I don't understand it,' I would do
it. It felt good. It felt like Americans believed I was capable of doing something important." Deep inside, though, she realizes in retrospect, María preferred to believe that she simply "worked hard to
excel," not that her peers sought her help because she is intellectually competent. When a teacher or anyone she respected commented on her intellectual ability she felt validated, and therefore
motivated, but also pressured to "do an even better job" so as not
to disappoint anyone. The ante rose with each confirmation. The
resulting anxiety often "robbed" her of quiet time and internal
peace. It did not allow her "to feel at home" in or out of school.

For most of us, that constant yearning for validation was paired
with a lingering fear that we would be ousted from the university,
that we would be "discovered as impostors who snuck in," Haydee
said. That attitude was clearly more prevalent in those of us who
grew up in lower socioeconomic conditions. We seemed to have
experienced our academic training as a covert activity, as if we
were conducting business behind most "people's backs." There

was always the relentless apprehension that the rest of Americans would find out that we were in academe, a place that was not meant for us. If they found us out, surely they'd kick us out. We felt like tricksters and thus any tidbit of validation fed us, but it also intensified our hunger for everyone else's approval and it compounded out emotional turmoil.

Temporary Closure

In the preceding pages, I have tried, in Freirean terms, to read the words and worlds, as they relate to becoming highly literate, of Dominican American academics teaching the humanities and social sciences in colleges and universities throughout the United States. I have focused particularly on the aspects we recurrently identified as the salient issues and motivators that impacted our wanting to pursue a doctorate. In identifying and naming those issues I have also mapped a significant part of our Dominican cultural heritage. But it is not enough to tell our stories, or to reaffirm that like each of us, those stories are shaped and negotiated by society/ies, and therefore they provide a significant window from which to view larger dominant and institutional ideologies. It is also crucial that I move the consideration of our experiences (beyond naming and telling) toward a critical understanding of the uniqueness of our condition.

There are a multitude of junctions and terrains in our internal geography, as well as unique peaks that mark our specific journey toward high literacy. Certainly, having important questions and pursuing meaning—enacting epistemic curiosity—in an existential sense is a major inclination transculturally, but for us in this study that quest is charged with ethnic melancholia, deep loss, shame, isolation, and feelings of deficiency and inadequacy. Like many other immigrants and minorities, we did not feel welcome in the United States. We did not feel at home. Our distinct cultural baggage exacerbated those experiences, including thinking that our Dominican Republic is an insignificantly small and politically powerless island as compared to the United States where (most of our parents believed) anyone can find treasures in the streets; and inheriting the mental effects of a thirty-year dictatorship and of the new (pseudo) democracy.

Whether or not we articulated those sentiments, our reality as immigrants signaled to us that we had to leave our homes in the D.R. because the U.S. was a much better place. Messages from our parents, family, and American people all around us declared that we needed to be grateful, a state of mind that Trujillo's tyranny had already taught us. Dictatorship trained our parents, who in turn prepared us, to feel beholden, to be silent and servile, to endure and resign ourselves to oppression. Likewise, his despotism also taught our parents and us to survive, to find subversive power, to resist unobtrusively, and to work very very hard.

It seemed obvious to us—no one had to remind us—that our parents left their beloved island in order to save us, in order to provide us with the political and economic prosperity that seemed impossible there. And economic wealth, our Dominican ethos had ingrained in us, could be gained through formal education, that very elusive privilege of the elites. We understood that our parents' task was to deliver us to the land of opportunity, but that ours was to acquire the rewards. And so, even if our language, culture, and general ways of being were not validated collectively or individually by mainstream society in the United States, even if we lived in emotional turmoil, we persisted in order to prove to our parents and everyone else in the States and in the Dominican Republic that we could endure, that we were not "cascaras the cocos," (common coconut husks that litter every nook and cranny of the Caribbean), and that, as my version of the American saying goes, we could make delicious lemonade out of rotten lemons.

Our stories reveal that we were strongly motivated to pursue high literacy and the professorate by the real need to make meaning out of chaos and by our intrinsic desire to belong. That suggests that our motivation was also rooted in enduring and in accepting challenges, in refusing to let institutions obliterate our individual hopes and needs for survival beyond living substandarly (economically or intellectually). It also implies that we chose to travel the high literacy road and to reach our ultimate professional destination, academe, because we believed it to be the socially sanctioned place in the United States where we could be quietly defiant, where we could find a measure of approval despite our histories, and where we could clandestinely re-create ourselves from inside out. Pursuing high literacy and the professorate may have given us the place (and occasion) for us to unpack our evolving understanding of both cultures; it may have functioned as the protective cloak we needed to survive as Dominicans and Americans.

Our stories affirm that acquiring high literacy is a process of discovering meanings and thus a process of shaping consciousness. Surely, as we illustrate, the mental processes by which knowledge is acquired, and the manners by which we integrate information and ways of being, correlate with the degree of exposure to the environmental ingredients that foster some skills over others. In other words, maybe all of us in this study were born with the cognitive skills to accomplish a high level of formal education, but without environmental triggers in the Dominican Republic and the United States, more than likely those skills would have remained dormant. That is not an earth-shattering revelation, but it is a reminder to all of us involved in literacy training that however difficult the task, if we are to succeed, we must recognize subjectivities and cultural uniqueness. We cannot think of providing any level of literacy as a blanket project.

Antonio and Teresita Ferreyra, people who had the courage to leave everything and everyone that was familiar, to work at dead-end jobs for too many hours a day, for too many years . . . precisely because they wanted their three children to have a solid formal education.

Antonio and Teresita Ferreyra at home in the Bronx, their three children's high school diplomas displayed prominently.

3

Parents

My mother died in 1991. Shortly after, I began to sort through my parents' apartment so I could move my father to my home (far away from the Bronx) where I was completing the doctorate. When I approached the bookshelf, its dark oak tones revealed as veneers in the early morning sunshine, I froze. All those books! Books I had collected from the moment we stepped off the Pan Am plane at Kennedy Airport. So many books—so many tangible things my parents gave me before and after leaving the Dominican Republic in the 1960s, things that undoubtedly helped me become highly literate.

On my fifteenth birthday, unable to provide a proper quince-añera party to mark my impending adulthood, as they would have done in the Dominican Republic, my parents opted for a trip to the local furniture store. I walked pensively around the narrow aisles, touching fabrics, smelling woods, sitting on various chairs in order to determine the level of comfort. They waited with the salesman who had taken the credit application. Finally, I decided on a queen-size sofa bed, a high-back tufted reading chair like the ones I had seen in illustrated versions of Jane Austen's novels, and the prize of my American birthday party, a shelf unit that would accommodate all of my books, records, pictures, journals, and painting materials. I pictured how it would cover one wall of our living room, how I would place the chair next to it, and a reading lamp conveniently behind it. The day our new furniture was delivered my parents left the textile factory early. They arrived at the same time a book salesman was about to knock on our door. I cannot remember his name, but I can see his white hair, furrowed face, clouded blue eyes, muscles stretched long to clasp bursting leather cases, the weight slightly doubling him as if he were a palm tree in a storm. I can see the numbers on his arm. I hear the silence when I told him that our neighbor had numbers too, and that she would not tell me about them. Slowly, pulling out his samples, he asked me to translate for my parents. "Se puede pagar mensualmente," I said, "very low monthly payments." Yes! My parents said they would buy the encyclopedia. It would be the last of my quinceañera presents.

The twenty-eight volume *World Book Encyclopedia*, plus a two-volume dictionary and an atlas, were delivered some weeks later. I waited until late that night for my father. Sure, he said, he would help me put my books and things into place. Maybe then even he could "absorb"(as if by osmosis) all the knowledge about America that they contained. It was up to me, he emphasized, to "eat" that information—me who could write and actually enjoyed reading. Years later in 1991, as I caressed the gold trims of each volume, as I dusted them for the last time before giving them to our church, I realized that it had been a tremendous financial burden to purchase that encyclopedia, but an investment, my parents believed—an investment worth as much as paying my Catholic school tuition.

Years after that, when I sat with Sandra recording our interview, she began to tell me about some ways her parents influenced her journey toward high literacy:

> What my mother did was really incredible. Back then there were a lot of door-to-door salespeople, and one day a salesman came selling the *World Book Encyclopedia*. My mother decided it would be good for us, that it would help us learn English. And this set of encyclopedia was put in a very important place in the middle of the living room. It is funny. I remember spending hours and hours just going through those books, just reading. It could also have been boredom, because I was not allowed to go out and play. My brothers were out running all

the time. They were allowed to come and go any way they wanted. But as a girl I could not. During the summer I was upstairs the whole time. After school I had to be home, so reading that encyclopedia was to me the only entertainment.

Me too! I said to Sandra. Me too. It wasn't just that I loved to read and learn; it was also that because I'm female my parents did not allow me to amuse myself if unsupervised. I could not leave our apartment to go play in the neighborhood. Thus, reading and writing at home became my major sources of recreation. I was intent on reading every page in each of those volumes. In fact, I finished all of "A" in one summer. But, I asked Sandra, what does our parents' behavior and their beliefs (and enactments) reveal about our journey toward high literacy and the professorate? What does their behavior disclose about our external landscape, the milieu in which we lived and the people who affected our literate development? How does considering the impact our parents had on us help us understand the construction of our ethnic and cultural identity, and perhaps more importantly, that construction's relationship to high literacy?

In this chapter my aim is to map those circumstances, those actions we (the participants in this study) recognized, in retrospect, as consequential. My aim is also to show how those factors relate directly to us becoming highly literate. Such mapping, drawn from both the etic (insider) and emic (outsider) perspectives, will help to clarify some of the ways we construct and perform our ethnic identities and how they intersect with issues of being/becoming highly literate. Our parents' influences on our literate growth are a distinctly recurrent theme easily identifiable in the fifteen hundred pages of our transcribed interviews. Those transcripts show that there are two salient themes regarding how our parents impacted us:

1) They ingrained us with the belief that acquiring a high level of formal education would provide us with a socially sanctioned identity and a sure way to make a living; their everyday enactments of those beliefs motivated us to pursue high literacy.
2) Their continual ability to engage in meaningful conversations about Dominican history (especially as it is intertwined with that of the history of the United States) helped us to become curious about

our cultural heritage, and thus to "ask important questions" we pursued as academic endeavors; what we learned during those conversations also provided us with a cultural marker, a lens through which we see our fissured identities.

Ingrained Beliefs

Despite their socioeconomic statuses, our parents (even Sandra's, who were not supportive of her wanting to attend university) contributed innumerably in material and other ways. But, most of us agree, their crucial influence in our acquisition (and enactments) of high literacy is rooted in how they revealed to us their attitudes toward formal education. Most of us explain that our parents' impact on our literate journey is complex and multilayered. There is no way for us to truly determine if their behavior and motivations were the same as we understand them to be as we reconstruct memories at this stage in our lives. Nonetheless, what truly matters, most of us agree, is how we perceived (then and now) their behavior, and that in reconstructing the events *we* come to deeper revelations about their roles in our development. For instance, when I asked Sandra to explain why it was critical when our parents bought encyclopedias for us, she responded:

> Well, now that I think about it, I realize that our parents' interest, investment, and financial sacrifice, the *World Book Encyclopedia*, reading and writing, all of that was significant because it opened the door to the world of America, a world that our parents and we revered. My parents had a sense that America was *great* and that Americans knew all this wonderful stuff that they did not know. They believed that and passed it on to us. Having *World Books* that told you everything about America was exciting. The key to American knowledge and to other things most people did not know was sitting right there in the living room, and you didn't have to ask permission from anybody to visit it. Whether or not they were aware of all those ideas is not so important; it is crucial that they bought the books for us.

I reminded Sandra that it seemed contradictory for her parents to spend so much money on an encyclopedia when later they did not support her attending college and graduate school. "Well," Sandra clarified:

> Both my parents wanted me to get a high school diploma. They were practical and wanted me to find a job and make money. Buying that encyclopedia was a pragmatic investment: my mother wanted us to be able to find information about our adopted country, to learn English and therefore to find a good job. That's all. It's hard to explain. In *Talking Back* bell hooks writes about how African Americans experience similar situations.

Sandra's comments explained the ambivalence of her parents, the frustration they must have felt.[1] My own father had similar reactions. He explained that he and my mother had seen my hunger for knowledge, and they wanted to feed me. They wanted me to learn everything I could about the United States, so that I could prosper and fit in. After that conversation I realized that my parents had recognized my love of learning early in my childhood. Each went about nurturing that love in their own ways. My father frequently purchased books for

---

[1] Sandra went on to mention how African Americans experience similar situations. She had been reading bell hooks' *Talking Back.* Later I looked up the passage where hooks describes leaving her small town in Kentucky for Stanford University:

> My parents had not been delighted that I had been accepted and adamantly opposed my going so far from home. At that time, I did not see their opposition as an expression of their fear that they would lose me forever. Like many working-class folks, they feared what college education might do to their children's minds even as they unenthusiastically acknowledge its importance. They did not understand why I could not attend a college nearby, an all-black college. To them, any college would do. I would graduate, become a schoolteacher, make a decent living and a good marriage. And even though they reluctantly and skeptically supported my educational endeavors, they also subjected them to constant harsh and bitter critique. It is difficult for me to talk about my parents and their impact on me because they have always felt wary, ambivalent, mistrusting of my intellectual aspirations even as they have been caring and supportive. (75)

me, even though he was not a reader. My mother made sure that I had a space of my own, and silence, where I could read or listen to music, even though she rarely had either for herself. Both ensured that I received my monthly allowance, despite our dire economic condition, because they knew I would use it to buy books, records, canvases, and painting materials. Later in my adolescence, they also recognized that it was essential for me to consume information about the United States (that is one reason they bought the *World Book Encyclopedia*). Reading those volumes was one of the strategies I used to survive and to feel less estranged.

Similarly, during our third interview Haydee told me stories about how her father often explained to her that he had struggled through school precisely because he did not want to repeat his parents' "problems" (not having a profession and thus "a dependable and honest way to make a living"). He could not perpetuate his family's poverty, being an only child and knowing he would have to support his future wife, children, and his parents, especially in their old age. They were going to rely on him, and, he figured, if he were to succeed he would have to get an education. That was a present theme in all family conversations when Haydee was growing up. That's how he taught Haydee and her siblings "responsibility," and how he "transferred," she claims, his "compulsion" to them. Haydee told me that her father's certitude inspired her to pursue the maximum amount of formal education, a doctorate, available:

> My father is at the very basis of my success. He was *the* one. He was the main figure pushing all of us to go to school and to become educated and to learn other languages and read and know about other cultures. His parents did not go to school, as you can imagine. He was very much aware of their economic problems and he didn't want his children to go through that.

Likewise, Clarisa's father believed firmly in the enabling power of literacy, and he too transferred his "passion" to his daughter: "He didn't want to die and leave us without resources. This was a priority in his life—to give us an education. He figured that if he left us money we could lose it, but if he left us an education there was no way we could lose our education. I guess my father taught me that if I went to school I would have a better life." In like manner, Antonio and Homero's fathers urged them to do well in school even before they started to attend first grade.

Both my parents also encouraged me to conquer formal education way before I set foot in a school. One source of motivation was a story my loquacious mother told about my taciturn father. He began to teach himself the alphabet at around age nine, when he was forced to leave my grandfather's farm and move to Santo Domingo, where he began to work as an errand boy for wealthy medical students at Universidad Autónoma. All of the families of students he served were rich, held prestigious social positions, and had completed high levels of formal education. It seemed to him, then, that attaining a high level of literacy would produce power, money, status, and prominence. Consequently, he venerates formal education, although he never attended school.[2] To this day it does not occur to my father that the students he served could attend university because they were wealthy, not the other way around. No matter, he and my mother (whose family was very literate and considered intellectual) taught me to virtually worship school and learning.

From early in my childhood both my parents accepted whatever jobs were available so they could pay my tuition at private schools. Each invariably demanded that I bring home excellent grades, and each consistently provided any money I requested for anything that had to do with school. They reminded me, most times without utter-

---

[2] Again, historically only the elite in Dominican society had ready access to formal education. In fact, every level of education for the masses of people on the island had been ignored until 1908, when President Cáceres designated "funds for the creation of schools," thereby increasing the number of primary schools from 200 in 1904 to 526 in 1910 (Moya Pons, *Manual de historia* 451, my translation). Higher education did not become a governmental priority until the 1960s, when (between 1966 and 1978) there was tremendous change. By 1978 Universidad Autónoma had three branches, and eight other officially approved private institutions were created. By 1983 private universities housed 50 percent of the total student enrollment (Escala 1, 45). In 1985 the country's population was 6.24 million; 123,748 of them were enrolled in universities: 30,892 in business and 17,139 in the humanities (UNESCO 1-41).

ing a word, of school's importance every day as they left for the factory, at night when they returned home exhausted, on the first of the month when the first thing paid was my school tuition, and the second was my allowance. He and my mother reminded me repeatedly that they emigrated primarily for our sake, my two siblings and I, so we did not have to work as errand boys (the way my father had), so that we could have "better food, a proper education," and therefore "decent" moneymaking professions, assets, and power. When graduate school seemed daunting, sometimes I would hear a loud inner voice reminding me that I could not disappoint my parents, that I could not dishonor their struggle by giving up.

Marina also explained that her family is not wealthy but that her parents reminded her systematically that they were able to live comfortably and to acquire material possessions because they went to college and became professionals. "They were right," she explained to me, because "access to any level of literacy on the island has always been linked to socioeconomic standing. And, symbiotically, access to an improved economic condition has also been linked to the attainment of literacy, especially after the death of Trujillo." She continued to clarify, and subsequently I researched that historically there have been only two clearly marked socioeconomic strata. At the highest level are the elites (an average five percent of the population), those who have enjoyed the major share of wealth, power, and the privilege to travel and attend world-renowned universities. They have tended to be white and of European ancestry comprised of several groups: older gentry, a business class that emerged around the turn of the century, landowners, bankers, professionals, and owners of light industries and tourist businesses, and those who gained great wealth by being part of Trujillo's regime.

The bottom stratum accounts for the overwhelming portion of the population. They tend to be darker skinned, have low-prestige jobs, or no employment at all, and of course very limited access to formal education (Leavitt 10). But there is a new, third, post-Trujillo stratum that has increased with improved access to literacy and (more complicatedly) with immigration (Pessar "Social Relations" 212). That increasing portion of the population, represented by Clarisa and María's families, have generally moved to the middle class by securing white-collar jobs. Once they have those jobs they go on to buy land and to participate in business ventures often funded by "income sent back home from various diasporic locations, predominantly the States" (Leavitt 11).

To the lower class, especially, tangible proof of academic (and any other) success (diplomas, awards, medals) has always been important. It is what was ingrained in the parents of participants in this study, and thus what they taught us. Homero explained to me, and subsequently I researched, that our parents placed such emphasis on us getting diplomas partly because that is what they learned from the dictator, the man who molded the core of their cultural sensibilities. Trujillo was known for weighing his jacket with all sorts of evidence that he was a great leader. In addition to honors from foreign states, the Vatican, and everywhere else, Trujillo conferred many awards upon himself. The list includes: Order of Military Merit; Great Cross of Benefactor of the Country; Collar of the Cross of Valor; Heraldic Order of Cristóbal Colón; Order of Trujillo; Order of Merit of the Air Force; Order of Merit of the National Police; Great Collar of Peace. He also gave himself official titles such as Meritorious Son of San Cristóbal; Benefactor of the Fatherland; First and Greatest of Dominican Chiefs of State; Restorer of Financial Independence; Commander and Chief of the Armed Forces; Father of the New Fatherland; Loyal and Noble Champion of World Peace; Champion of World Peace; Chief Protector of Dominican Culture; Maximum Protector of the Dominican Working Class. Scholar Gare Joyce writes that Trujillo's "influence upon the Dominican agenda is still obvious three decades after his death" (162). Homero reiterated that it is logical that our parents would push us to win academic accolades.

Like most of our parents, Marina's mother and father believed (and had lived) the notion that acquiring high literacy would provide her with external and internal riches. Her father, the first in his family to attend university, is an attorney and professor. Her mother is a high school teacher. Both live "in between two islands: the Dominican Republic and Manhattan," and both taught Marina to value and use education as a vehicle for economic mobility and personal growth. Like Marina's mother and father, all of us in this study, to varying degrees, heard that message. Our parents exhorted the virtues of formal education. Sometimes they did so unintentionally, as Ramón's poignant story illustrates:

> My father wasted a lot of money on liquor, money he should have spent on his kids. He drank a lot. He also spoke a lot while he was drinking, and the subject of his conversation was usually his read-ings—just basically sharing his reading with the neighborhood. He was not really a model in the sense of guidance, but he was inspira-tional intellectually. He knew his Plato, his Aristotle, Shakespeare. He always talked about the Lake poets. When I went to school Aris-totle was a familiar name. And my mother too. She was of peasant extraction. My mother wanted to become an opera singer. I remem-ber hearing her produce melodies. So from infancy I really had a sense of things that were important, of the body of knowledge, the humanities as an area that was crucial, that was worth being familiar with and worth knowing and being proud of knowing.

Clarisa's father taught her "to do things with literacy that im-proved" her life. He read, sometimes to her, "every night, even if it was just the newspaper." And both of María's parents modeled liter-ate acts, what can be done with literacy, from the time she was a child.

> It was there just through their life, their action. You know, they val-ued reading and writing and I saw that. My mother used to write many letters back home, all the time, and I used to see her writing. I used to see my father always keeping records of everything. He had notebooks upon notebooks where he logged every penny he spent. He would describe it all. I used to watch him. But most of all it was his reading, reading aloud to us, that I think made such an impact on me.

An overwhelming majority of participants in this study said that of the two parents mothers modeled literate behavior most often, most intimately, and from early on, probably because children spent more time with them. Raising kids, their most meaningful obligation, in-cluded teaching basic reading and writing (usually in Spanish), even if they themselves were only functionally literate. Therefore, mothers made a more striking imprint on our literate development.

My own nascent love of words, language, art, music, and literate behavior was certainly instilled in early childhood by my mother when we still lived in the D.R. My memories are vivid. I can still feel early sunlit mornings in the garden, my mother bending, her long ebony hair draping my shoulder, her bronzed hand cupping mine as we traced letters. And colors. I see the cobalt ocean blues and flushed bougainvillea purples she taught me to capture in drawings. I hear suspenseful stories she whispered at bedtime, or requested I invent for her. Those were such pleasant peaceful moments in the midst of threatening bullets and frenzied planes buzzing over us! It seems logical that later I (like Marina, María, and Clarisa) would find fulfillment in literate behavior and would grow up yearning to learn.

Laura also learned to find joy in literacy, reading especially, which her mother taught her to do before her fifth birthday. All of her life Laura watched her mother read voraciously, chiefly the staples in the Dominican school curriculum such as *One Thousand and One Nights,* Hugo's *Les Miserables,* and Dumas' *El Conde de Monte Cristo.* Some mothers (for instance, Sandra's) who were only functionally literate read profusely illustrated popular romances (novellas), and comic-book-like versions of great works of literature. Other (middle-class) mothers owned books. Flor's mother had a "huge bookshelf full of novels and a large collection of Trujillo's writings" in their Santo Domingo home. She and her women friends often exchanged their collections. "Once," Flor said during our first interview, Flor "stole" Lawrence's *Lady Chatterley's Lover* from her mother's bookshelf and read it (in Spanish) without her parents' permission. Since then, "escaping" into the world of books has been "an enticing" experience for Flor.

Second to mothers, most female participants claimed, grandmothers encouraged us, showed us literate behavior and also made memorable impacts. They too were charged by custom, on the island and in the States, to teach us basic literacy, and hence were often the first to instill an affinity that lasted a lifetime. Flor's grandmother bought books for her, and when Flor emigrated she continued to send reading material along with lengthy letters filled with "beautiful calligraphy, beautiful ideas, metaphors, you know." Flor said that her grandmother gave her "what no one else did—not my children, not my husband, not my teachers, not my mom." And that is "the belief that literacy was important, nourishing," and that Flor "could complete whatever level of American formal education" she desired. Flor said to me:

> When I told my grandmother that I wanted to do a Ph.D. she said it was the least I could accomplish. And when I did research for my dissertation she ran all over the Dominican Republic to get me the books and mail them to me. She was in her eighties.

Participants in this study affirm that (even if unintentionally) from early in our childhood our parents ingrained us with the belief that formal education is desirable—the more the better—and a "sure way" to increase social and economic status. However mixed that message was sent, particularly to the women, however complex their enactments of that message, we accepted it as true. Hence, believing our parents' notions led us to value and seek high literacy, and to enter a profession that reifies all those precepts. We truly (if not naively, particularly at a young age) believed that formal education would empower us internally, externally, socially, economically, and most certainly in terms of creating a presence for us, an identity.

Engaging Conversations

A startling majority of participants said recurrently that yet another significant aspect of our parents' influence in our educational journey is the conversations they had. Marina told me that while growing up her family dinners were always "filled with animated conversation." "That was crucial," she reiterated, "my house is the center of discussion. My interest in politics and my own academic research comes from that. It's been essential to have an informed family" who modeled literate behavior and engaged in substantive conversations. Intentionally or not, most participants agree, our parents' conversations provided us with one vital lesson: a basic understanding of Dominican history, especially as it relates to the history of the United States. However fractured, however many gaps we had to fill in, conversing with our parents (and sometimes with other family and community members) gave us the course material that was missing in our American school curriculum.

Hearing and participating in our parents' conversations about Dominican history was particularly meaningful for those of us who had not attended schools on the island where the curriculum (though it favors Spanish history) furnishes the foundation of Dominican history and thus an affinity with things "Dominican," and an identity. Having some knowledge of that history functioned (when we were children and still now that we are adults) as a cultural marker that helped forge a substantial aspect of our ethnic identity. Their conversations engendered a fierce curiosity about our history. It pushed us to seek information in our schools. That need was heightened by the fact that although there were many courses on "Puerto Rican" and "Latin American" issues, there was no such thing as a "Dominican studies" undergraduate or graduate course in any of our schools.

Dilia explained to me in detail that she deliberately sought to learn about Dominican history when she was an undergraduate, mainly because conversations at home incited curiosity and gave her a general outline that she "longed to flesh out" in order to "fully understand" her "whole cultural identity." She also told me a bit about her parents' conversations and about how they helped to shape her notions about U.S.-D.R. relations. Dilia's parents had a ritual for every 27 of February, Independence Day in the Dominican Republic.[3] They made special meals and decorated the table with Dominican flags. Dilia is not sure where that tradition started, since she does not remember anyone on the island doing such things. She explained to me that her parents' behavior was probably "a reaction" to being confronted with the furor of July 4th in the States. No matter, Dilia said, her parents' "idiosyncrasies" served her well because she learned about the island's history—"for starters," that Dominicans celebrate independence from Haiti, not Spain ("something," she said, "to think about if

---

[3] February 27, 1844 is the official birth of the Dominican Republic as a sovereign nation. It is the moment when patriots Juan Pablo Duarte, Ramón Matias Mella, and Francisco del Rosario Sanchez led the fight and won freedom from Haiti, but independence has always been relative for the Dominican Republic, particularly when seen from the perspective of its relationship with the United States.

you put it in the context of Dominicans' hatred of Haitians").[4]

Homero described to me how conversations with his parents taught him the rudiments of Dominican history and "planted" in him a "desire to learn more." During our first interview he clarified that in those conversations he learned that the United States' direct involvement with the Dominican Republic did not start in 1844. It had begun at the end of the eighteenth century, when the Dominican Republic, then a colony of France (since 1795), was called Saint Domingue. That is when the United States first saw that eastern part of the island as commercially viable. Homero pointed me to the work of Dominican historian Frank Moya Pons, who writes that at the end of the eighteenth century the United States "opted to supply themselves with sugar, molasses, wood and hard liquor from the French colonies, especially from Saint Domingue" (*Manual de historia* 163, my translation). Dominican colonists were already frustrated with the fact that most of the profit went to French landowners, and thus there were rumblings of insurrection. The United States government, seeing how it could gain if Saint Domingue became independent, supported their rebellion.

In 1697 the island was divided between France (the western side) and Spain (the eastern side). The Spaniards began to explore Latin America and to ignore Hispaniola, so that by 1795 the French controlled the entire island. Slaves rebelled and the western side became an independent country, Haiti, in 1804. In 1805 Haiti invaded the eastern side, which fought and in 1809 became Saint Domingue. Spain ruled Saint Domingue once again between 1814 and 1822 when Haiti overran and ruled it until 1844.[5] Slavery was abolished

---

[4] Again, in the D.R. the middle and upper classes, especially, have historically identified with Spain. That is yet one more reason why Dominican historians "have portrayed the Haitian occupation—in which slaves were freed and Afro-Dominican culture thrived—as a brutal nightmare. Accordingly, Dominican nationalism developed in opposition not to Spain but to Haiti and is still animated by fear and denial of Afro-Caribbean culture. The *negritud* movement, so influential elsewhere in the Caribbean, had little impact in the Dominican Republic" (Manuel 98).

[5] Ethnomusicologist and historian of merengue music Paul Austerlitz makes an astute observation about the ideology underpinning self-identity/naming

and in 1822, Haitian leader Jean Pierre Boyer invited blacks in the United States to settle on the island. He offered free passage, land, temporary support, and full citizenship rights. The first boatload of African Americans arrived in Santo Domingo in 1824. By the end of 1825 there were 6,000. Some returned to the United States; some died of various illnesses; and many stayed in Samaná and Puerto Plata. English is still spoken in those communities (Torres-Saillant and Hernández 13).

Indeed, as I confirmed after discussing Dominican history with Homero, Dilia, Carmen, Clarisa, Laura, and María, the United States had yet another basis for intervening in Dominican affairs. In December 1823 President James Monroe issued a message to Congress ("a warning to Europe, really," Dilia said), known subsequently as the Monroe Doctrine. It was the first time the United States officially expressed interest in Latin America. President Monroe did not ask for or receive international ratification for that message. Nonetheless, he spoke as if the leaders of Latin American countries had given him authority to admonish European powers, specifically Portugal and Spain, not to try to reimpose rule over newly independent nations, like the Dominican Republic, in the Western Hemisphere. Any attempt would be considered an affront to the United States. Monroe wrote:

> We owe it, therefore, to candor and to the amicable relations existing between the United States and those powers to declare that we should consider any attempt on their part to extend their system to any portion of this hemisphere as dangerous to our peace and safety. With the existing colonies or dependencies of any European power we have not interfered and shall not interfere. But with the governments

---

in the early history of Haiti and the D.R.: "By choosing to name their country *Haiti*, said to derive from an indigenous word meaning 'mountainous land,' Haitians express an anticolonial posture. By contrast, the Dominican use of a European name (La Repúbica Dominicana, or The Dominican Republic) as their country's official designation and an indigenous name (Quisqueya) as a vernacular one reflects mixed feelings rooted in colonial experiences (*Merengue: Dominican* Music155). It is notable that Columbus named the island Hispaniola, 'Little Spain.'"

who have declared their independence and maintained it, and whose independence we have, on great consideration and on just principles, acknowledged, we could not view any interposition for the purpose of oppressing them, or controlling in any other manner their destiny, by any European power in any other light than as the manifestation of an unfriendly disposition toward the United States. (323)

The implicit threat to Europe was: "if you interfere with independent countries on this hemisphere, the United States will retaliate." That warning, Dilia said during our second interview (and scholarship confirms), has been used by the United States to "justify their involvement in Latin America, and essentially to violate the sovereignty of many Latin countries, among them the D.R." As Homero explained when we discussed his struggles with feeling like an outsider in the U.S., the Monroe Doctrine has sustained a very intimate relationship between the two countries, one that was initially intensified a year after the D.R. was born and its first leader, General Pedro Santana, desperately sought alliance with the United States.

In 1844 the Dominican Republic declared emancipation from Haiti, but in 1849 the country erupted into civil war. England, France, and the United States mediated and a president was elected. By then instability and the war had devastated the economy. Recognizing its commercial and naval value, particularly the Bay of Samaná, the United States government, with the help of President Santana, became more aggressive in its attempt to control the politics of the country. In 1845 President James Buchanan appointed an agent, John Hogan, to attend to business on the island. In 1847 Hogan's follower, Francis Harrison, suggested that the D.R. be annexed to the U.S. The succeeding U.S. president, Zachary Taylor, pursued the proposal and sent a commissioner, Benjamin E. Green, to advance the interests of the U.S. Green offered to "warn Haitians" against invading if the D.R. would give the Bay of Samaná to the U.S.[6]

---

[6] There was much manipulative activity in other Latin American countries at the time: in order to "protect" U.S. interests, the CIA helped to install several puppet governments in what became known as "banana republics." For example, in 1854 Nicaragua was invaded because someone insulted the American minister; in 1855 Uruguay was invaded because there was an at-

After President Taylor's death, President Millard Fillmore sent Robert Walsh to Santo Domingo, then in 1853 Secretary of State William Marcy. In 1855 President Franklin Pierce sent General William Cazneau with instructions to convince the Dominican president to cede the Samaná peninsula. In return the U.S. government promised political, military, and economic support. President Santana gave Cazneau a generous plot of land for white U.S. citizens to launch a colony.

Discussing Dominican history and its relationship to that of the United States with the participants in this study led me to recall my own parents' conversations about it. More importantly, I believe, those interviews prompted me to research and fill in the gaps in my own understanding, to know, for instance, that the D.R. lost its sovereignty to Spain in 1861, but recovered it after the War of Restoration in 1865. Even though European leaders objected, President Franklin Pierce continued to garner support for pursuing total control of Samaná by involving the American populace and assuring them that the D.R. had rich natural resources, that it was a new Eldorado, and that the U.S. had a right to it. The issue gained general attention. For example, in 1860 W. S. Courtney wrote in his book *The Gold Fields of Santo Domingo*:

> the fact has become palpable of recent years, that if the colossal resources of the Dominican part of the Island are ever fully developed, and rendered subservient to the interests of humanity as well as to the certain and abundant opulence of those who undertake it, it must be done by the Anglo-American. (quoted in Torres-Saillant and Hernández 18)

"Anglo-Americans think they have a right to our country just because they are Anglo; that's the history," Laura said emphatically when we talked about significant conversations she had at home while growing up: "I remember that my parents talked about it all the time. I think the U.S. has always held the power. The D.R. has been their backyard. Just look at what our revered President Lincoln did."

---

tempted revolution in Montevideo.

Laura and I talked about 1861 when President Abraham Lincoln formed the American West India Company in New York. Its aim was to stimulate migration—specifically of blacks—to the Dominican Republic.[7] The prospectus declared that the United States held ownership of extensive lands near the Ozama river, a fertile area deemed favorable "for the introduction of a large number of agricultural homeless laborers from the U.S. for whom the U.S. government feels a responsible interest and who would find there a most desirable home" (quoted in Torres-Saillant and Hernández 18).

In 1866 Secretary of State William H. Seward was sent to the D.R. to arrange a commercial treaty for Samaná. In May 1868 President Báez agreed to sell the Samaná peninsula to the U.S. and then went as far as to recommend once again that the entire country be annexed. But under the leadership of General Gregorio Luperón, the Dominican people objected and carried on an armed resistance. American warships intervened in support of President Báez.

President Ulysses S. Grant also wanted to control the D.R. In 1871 he addressed the U.S. Congress: "the acquisition of Santo Domingo will furnish our citizens with the necessaries of every day life at cheaper rates than before; indeed, it is confirmed by the report that the interest of our country and of Santo Domingo alike invite the annexation of that Republic" (quoted in Torres-Saillant and Hernández 21, 22). Faced with economic and political instability and the threat of an invasion by Haiti, the Dominican government again agreed to ask for annexation. But President Grant could not get enough legislative backing: the U.S. Congress refused predominantly on the grounds that Dominicans were too different culturally and linguisti-

---

[7] Reading Macedo's *Literacies of Power* (70) reminded me that Abraham Lincoln's often-quoted phrase "government of the people, by the people, and for the people" was not meant for those African Americans he was trying to displace out of the United States. Lincoln also declared: "I will say, then, that I am not, nor ever have been in favor of bringing about in any way the social and political equality of white and black races. I as much as any other man am in favor of having the superior position assigned to the white race." (Macedo quoted from page 184 of Howard Zinn's *A People's History of the United States*. New York: Harper Perrennial, 1980.)

cally; but one senator, Charles Summer, fought against annexation because he believed it was an opportunistic, mercenary, and immoral act (Moya Pons, *The Dominican Republic*, 376). In 1891 the U.S. government again endeavored to negotiate control of Samaná. It finally succeeded in 1893 when the San Domingo Improvement Company was established and with it the beginning of direct U.S. financial, economic and political control of the country (Moya Pons, *The Dominican Republic* 420).

"Our countries have always been intimately linked, so theoretically I should not feel estranged in the United States. Look," Ramón tried to make me realize,

I feel isolated living in the U.S., but I have a right to be here. Historically the American government has worked to keep us at arm's length: close enough to control us but far enough not to accord us the respect we deserve. They have always meddled in Dominican politics and culture. And the sad thing is that the Dominican government has consented.

Indeed that is true. In 1904 the D.R. agreed to let the U.S. take over its debts and to assume the right to occupy the country if U.S. interests were threatened. That action reinforced the Monroe Doctrine and Theodore Roosevelt's belief that "it was the moral obligation of the U.S. to act as political tutor to Caribbean countries in order to teach them to govern themselves until they matured" (Moya Pons, *Manual de historia* 460, my translation).

In 1914 President Woodrow Wilson attempted to gain full control of Samaná. His "Wilson Plan" consisted of threatening to send U.S. forces stationed in Guantánamo, Cuba, if the Dominican Republic did not resolve its economic and political instability. That threat became a political and military invasion in 1916: the "Marines occupied the Dominican Republic to protect American corporations' investments in the country's plantations. These plantations provided fresh fruits and vegetables to American markets during the winter" (Leavitt 7). President Wilson further justified the invasion by claiming that there were pro-German activists and a center for German operations on the island. That, he assured Congress and the American public, would endanger the United States' involvement in World War I and jeopard-

ize the work being done in the Panamá Canal and other places in
Central America.

The occupation ended in 1924. After the United States had installed a series of puppet presidents, on August 16, 1930, Rafael
Leónidas Trujillo Molina, who had been groomed by the United
States, was fraudulently elected president. Trujillo was "elected" four
more times and then his handpicked "presidents" were elected to keep
up the appearance of a democracy. His dictatorship lasted until he
was assassinated, with the approval and assistance of the United
States, on May 30, 1961. All of the parents and some of the participants in my study lived through some part of that dictatorship. All of
them say that during those thirty-one years the United States and the
world chose not to see Trujillo's brutal tyranny.

Like many of us, Flor has vivid memories of her parents' hushed
conversations about Trujillo and the state of the country during his
reign. She was ten years old, and still living in Santo Domingo, when
he was killed, and her family had to scurry about in fear. Today she
calls herself a "survivor of his despotism." "I *lived* that history," she
says proudly; "I remember the chaos on May 30, the destruction of
anything and anyone that was slightly connected to his regime. People running scared, some leaving the city to hide in the campo."

Laura too remembers hushed conversations, and she was just an
infant. Shortly after Trujillo's death her family went to live in Puerto
Rico. "There" she said,

> we could talk without fear. There my reserved parents talked up
> storms with us kids. Sometimes they frightened us into obedience by
> threatening to send us back to the aftermath of Trujillo. I did not
> know Dominican history clearly then, but I felt it, deep in my gut.
> My parents taught me to feel it.

Laura "knew" there had always been poverty in the country, and that,
according to her parents, it was because the United States would not
leave the D.R. alone. "And now there I was, in Puerto Rico, a country
also manipulated by the U.S. Then," she said, shaking her head as if
to emphasize the irony, "I became an American citizen, a citizen of
the same place that had damaged my native home."

Like a few other participants, Laura learned about Dominican history through an immigrant's ear, which, she said, was productive because she heard different versions of the same thing and thus "really had to use" her "critical thinking skills." Her parents yearned daily for the home they left behind. That longing intensified their interest in any information about the D.R. Soon, Laura became part of her parents' ritual: they sat in front of the television together and watched the news on Spanish-speaking channels, or they sat around the radio, or around her father who read aloud from several newspapers. Invariably, they commented on what was happening. That's how Laura learned much of Dominican history after Trujillo.

The first democratic national elections since Trujillo's takeover were held in December 1962. Juan Bosch won and was installed as president in February 1963. But fearing his socialist leanings, the U.S. government helped the Dominican military to overthrow him in September 1963. A de facto government ruled until April 24, 1965, when a nationwide popular demonstration calling for Bosch's return helped depose the de facto president. Opposition to Bosch's restoration led to civil war and the second occupation by the United States. Initially, President Johnson sent 405 Marines to cover the evacuation of American citizens. A buildup followed and then a full intervention by a total of 42,000 troops. They set up an interim government, arranged elections for June 1966, and "suggested" that Joaquín Balaguer (who had served as president and vice president during Trujillo's regime) be elected.

Balaguer won and promptly proceeded to amend Bosch's 1963 constitution that guaranteed civil rights. Balaguer ruled for the next twelve years, a period many call a quasi democracy or neo-Trujillismo. During the first year of his rule "over 1000 Dominicans were assassinated for political reasons (and many more imprisoned and tortured) between 1966 and 1971"; the first six years of his government "were dedicated entirely to the most ferocious repression known in Dominican history, exceeding several fold that of Trujillo's tyranny" (quoted in Pacini Hernandez *Bachata* 105).

Laura also remembers that in the late 1960s, when they lived in Puerto Rico, her family began to talk openly about family planning. When she visited Santo Domingo she heard conversations all around her: "This country would be richer if we stopped having so many kids; Juanita got the 'operation' and it didn't cost her too much money; yes, Silvia got her tubes tied and now she's always nervous." There were rumors everywhere, Laura recalls. And with good reason: beginning in the late 1960s the United States pushed family planning all over the Dominican Republic (like they had done in Puerto Rico a decade earlier during "Operation Bootstrap"). The plan was not implemented because Dominicans feared overpopulation. Family planning "was part of a long-term U.S. foreign policy on population control, directed particularly at areas receiving U.S. investment" (Torres-Saillant and Hernández 41). The U.S. effort was so successful that in a decade (1975-1986) the use of family planning by women between fifteen and forty-nine years of age rose from 20 percent to 31 percent, and "among women who were living with a man (married or not married), the proportion grew from 32% to 50%" (quoted in Torres-Saillant and Hernández 40). By the late 1980s permanent sterilization had become the most popular contraceptive method used by Dominican women.

Population control was part of the country's new freedom, and President Balaguer complied with the United States' approach. He also allowed substantial new foreign investments because his aim was to modernize the Dominican Republic through land reform and industrialization. Implementing that goal forced large numbers of people to move from the countryside to Santo Domingo where (between 1960 and 1970) the population rose from 370,000 to 669,000 (quoted in Pacini Hernandez, *Bachata* 105). Thousands of displaced rural people crowded the cities in search of employment. Economic and political conditions worsened, and as the United States needed cheap labor at home, both the Dominican and U.S. governments loosened emigration restrictions. The relaxation was "clearly a result of a tacit agreement between the U.S. and the Republic to facilitate emigration as one method of reducing internal tensions. The U.S. beefed up its consular forces and expedited processing of visas" (Spalding 54).[8] These

---

[8] Torres-Saillant and Hernández also write that the U.S. and the D.R. acted in unison: "Political dissidents received visas to travel to the United States. Others would apply for a passport and the government would simply grant it. In 1959, 19,631 people applied for a passport and only 1,805 got one; in 1969, every one of the 63,595 petitions received approval. The magnitude

push-and-pull factors prompted the two major waves of emigration to the United States: the first in the mid-1960s, the second in the mid-1970s.[9]

After that, several participants told me that they noticed a change in conversations at home; yet another major theme began to be discussed: how to get a visa. Half of the participants in this study arrived with the first wave, many leaving most family members back in the Dominican Republic, and they recall that talk about "the visa" was relentless. There were songs about it, parents planned and saved pennies, younger siblings cried on the phone when told they had to wait another year until they could join family in New York. There was constant talk about the economic and political conditions in the country. "The whole scene was an intense way to learn history," Antonio told me.

In 1978 Balaguer rigged his fourth election by ordering the army to suspend the counting of ballots. After President Jimmy Carter's warning, however, he accepted the victory of Antonio Guzmán. That transition was smooth mainly because of President Carter's human rights policy (Espinal "Between Authoritarianism" 154). By 1981 decreasing births and increasing migration out of the country was triggering important societal changes. In 1981 the population on the island was 5.6 million; in 1993 it was 7.1 million: that is a 1.95 percent growth rate, substantially less than the 2.9 percent growth of the1960s and 1970s. Economic conditions worsened.

Balaguer was defeated once again in 1982 by Salvador Jorge Blanco, but he (then elderly and blind) narrowly "won" the 1986, 1990, and 1994 elections. (In 1988 ex-president Blanco was convicted in absentia of corruption.) The 1990 election was monitored by a group of international observers led by former president Carter. His

---

of the Dominican exodus after 1966 would suggest that the doors opened to expel surplus labor as well as dissidents" (40).

[9] Less than 10,000 Dominicans had immigrated to the United States before Trujillo's assassination. They were mostly members of the elite and political exiles, because he controlled emigration to "insure abundant and cheap labor," and "to limit contact between the Dominican Republic and other countries (e.g., Cuba and Venezuela) that were experiencing agitation for democratic reforms" (Leavitt 7-8).

verdict was ambiguous: Carter "declared that there had been some irregularities linked to errors in the computing system, but that by and large, the elections had been fair" (Espinal "The 1990 Elections" 139). The opposition party, PRD (Partido Revolucionario Dominicana/Dominican Revolutionary Party, social-democratic), demanded a recount of votes. The recount was favorable to the PRSC (Partido Reformista Social Cristiano/Social Christian Reformist Party, conservative). Balaguer remained president, but the abnormalities noted in the counting served as the basis for modifying the constitution so that new elections could be held once again in June 1996.[10] In that second election an absolute majority of votes would be required, otherwise a second round of votes would determine the winner from the two parties with the most votes in the first round.

Our parents' conversations about Dominican current affairs helped to inform those of us in this study in ways that schools in the United States did not. Many of the participants identified that theme as recurrent and thus significantly formative. One participant, María, noted that her own two children would more than likely experience the same phenomenon. And indeed, when I arrived at María's house to interview her for a second time in 1996, she and her mother were talking, in front of the two children, about what had been going on regarding Peña Gómez's physical appearance. I joined in.

The major candidates in the 1996 elections were Dr. José Francisco Peña Gómez, representing the PRD, and Dr. Leonel Fernández Reyna, representing the PLD (Partido de la Liberación Dominicana/ Dominican Liberation Party, founded by Juan Bosch in 1973). The media paid particular attention to the candidates' ethnicities, often pointing out, sometimes ridiculing, Peña Gómez's more African features. They also paid attention to each candidate's predilection for outside influences. Much was made of the dispute about whether or

---

[10] Under the constitution (patterned after that of the United States), the Parliamentary branch of the government constitutes the Congreso de la República (Congress of the Republic) which has two chambers: the Cámara de Diputados (Chamber of Deputies) with 149 members elected every four years by proportional representation in each of the provinces; and the Senado (Senate) with 30 members elected every four years in single-seat constituencies.

not they should engage in a public debate, the way it is done in the United States and other developed nations. Peña Gómez refused; Fernández Reyna complained, especially in a speech delivered on June 18, 1996. He said:

> In the United States it is an established practice that presidential and vice-presidential candidates participate in various debates. Likewise, this practice is normal in European countries, and we must remember that very recently there was a debate in Israel between the hopefuls for Prime Minister, Simón Péres and Benjamin Netanyahu. In Latin America, as democracy consolidates, the practice of having debates is being more widely used. It is useful to remember the famous debate between the current president of Peru, Alberto Fujimori and writer Mario Vargas Llosa, as well as the one between the present president of Mexico, Ernesto Zedillo and Cuahutemoc Cárdenas y Diego Fernández De Ceballos. [My translation][11]

In the first round Peña Gómez (PRD) received 45.9 percent of the votes; Fernández Reyna (PLD) 38.8 percent; and Jacinto Peyando (PRSC) 14.9 percent. The PLD and PRSC formed a coalition, and Fernández Reyna won the four-year term (along with vice president David Fernández Mirabal) on the second round with 51.25 percent of the votes. (Peña Gómez obtained 48.75 percent of the votes; he died in his home on May 10, 1998.) Fernández Reyna was sworn as president on August 16, 1996.

Fernández Reyna, who had served as national director of the PLD and whose "teacher and spiritual father," as he calls him, is Juan

---

[11] "En los Estados Unidos es una forma establecida el que los candidatos a la presidencia y al viceprecidencia participen en uno varios debates. Asimismo, esta práctica es normal en los países europeos, y recordamos que muy recientemente se produjo en Israel un debate entre los aspirantes a Primer Ministro Simón Péres y Benjamin Netanyahu. En América Latina, en la medida en que se consolida el proceso democrático la práctica del debate se está generalizando, por lo cual vale recordar el famoso debate entre el actual presidente del Perú, Alberto Fujimori y el escritor Mario Vargas Llosa, así como en México, el del actual Presidente Ernesto Zedillo, Cuahutemoc árdenas y Diego Fernández De Ceballos."
(http://www.codetel.net.do/Leonel/discurso10.html)

Bosch,[12] was born in the Dominican Republic on December 26, 1953. He lived in New York City during infancy then returned to Santo Domingo to attend Universidad Autónoma, where he studied law until 1978, when he earned a doctorate. He is fluent in English and French. His platform included a call for socioeconomic, technological, and environmental changes. Since it was estimated that in the year 2000 there will be 20 million inhabitants in the 76,192-square-mile island, he paid special attention to resolving deforestation, unemployment, migration, and Haitian border issues.

"And so," Ramón said emphatically, "participating in all those conversations taught me that we Dominicans are entitled to be in the United States." He continued: "just get to know our history, the one learned at our parents' knees," because "certainly Americans won't teach our version." And the "important" part of that version is that "it proves Dominicans have a place" in the United States. Ramón pointed me to scholarship done by Torres-Saillant and Hernández, who reaffirm that there has been a Dominican presence in the States since the nineteenth century, though prior to the 1960s it consisted mainly of light-skinned "government agents, diplomats, adventurers, entrepreneurs, or students from wealthy families" (104). (Antiblack sentiment in both the States and the D.R. favored light-skinned visa applicants.) For example, in the 1830s, the founding figure in Dominican nationhood, Juan Pablo Duarte, lived in New York City. And President Buenaventura Báez visited New York various times. Common folk like Captain José Gabriel Luperón and Juan de Dios Tejada also immigrated to New York.

There were also prominent academics, for instance, siblings Pedro and Camila Henríquez Ureña. Pedro left the island at age sixteen in 1901 in order to study at Columbia University. In 1916 he began graduate studies (while he also taught) at the University of Minnesota in Minneapolis. In 1918 he received a doctorate in philology. That same year, Camila, who had also been attending the same university,

---

[12] Bosch is also a scholar. His two most popular books are *De Cristóbal a Fidel Castro: El Caribe, frontera imperial* and *Composición social dominicana: Historia e interpretación* (both published in Santo Domingo by Editorial Alfa y Omega in 1986).

earned an M.A. in Spanish literature. He went back to the Dominican Republic and twenty years later, in 1940, returned to Harvard University as a Visiting Professor. Camila stayed in the United States and taught literature at Vassar in Poughkeepsie, New York, from 1941 to 1958 (Torres-Saillant and Hernández 107-111).[13]

Other participants echoed Ramón's sentiment about the influence of our parents' conversations regarding Dominican history: those conversations helped us to feel that however hard we had to fight for it, we have a "rightful place" in the United States: "We belong in this American soil as much as anyone else," María said several times during our interviews. Laura too said the same thing and added that the United States was part of her life while she lived in Santo Domingo. She could not escape it: after Trujillo's death American values, institutions, ideology, products, and popular culture were more blatantly present in Dominican culture. Now those aspects are hardly noticeable as being foreign. Streets are named after Kennedy, Washington, and Lincoln, and people frequently travel back and forth, thus changing both societies at home and the U.S. To further solidify that exchange and the sharing of histories, in 1996 the Dominican Constitution was amended to decree that all people born in the D.R. have the same citizenship rights even if they are citizens elsewhere. Dominicans now have cultural *and* political duality.

These are crucial issues learned primarily because we heard our parents talking. Even if unintentionally, those conversations provided us with the basics of Dominican history, especially as it intersects with that of the United States. And thus, "seeds were planted," as Antonio said, that grew into curiosity about diverse issues, among them our cultural heritage. That curiosity led us to ask the "important questions" that most of us continue to pursue as scholarly endeavors, and that therefore contributed to us seeking higher education/literacy, and to acknowledging and unpacking our condition.

---

[13] Julia Alvarez's current novel, *In the Name of Salomé*, fictionalizes the lives of Salomé Ureaña, the Dominican Republic's best-known female poet, and her daughter Camila who lived a more private life in the United States.

Temporary Closure

My aim in this chapter has been to map what participants identified as our parents' salient convictions and behaviors and their influence on our sense of self and therefore on our journey toward high literacy and the professorate. I began by delineating how our parents ingrained in us the belief that acquiring a high level of formal education would provide us with a socially sanctioned identity and a sure way to make a living. I continued with a description of their enactments, their conversations, and how they motivated us to pursue high literacy.

Except Sandra, all of us in this study maintained that our parents' principles imprinted in us a desire to seek knowledge (particularly anything having to do with the States), to find answers in books, teachers, and school, and to want literate ways of being, and the life of the mind. Our own living of the immigrant experience compounded that lesson, including those of us that were born and raised in the States. That immigrant experience required that we negotiate and mediate at least two cultures and ways of being. It necessitated that we gather information, more than "a real American" would have to know, because we were the ones who had to prove that we belonged, and that we had a right to be in school and in American society. We were the ones who had to provide the evidence that would convince others that indeed we could measure up.

We may not have realized it as it was actually happening, but by the time I conducted interviews, most participants explained, we understood that (in differing degrees) each of us had attempted to comprehend our diasporic existence. It is part of what pushed us toward books and scholarly behavior. Wanting to fill in the gaps (in our history and in our positionality) provided many of us with occasions to do research in college and graduate school.

Right or wrong, simplistic or not, our parents taught us what they learned in Dominican society—that we would be less vulnerable, that we could "belong" in American (and any other) society (at least in terms of socioeconomic class) if we acquired high literacy. Obtaining any level of literacy, the higher the better, meant that we could have access to the knowledge and power that would prevent us from being alienated or diminished.

Our parents' attitudes and beliefs also provided us with a Dominican sense of self, home, and culture that nourished us especially when it was "often derided by American society," as Laura affirmed during each of our interviews. Antonio explained it this way: "I was taught to believe, I saw my parents and family believing, that formal education is the 'salvation' for anyone who must run from an impoverished dictatorship. It's the key, the way out." Those messages from our parents served to establish a sense of history. And in the States where we had to confront problematic messages about our worth as individuals and as a particular immigrant group, our parents' "gift," as Haydee calls it, functioned to help heal our sense of inadequacy and the emotional turmoil we experienced as children and now as adults.

Stories about our parents' influences help to clarify who we are. As most of the participants in this study affirmed, at the core they elucidate the "condition" we brought to American schools. They show that we entered colleges and graduate schools still unpacking a legacy of physical and psychological tyranny, "freedom" lived in a pseudodemocracy, poverty, racial, and ethnic dissimulation, and the relentless corporeal and emotional assaults that are inherent in living life on the cultural margins of society in the United States. Most of us in this study maintained that in complex and multilayered ways our parents' legacy (their beliefs as learned in Dominican society) is one of the factors that "empowered us," as Laura reminded me, "to focus almost exclusively on literacy." Tangible evidences of our academic success (diplomas, awards) were important to our parents, but they also forced us to face an intense sense of dislocation and isolation at home and at school, myriad labels and preconceptions assigned to us, and the need to prove that we are competent, not impostors, and thus deserve to be in the academy.

Dulce María dressed for eighth grade graduation from Catholic school. The event cost money, the least of which was buying the cap and gown, but Antonio and Teresita made sure it was available.

Dulce María. Cultural markers I chose consciously during adolescence: Dominican and American music, Hollywood cinema, long cool hair, tight jeans, books and art . . .

Dulce María in high school, where most teachers cared about each student and felt free to create opportunities that emphasized the arts and ideas as vital aspects of everyday life.

4

Professors

The huge Montana sky enveloped all of it: the hill where I stood, the monument, the multitudinous white crosses rising out of swaying summer grass, and the tourists meandering out of large air-conditioned buses down toward winding trails past the rattlesnakes. I sipped water from my bottle and tried to shield myself from the scorching sun. I hadn't felt that despondent in a long, long time. Death loomed visibly, but only the death of Custer's men. Where were the grave markers for all the slaughtered Native Americans? Why was there such a tremendous memorial built to the very man who killed them? Why had this event been presented in my American history classes as if it had been a Hollywood movie where strangely the guys in black defeat the guys in white?

Little Bighorn Battlefield National Monument commemorates Lt. Col. George Armstrong Custer and 263 members of his immediate command who perished in a clash of cultures. It happened in the valley of the Little Bighorn River on June 25, 1876—the exact spot where I stood spiritually weighed down 123 years later. Soldiers and attached personnel of the U.S. Army had marched from near Bismarck, North Dakota, in search of Indians thought to be gathered under Sitting Bull, Crazy Horse, and other leaders of Lakota and Cheyenne warriors. Reportedly, about 2,000 of those warriors awaited Custer. They aimed to fight against the encroachment of white civilization and thus to protect their families and land and to preserve their traditional way of life. On the evening of the 26th, having accomplished their greatest victory, the Indians withdrew. Supposedly, only 100 died, their bodies picked up by survivors, so that, a tour guide explained, there is no way to mark where they fell. Soon after, the remainder of the community was subjugated and confined to live in reservations.

Walking the trails, I wondered where exactly a Native American might have been shot, where his throat might have been slit, where his blood might have spilled, and more pressingly, why my professors had abated their courage and perspective. Logically, it seemed to me, that monument should have been built to honor the Indians, not Custer. But that's not the case. In fact, it was only in December 1991 that a law was passed to change the name from "Custer" to "Little Bighorn Battlefield." That law also authorized a national design competition and construction (once enough donations had been collected) of a memorial for the Native Americans. In 1999 the project had not been started.

Back in Virginia revising this chapter, I thought about the power that formal education has in creating and reshaping a collective conscience. The history of access to and denial of education in the United States explains, for example, why at the end of this century 20 percent of all Latinos are still dropping out of high school. In 1980, around the time I was graduating from twelfth grade, 72 percent of New York Dominicans age twenty-five or older failed to complete high school. In 1990, when I was already in graduate school, only 8 percent were completing college or more (as compared to 29.9 percent of the overall population in the city) (quoted in Torres-Saillant and Hernández 72).

I had already identified professors' influence as a salient theme in the 1,500 pages of transcribed interviews with participants in this study. But given those statistics and my awakening at Little Bighorn Battlefield, it seemed even more imperative to examine how teachers and professors marked those of us in this study. What did they do to facilitate our successful journey to high literacy and the professorate? Initial analysis of all the interviews I transcribed indicated that participants in this study talked recurrently about their professors' influence. I had already traced the salient themes and noted that a few of us "were not lucky enough to encounter supportive professors," as Dilia said.

Dilia had many "negative" experiences. Her sense of deprivation and inadequacy intensified in graduate school, because, she told me, most professors treated her "condescendingly." "Being bilingual and bicultural was not an asset," she wrote on the margin as she read the transcription of our first interview, "not if you were of Spanish heritage and spoke like a New Yorker." Professors at the predominantly white institution where she completed graduate school "talked" to her as if she had "just stepped out of a Brooklyn ghetto," as if she "had been misusing welfare funds." Those words were never spoken to her face, Dilia specified, but she "saw them written on professors' faces and attitudes."

Ramón endured similar circumstances in a different institution. He believed that his academic work and intellect were judged according to the way he pronounced English. His pro-fessors "confused fluency with intelligence" and "predetermined" that he did not know standard English because he spoke with a heavy accent. Ramón felt that several of his professors "punished" him. The only time Ramón protested a low grade, the professor acknowledged: "yeah, maybe I was a little thrown off by your accent." "Soon," Ramón said to me,

> I realized that if you take certain liberties with language and you are not a native writer, a native speaker [of English], it is not seen as creative. It is seen as a fault of some kind. I was doing turns of phrases, saying things in an unusual manner, playing around with syntax. But invariably when I got a paper back from the professor I would see all kinds of stylistic corrections that I did not agree with and that I thought were unnecessary. I learned that when given to choose between a mistake and creative smart use of the language, professors would see a mistake, because otherwise they

would have to grant me the ability to do that sort of thing which would not be compatible with the way I speak and look.[1]

Ramón and Dilia affirmed that those kinds of messages sent by professors and the academy were demoralizing and led them to question their ability "and right to be" in a graduate program." Dilia told me this story during our first interview:

> I went to speak with one of the professors about getting a Ph.D. in psychology, and she said, "no, don't think about doing a Ph.D. You're just a Masters student. Hispanics don't do well in psychology." And I believed her. I believed her. I said, "well, okay I'm going to take literature instead. After all, I don't have what it takes to study psychology."

To this day Dilia wonders if she should "remake" herself and "take up psychology." She did complete a doctorate, thus now believes that she indeed had the academic wherewithal to succeed. But that professor, and the "entire general atmosphere" in her department, made her feel "incapable," out of place, "like an impostor" in the academy. Years later, as we sat in her office, framed Ph.D. in Spanish literature behind her, Dilia clarified that

---

[1] Recently, while teaching bell hooks' *Teaching to Transgress*, I was struck by one of her utterly candid stories, because it resonated with Ramón's experiences. hooks writes:

> In graduate school I found that I was often bored in classes. The banking system of education (based on the assumption that memorizing information and regurgitating it represented gaining knowledge that could be deposited, stored and used at a later date) did not interest me. I wanted to become a critical thinker. Yet that longing was often seen as a threat to authority. Individual white male students who were seen as "exceptional," were often allowed to chart their intellectual journeys, but the rest of us (and particularly those from marginal groups) were always expected to conform. Nonconformity on our part was viewed with suspicion, as empty gestures of defiance aimed at masking inferiority or substandard work. . . . As we constantly confronted biases, an undercurrent of stress diminished our learning experience. (5).

she was "hurt" by that professor's comment and his stereotyping of her potential. She wanted "and needed" his validation. She wanted his concrete help in addressing whatever weaknesses there were in her academic performance.

When I told Dilia that other participants in this study, Flor and Sandra, for example, used such affronts as an impetus to achieve, she explained that she had arrived in New York at age fourteen. She had survived by being "a good immigrant girl, obedient, docile, obliging." Back then, she admitted, she used to believe that the United States was the greater of the two countries (else why did she have to leave her own nation?), and that Americans "knew better" (so why would she "dare" challenge a professor, a male one at that, she being "just an immigrant woman who had much catching up to do" in order to reach the "lowest part of American standards"). During that interview Dilia talked about still feeling anger, shame; she still blames herself for "not being strong enough" and for not pursuing the discipline she really loves. It has taken her "too many years to grow out of that state of mind." Becoming/being highly literate, reading and writing, and understanding her experiences from a scholar's perspective have helped her to "grow out of the gloom" she has "suffered."

Notably, Ramón and Dilia's stories are *not* recurrent in our transcribed interviews. The opposite is true. Most of us in this study made resounding affirmations about our professors' productive imprint on our journey toward high literacy and becoming academics in the humanities and social sciences. We claim that our professors in undergraduate and graduate careers were propitious in that they modeled high literacy for us. That was a particularly vital impact, especially for those of us who are the first in our family to complete college and graduate school. Analyses of the transcripts also reveal that there were other more resounding influences. In this chapter my aim is to map the two factors that participants in this study repeatedly identified as salient:

1) Professors made a solid difference in our academic journey by taking an interest in us as individuals, and by respecting and validating our work and cultural backgrounds.

2) Professors also facilitated our journey by providing the information that helped us navigate academe, and by infusing their
courses with scholarship by and about Dominicans.

Taking an Interest

In *Teaching to Transgress* bell hooks describes "engaged pedagogy" as teaching that extends beyond simply providing information and includes respecting and caring for each other's souls.[2] She
says that teaching "in a manner that respects and cares for the souls
of our students is essential if we are to provide the necessary
conditions where learning can most deeply and intimately begin"
(13). Similarly, John P. Miller, author of *Education and the Soul*,
writes that the most important element in soulful learning is the
teacher's soul:

> The Teacher's soul must be nourished if the student's soul is to
> develop. There is nothing that our students desire from us more
> than our attention, our authentic presence. . . . Two qualities that
> the soulful teacher can usually bring to the classroom are presence
> and caring. Presence arises from mindfulness where the teacher is
> capable of listening deeply. . . . Closely related to presence is car-
> ing. The caring teacher relates the subject to the needs and inter-
> ests of the students. (10)

---

[2] As I revised this chapter, I was also teaching hooks' book to my Composition Theory graduate students. And for my own growth I was also
reading Robert Sardello's *Facing the World with Soul*. He helped me to
understand the relationship between teaching, learning and the soul. For
instance, he writes that our physical beings, who we perceive ourselves
to be (ethnically, culturally, etc.), plays a central role in how we teach
and learn. Sardello explains that reducing teaching and learning to the
mere act of transmitting knowledge prevents the soul from growing. That
"banking" approach (as Freire terms it) "assumes the learner to be without body, to be anybody and nobody. To learn through soul, one must see
through the eyes of the heart, love the subject matter as one sees the
teacher loving it" (54). That is, Sardello maintains, teachers can and do
make productive impacts when they are genuinely interested in their students, their worlds, their views.

hooks asserts that engaged pedagogy is successful when professors understand that there is "a sacred aspect" to teaching and that their "work is not merely to share information but to share in the intellectual and spiritual growth" of students (13). They are not to "offer them information without addressing the connection between what they are learning and their overall life experiences" (19). If professors are to empower students, hooks writes, they must be "healers"—that is, "be actively committed to a process of self-actualization that promotes their own well-being" (15).

That comprises part of what she means by "education as the practice of freedom." Professors who take an interest, especially in students like us in this study who have been traditionally marginalized in and out of academe, begin to enact the kind of education hooks describes:

> As a classroom community, our capacity to generate excitement is deeply affected by our interest in one another, in hearing one another's voices, in recognizing one another's presence. . . . To begin, the professor must genuinely *value* everyone's presence. There must be an ongoing recognition that everyone influences the classroom dynamic, that everyone contributes (8).

Almost all of us participants in this study maintain that we were "lucky" enough to encounter such engaged and caring professors who consequently helped ease our way through college and graduate school. We met professors who took an interest in us as individuals. Those who talked with us, who respected our work and cultural heritage, who saw us as complex human beings with much to contribute—those who became mentors—they made memorable contributions in our development. César (more so than Ramón) found such mentors. César and Ramón felt disconnected from their parents, home community, and graduate school peers (who were predominantly European Americans of higher socioeconomic status). For César and Ramón, significant professors generally functioned as mediators of those three groups of people. But professors who made a long-lasting impact, they said, did more than that. Those professors were genuinely interested in them. Those professors spent time getting to know students. They dedicated energy to talking about scholarly matters and other intellectual interests; and they were critical but also respectful of students' academic work and cultural heritage.

For example, during our first interview, César explained that while in graduate school he believed that his parents did not care about his scholastic life. They "didn't know" what he was doing, and were "disconnected" and "uninvested" in his pursuits. It took long discussions with one professor, and "much reading on the topic of higher education and socioeconomic class," for César to fully understand that his parents felt estranged from his activities at school, and that he needed to be more patient in, for instance, explaining that studying for his qualifying exams could be as demanding as the physical labor his parents defined as "honorable work."[3] César's mentor helped him realize that his barely literate parents valued different modes of behavior, and that those modes are not necessarily less worthy or complex. In their exchanges César was reminded that

---

[3] In a subsequent conversation about the different ways our parents and professors define "work," and about what we could personally learn from both groups of people that would help us to be effective teachers, I offered César a passage from *Teaching to Transgress*, where hooks explains that "engaged pedagogy" asks professors to work diligently at their own self-actualization. That means that we need to truly examine epistemological confluences such as the one César encountered regarding his reading not being "work." hooks writes:

> Our romantic notion of the professor is so tied to a sense of the transitive mind, a mind that, in a sense, is always at odds with the body. I think part of why everyone in the [academic] culture, and students in general, have a tendency to see professors as people who don't work is totally tied to that sense of the immobile body. Part of the class separation between what we do and what the majority of people in this culture can do (service, work, labor) is that they move their bodies. Liberatory pedagogy really demands that one work in the classroom, and that one work with the limits of the body, work both with and through and against those limits: teachers may insist that it doesn't matter whether you stand behind the podium or the desk, but it does. (138)

his parents did not participate in his intellectual pursuits also probably because they were usually exhausted from working several shifts, because they did not speak English (César's dominant language), and because they felt inferior, in awe, and as if they had little to offer him.

In the same way, Haydee said that in graduate school conversation between her and her parents diminished, not just because they were too tired from working or too busy attending to endless tasks, but also because much of what she was learning in school was foreign to them. It was "painful," Haydee said, to "feel acutely divided from them." Yet, she also "felt gratified" because in completing graduate school she was living her "dream." Nonetheless, as soon as she got home she "had to forget about . . . let's say Sor Juana Inés de la Cruz, the only Latina" she had learned about in her all-American curriculum. Sor Juana, a nun born in the late 1500s in colonial Mexico, was an important model for Haydee. She personified a steadfast pursuit of formal education and intellectual growth—despite the church and her society's attempt to first deny and then censure her ideas.

When Haydee wanted to discuss Sor Juana with her parents she felt like a "teacher," not a family member, a role reversal that made her uncomfortable since she could "see" that "*they*" felt inadequate." At the same time Haydee also "saw their pride and admiration," because, after all, she had managed to "succeed in an American school." No matter how Haydee dealt with the situation, she "felt torn." That kind of "emotional distraction" kept her awake for many long nights, but as she began to talk about it with several professors (in and outside the classroom), she began to understand the complexity of her circumstances, and thus to "separate" herself from "the pain."

Ramón too told me that he felt distant from his parents and the other Dominicans in his New York City neighborhood, most of whom were poor and minimally literate. The more education he "garnered under his belt," the more he perceived himself as "an outsider." "When I got to the community I had to forget about George Herbert and James Joyce because the compulsions there were different. I had nobody in my community that I could share this knowledge with," he said sadly during our second interview. In graduate school Ramón felt equally removed and isolated from his peers and the academy, "sort of lost in the wilderness." Now, he said, he knows that "social class had a great deal to do with" what he experienced then. His being a university student separated him from family and friends. His low economic status marked him as an "other" in school. For instance, invariably, he could not purchase all of the required books. Oftentimes, he "ran around" to borrow them from multiple libraries: "It was exhausting just to keep track of what books were due when and where."

Now, Ramón believes that one of the "fixed obstacles" was "trying to balance" his classes with his jobs. He worked too many jobs and therefore could not dedicate much time to studying. Inasmuch as he "was going to school in the evening, a criterion for which courses to take was their degree of difficulty." "One summer," he admitted,

> I studied Ancient Greek. To me that was wonderful. I think that is really when I learned what I was capable intellectually. Now I realize how crazy it was, because what that meant was that I didn't earn any money that summer. It may have been the remnants of student loans that kept my wife and me going.

Ramón had no choice but to work at least two jobs at the same time he was trying to finish graduate studies. He had to pay tuition and all of the other expenses incurred at school. He had to contribute to the upkeep of his parents and siblings, and when he married he also had to help support himself and his wife. Exacerbating all that financial stress was the reality that he did not have a separate "space to study." "Sometimes," he told me during our last interview, "I feel that that's why I married. I remember I couldn't study at home." He explained that "on Sundays the [college] library closed before" he "got out of work," but that he "went there anyway because on the way" he "would study two hours on the train." And when he could not go to a library, he "went to the parks—you know, on warm days—to study there."

For Ramón as for most of the other low-socioeconomic participants in this study, pursuing high literacy was a double-edged sword: it disassociated him further "from the family and home communities" he loves, and at the same time intensified his awareness of being economically dispossessed. He "constantly felt like an intruder" and "an impostor" both at home and at school. During our second interview he clarified:

> I changed. I wasn't like my family and community, so I was an outsider. I was an alien in school too. In terms of social economic condition I was not comparable to my classmates who were waiting for the check that mommy would send from other states. I had the experience of someone who worked for a living from as early as age ten. Consequently, I felt different too because I did not think the way they did. I felt like an outsider.

"That is why," he stressed, "it was important for me to connect" with at least one professor. Although he never developed a "truly mentor-type relationship" with anyone specifically, throughout his graduate experience Ramón found a couple of professors who were usually available during office hours and after class. They talked about course content, general intellectual topics, and sometimes other issues weighing on him (such as how to deal with the multiple demands in his life and still do well in his classes). Exchanging ideas allowed him to place his personal experiences in a scholarly context, and thus to understand them in new and profound perspectives. For instance, he realized that class is not just about money; class is also about "the way you see the world, the words, the ways you make meaning," what you value, the processes you engage. "Slowly," Ramón said, discussing ideas with his professors allowed him to feel less estranged and "more empowered." It helped him to "develop a public voice" and to begin to think deliberately about his and other nontraditional students' position in the academy. Consequently, his experiences in coming to consciousness about the role of class in the academy (and his investment in analyzing it) turned into a topic he has pursued in his scholarship.

Another participant in this study, Flor, was lucky to find two professors who inspired her. She told me that without them she "would not have made it even through *college*." As an undergraduate she was motivated by a female professor who critiqued her assignments with more than just a grade. That professor built up her confidence and encouraged her to go on for a graduate degree:

> My husband was a student of hers too. I remember getting back my first paper. She wrote this really long personal comment about the two of us and how she saw my work. And so I decided to major in English also. I think that for me the encouragement stemmed from her recognizing that I could write in this new language. That was the language of the powerful, sort of the key to the kingdom. The fact that she acknowledged that she liked my work, that motivated me. That helped me to go on.

Similarly, Sandra, who had very little, if any, parental and familial support, affirmed that she would not have been able to complete any level of literacy without the many teachers and professors who supported her from early on:

> As I go back I can think of that science teacher. I don't know why she recommended me, but of all the students she had, for whatever reason she recommended me and that made a difference. Somebody noticed something. I really believe in the power of an individual to see something and provide an opportunity for somebody else. I believe people need to feel special. If your family doesn't make you feel special, hey, that's horrible. But if a stranger, if a school system, if somebody else can believe in you, it can substitute. It can really substitute for what's missing within the family.[4]

---

[4] In another conversation I mentioned to Sandra that published scholarship on Latinos' experience in the academy confirms her own. For instance, A. Reynaldo Contreras, a Chicano professor, writes:

> It was in the eleventh grade when a counselor informed me that I did exceedingly well on a standardized test and suggested I take the SAT examination. At the time, I had no idea what the SAT was or the implications of taking the test. I took the examination. When the results returned, the same counselor asked me if I had given any thought to attending college. I had not. I thought college was where rich kids or children of professors went after high school. (112)

My own experience in college (not graduate school) is similar to Sandra's. I wanted desperately to attend university. I fantasized about it while I was in high school and through subsequent years when I worked before becoming a full-time student. In retrospect, I identify three major reasons why I felt deeply passionate about acquiring high literacy: (a) I was starving for knowledge; (b) I wanted certification from American society; (c) I wanted to be affirmed as a competent member of that highly literate minority my father described as (therefore) having power and prestige. I suppose I also wanted a "profession" that would allow me to live differently from how I grew up (less harried, less consumed by finding ways to survive).

From early in childhood I have known that I wanted to be a writer. I have always kept journals, and all of the aspects of composing and arranging ideas have always held my preoccupation. Nonetheless, in high school I imagined myself in various vocations. At different times I wanted to be a newspaper reporter, a marine biologist, an art historian, then an archaeologist, a traveling botanist or botanical illustrator, an anthropologist, a translator who wandered everywhere. Any job that allowed me to write, enjoy the arts, and explore unknown corners of the world seemed to be for me. But those longings were deferred.

I also ached to get away from my parents' traditionally Spanish authority, which at the time I perceived to be unjust and oppressive. Leaving for a university far from home where I could live as an American seemed to be the logical answer. But there were complications: there was little money to support that ambition; my parents would not accept me living on my own; and four years seemed to be an interminable amount of time for me to attend the local college and "wait to start my own life" (as I thought of it back then). Suffice it to say that I didn't start a four-year college until a few years after graduating from high school. But when I did, the world of ideas exploded inside me, and I didn't know what to do with it. A professor who showed interest in my academic development helped me sort the parts.

I did not return to college with a plan to become an English professor. Primarily, I wanted to learn—about literature, arts, history, many cultures, languages, flowers, the world in our oceans, music, theater. My prime motivation for attending college was to feed my hunger, but I was also practical: I figured that I could gain knowledge and find some way to use it to make enough of a salary to live comfortably. Perhaps, I considered, I'd teach English in high school. I thought only about graduating from a four-year humanities program. That alone seemed like a huge goal. Continuing to graduate school was not even in my dreams, not until I was almost ready to graduate and a professor reacted very enthusiastically to my mentioning that I was considering a master's degree. Had it not been for Carol Sicherman, my favorite English professor, who had long been interested in my academic development, I might not have continued.

I took many of her classes, not just because the topics were always fascinating (e.g., "Postcolonial African Literature"), but also because she was demanding. She required that I do my best *and* showed me how to accomplish that task. In one of her classes I memorized the beginning of Chaucer's *Canterbury Tales*, and I recited it in front of everyone. I practiced writing sonnets. Doors to noncanonical literature and cultures were opened to me. I traveled far and wide in the universe of ideas she brought to our classrooms. And all the while she consistently made me feel that I was important, that my ideas (stated orally or in the many written analyses she assigned) were valuable and worthy of being expressed. She praised me as well as corrected me, often in very warm and congenial ways (e.g., "don't try making your living as a sonneteer"). She read my work respectfully and marked it copiously. Carol frequently offered me books to read, music to hear, movies to screen—things to do that showed me that she was interested in me as an individual. That helped to stretch me intellectually and emotionally.

But what is unique about her interest, what helps to distinguish Carol from my other professors, is that she respected and was interested in my hybrid culture. She wanted to know about my experiences emigrating and about the Dominican Republic. She was genuinely curious and invested in learning about the island, and she often asked me to make connections with my history and the content in our classes. Consequently, although my memories were vague (and thus I usually had to research before answering her), she regularly made me feel as if I had important information to teach her about a place and condition that no one else seemed to value.

Like other professors for a few of us in this study, Carol Sicherman made an impact primarily because as a representative of a major American institution she showed interest in me as a unique whole human being with a complex life that she acknowledged as being inestimably rich. Those of us who met such mentors affirm that having that kind of recognition and support, having at least one professor value our academic development and our cultural heritage, helped to make us feel in place in the academy, helped to encourage us to pursue high literacy and to feel less alienated, particularly during difficult times. They helped us answer those existential questions: Who am I? How do I see and experience myself? Those interested professors enabled us to understand that we ought not to determine our ethnic identity solely by physical appearance, socioeconomic status, material possessions, our roles in life, worth in relation to others, the sum of our memories, or even acquired level of literacy.

Providing Information

Although our professors' interest in us was crucial, their more instrumental influence is rooted in the ways they exposed us to opportunities and helped us navigate the maze that is graduate school and academe—the ways they became resources for us. They also made a tremendous difference when they infused their courses with scholarship by and about Dominicans anywhere in the diaspora. Those are recurrent topics in the 1,500 pages of our interviews that I transcribed and analyzed.

My experience with Carol Sicherman is only one of the many stories appearing in those pages. Like other professors in participants' narratives, Carol is noteworthy because she took an interest in my Dominican cultural heritage and me but, most memorably, because she also became a resource by providing me with a wealth of information. Two such bits of data were advertisements to spend time studying in Madrid, Spain, and in Oxford, England. She then proceeded to help me fill out the applications, and several others for accompanying scholarships, and to write letters of recommendation. As I completed the master's she did the same thing to help me continue with a doctoral program in another state. Had it not been for Carol's belief that indeed I could make it through a doctoral program, her support and guidance, and her diligence in writing letters of recommendation, I probably would not have been accepted at the school of my first choice. Certainly, there was no one in my personal circle of family and friends who could offer guidance, since none had attended graduate school. Carol encouraged me and gave me practical information.

Another participant in this study, Sandra, is the premier example of what happens when a professor invests in students as individuals. "Miraculously," Sandra told me, she had "made it all the way through" college and was about to complete a master's degree. She desperately wanted a doctorate, but "deep inside" she did not really have the confidence, nor was she familiar with the process. She was afraid: "I felt that getting the master's was *waaaay* beyond what I had ever expected. I felt like the gravy was already there, and that I couldn't do anything else." But then a professor insisted that she not give up. He gathered information and numerous applications, presented them to her, and offered help in filling them out. Sandra was astonished.[5] She figured that she "at least better try because he apparently saw something" in her, that perhaps she had not seen in herself.

---

[5] A. Reynaldo Contreras's experiences are, again, very similar. In an article he writes that while he was in the Peace Corps his director suggested that he attend Stanford for a master's degree:

> This suggestion startled me. I had never aspired to go beyond a B.S. degree. Even becoming certified as a teacher was going beyond my expectations. Now being told I could succeed in completing a master's degree program was intriguing. I had no idea what Stanford was like or where it was located. . . . I applied . . . three months later received notice [of admission]. Yet Stanford University and attending Stanford University were abstract notions to me. (119)

Years later Sandra felt similarly overwhelmed about having to write a dissertation. She doubted her intellectual and emotional ability, her stamina and determination. Ingrained fears paralyzed her. She was tired of fighting in order to acquire the level of literacy she believed in her "gut" she "deserved." She was confused by the requirements, daunted by the prospect. "Working on a dissertation seemed like such a major obstacle," she said to me in exasperation during our first interview, "and writing has never been my real strength." Fortunately for Sandra, at that very disruptive time, during her last semester of classes, the university appointed a new faculty member in her department. Sandra's face brightened when she explained that he was a Puertorriqueño who "singlehandedly" got her through the process:

> I wasn't sure if I wanted to do it. Working on a dissertation seemed like such a major obstacle and writing has never been my real strength. It was difficult to set up a dissertation committee: you find yourself dealing with the rare minority professor whose standards were so high (they were going to use you to prove something to the world) or whose standards were so low that it was a joke. I found that the supporting mechanism really wasn't there. But then it turned out that the university appointed a Puerto-rriqueño who came during my last year. I honestly have to say that he single-handedly . . . negotiated the system for me.

It made a "difference" to her that he spoke Spanish, that he was familiar with Dominicans' culture and the history of their migration to the United States, and that he personally had also struggled to make it through graduate school. She felt a camaraderie with him that was solidified once he clarified that he was available to help her, that he'd been around academe long enough to let go of "the pressure to prove anything," that he would animate her, read and value her work, make suggestions, guide her, and provide the expertise he gained during his own quest to acquire high literacy and tenure. Consequently, Sandra felt less alone, "safer," and galvanized.

Mentoring from a professor with whom she identified was crucial for Sandra. She needed that kind of support, not just because she felt isolated from the process and the academy, but because she felt culturally alone.[6] Finding comradeship with a Latino who shared some of her cultural background, who had experienced and survived the same ordeal, and who knew the system helped her to persist. Years later, during our interviews, like most of the respondents, Sandra affirmed that sometimes a single professor can make "a world of a difference":

> generally all graduate students need a professor's support, but I believe that immigrants and women need it most, because they are the least familiar with higher education and they feel removed, so they need guidance.

Even Carla, whose family is overwhelmingly highly literate, and whose high socioeconomic status predisposed her to feel less alienated from access to formal education and the graduate school experience, echoes Sandra's belief that we needed just one professor to provide information, to be a resource, and to thus be the catalyst for us to persist in seeking high literacy. Carla is convinced that key teachers and professors helped to determine her academic success and that therefore a major effort must be undertaken to increase the pool of Latino professors: [7]

---

[6] The Dominican experience echoes that of other minorities. One study conducted in the 1980s revealed that all minority graduate students face deep isolation, and that many "feel they must prove they have a right to be in graduate school in a way that white graduate students don't. Meanwhile, they hear rumors about the 'bidding wars' for minority professors but don't always find themselves so eagerly sought" (Magner A19).

[7] Unfortunately, there was no real presence of Latino professors anywhere in the States. In the mid and early 1980s Latinos comprised only 1.6 percent of the U.S. professorate. In one rare article that addressed the issue, "The 'Barrioization' of Hispanic Faculty," the author, Hisauro Garza, explained that "the presence of minority faculty" on campus was "the most underrepresented group in academe," "alarmingly inadequate," and "slight compared to their representation in the population" (*Educational Record* [Winter 1988]: 122-24).

I found this teacher at this school and this teacher at that school who would read what I wrote, encourage me, take the time out—those little ways that you get nurtured, especially as a girl where you don't feel like you're taken seriously. I think it was my teachers. I think that that's really what most encouraged me.

Expanding the Canon

Most of us also note that professors also facilitated our journey toward high literacy and the professorate when they expanded the traditional canon, when they infused their courses with works by and about Dominicans (and other U.S. Latinos). Dilia explained why that was so significant to her. She said that throughout her experience in higher education she did not encounter one single course that focused strictly on Dominicans or U.S. Latinos. That omission made her feel unwanted, frustrated, and discouraged. She clarified:

> You see, not being represented in the curriculum creates a negative impact on our lives. Unconsciously we develop low self-confidence and we begin to think that our heritage and culture are not worthy of an American classroom. We begin to equate ourselves with undesirable things. Then we begin to hide ourselves. You think, I can't speak my language; I can't expose my culture because it's not good enough. If I do I'm going to be rejected—or worse, punished. On the other hand, an inclusive curriculum that represents your culture motivates students at any level. I know I would have benefited from seeing courses about my native home, especially in graduate school when I began to consciously think about my identity. I think I would have received a message that said, "you fit somewhere; you're connected." You know, I would have felt that *my* culture in the States and on the island is valuable. I would have felt less demoralized.

Flor too said that there was nothing about Dominicans in the curriculum. She emigrated at age ten, and she had attended school sporadically in Santo Domingo. Hence, she already had a general awareness of Dominican subjects. That knowledge, heightened by her desire to learn more, allowed her to notice the blatant omission of Dominican topics in the States early in her scholarly development.

Flor also told me that the situation is changing, at least in
Kindergarten through twelfth grade in New York City. And indeed,
research indicates that there are changes. Dominicans constitute "the
largest share of the students entering the New York City public
schools since the 1980s," and for that reason, there are greater
numbers of Dominicans studying education and, "upon graduation,
seeking instructional and administrative positions in the public
schools"; already there are "some Dominican school principals"
who are beginning to "influence the system" (e.g., curriculum
design and instruction) and helping to make schools "more
responsive" to the specific needs of Dominican students (Torres-
Saillant and Hernández 72).

In New York City, where Dominicans constitute the largest
Latino subgroup, the current situation seems "a little less dishearten-
ing," Flor claimed during our last interview and research confirms,
than when she attended graduate school. Recently, one institution
took action:

> six of the City University campuses have created Dominican heri-
> tage survey courses. Some of the colleges have hired Dominican
> faculty, and the university has sponsored the creation of the
> CUNY Dominican Studies Institute, a research unit of the univer-
> sity housed at the City College campus. The purpose of the Do-
> minican Institute is to create instruments of knowledge that will
> enhance the possibility of communication and will diminish the
> chances of tension between Dominicans and non-Dominicans in
> the United States. (Torres-Saillant and Hernández 88)

Thus, although questionable because of the recent massive budget
cuts, there is tangible evidence that today Dominican students may
not have to experience what the participants in this study did in the
early 1990s and 1980s (and before) when they attended college and
graduate school. There wasn't much of a support system then,
particularly outside of New York City. That is one reason, many of
the participants in this study affirmed, that caring professors were so
instrumental, especially those who included works by and about
Dominicans in their courses. That is one outstanding way they
energized us.

"Reading and writing about ourselves and our cultural heritage does more than authenticate us," Flor maintains; "it helps us to grow personally and professionally." Carla added that scholarship, literature in particular, by and about Dominicans (and other transcultural people) is a "powerful model and a formidable motivator." She said resolutely:

> When you read about yourself, when you see yourself in print, hey, you feel proud of who you are; you see yourself as an asset, not as a dead body you're hauling around and trying to hide in the closet. You feel vital, important and wonderful.

Flor believes similarly. A professor (who later became her mentor) "changed" her life when he acknowledged her cultural heritage: "He was a Puerto Rican. My last semester, after I told him I was born in the Dominican Republic, he gave me a copy of *Hay un país en el mundo*, that collection of Pedro Mir's poems that was published in Cuba in 1949."[8] Flor was so "invigorated" that she went on to write her doctoral dissertation on Dominican poets and writers. Now that she's a professor herself, Flor has made it her "mission" to infuse her own courses with scholarship by and about Dominicans throughout the diaspora. In fact, during our first interview she shared her favorite poem with me, one that I did not know. "Yania Tierra," by Aída Cartagena Portalatín, the premier woman poet of the Dominican Republic, is a documentary about the history of the D.R., particularly about the many women who fought fiercely for the island's freedom since before the arrival of Christopher Columbus.

---

[8] Pedro Mir, named National Poet by the Dominican Congress in 1982, was born June 3, 1913, in San Pedro de Macorís. His father was Cuban, his mother Puerto Rican. He was forced into exile in 1947; he returned from Cuba to the Dominican Republic in 1962. He has become known in the English-speaking academic community (at least in New York) in recent years. In 1991 he was awarded an honorary doctorate from Hunter College, CUNY. That same year he was the subject of a conference held at Hostos Community College in New York.

The women include Anacaona, the indigenous cacique of Jaraguá, one of the six chiefdoms of the Taínos. This puissant queen
was reduced to being a slave and forced to serve the Spaniards.
Despite that, she rose to lead a heroic rebellion, which, although
unsuccessful, remains legendary in Dominican consciousness.
Other women whose voices are heard in this poem include Cleofes
Valdez de Mota, who was killed because she opposed the Spanish's annexation of the D.R.; the Andújar sisters, who were murdered because their father participated in the resistance against
Haitian troops in 1822; and like them, the Mirabal sisters (of whom
Julia Alvarez wrote in her novel *In The Time of the Butterflies*),
who were slaughtered in 1960 by Trujillo because they defied his
tyranny.

During that interview, Flor pulled a copy of the poem and read
me the following part, the last lines, which are a call to all contemporary Dominican women to continue the struggle for self and national autonomy:

Yania se desconcierta del juego y las apuestas
Con el cordón umbilical atado
El macho que rechaza
Es devuelto con retrato de esqueleto
Sin derroche/tan cierto
Que su estirpe respetan las Manuela
Las Olaya las Josefa
Es la Historia/Luto negro
Grita el cojito con alegria y pena
Indias/negras/blancas/mestizas/
Mulatas/las aman la justicia y el
Amor con respeto ¡venid!
¡Ea! ¡Mujeres!
¡Ea! ¡Mujeres!
¡Soltad los pájaros de la esperanza!
¡Ea! ¡Mujeres!
¡Soltad Palomas![9]

---

[9] The poem was originally published in1981. I quote from the bilingual
Azul Editions (Washington, D.C.) translated by M. J. Fenwick and Rosabelle White, published in 1995. The English translation follows:

Listening to Flor read part of that poem enlivened me and led me to learn more about courageous Dominican women. Perhaps more significantly, once I found a translation of Portalatín's work, it led me to include it in many of the courses I teach.

Ramón too claimed that one professor is particularly memorable simply because he included works by and about Dominicans in his courses. Reading Mir's poetry in a class was an energizing experience. He said that the "proper introduction" of the Dominican poet sanctioned the poems, Dominican culture, his interest in it, and essentially himself as a Dominican American man. Studying Mir's text in an American university classroom fueled his desire to complete his doctorate and to engage in scholarship that would continue to authenticate him and his heritage. He said to me:

I remember the teacher playing the poems of Pedro Mir, the record, *Hay un país en el mundo* in particular.[10] I remember being

---

Yania is disconcerted by the game and the stakes
With his umbilical cord attached
The man who fights back
Is returned a skeleton
No waste/so certain
That his offspring will respect the Manuelas
The Olayas the Josefas
It is history/A black mourning
The cripple cries with joy and sorrow/
Indian women/ Black women/ White women/
Mestiza women/ Mulatta women/Justice and
Love them with respect come!
Come on! Women!
Come on! Women!
Release the birds of hope!
Come on! Women!
Release the Doves!

[10] Although *Hay un país en el mundo* is widely known by peasants, students, intellectuals, and politicians on the island, Mir's essay "Tres

very moved and feeling pride and ownership—not just intellectually, because obviously everything that you know is yours. I felt that I come from there [the D.R.], and that Mir is as much worthy of intellectual inquiry as anything else.

During that same interview, Ramón recited the opening lines of the poem:

Hay
Un país en el mundo
Colocado
en el mismo trayecto del sol.
Oriundo de la noche.
Colocado
en un inverosímil archipiélago
de azúcar y de alcohol.
Sencillamente liviano,
como un ala de murciélago
apoyando en la brisa.
Sencillamente
Claro,
Como el rastro del beso en las solteras
Antiguas
O el día en los tejados.
Sencillamente
Frutal. Fluvial. Y material. Y sin embargo
Sencillamente tórrido y pateado
como una adolescente en las caderas.
Sencillamente triste y oprimido.
Sinceramente agreste y despoblado.[11]

---

leyendas de colores" (1969), is probably a more effective piece to share with students, because, as literary critic Berroa writes, in it Mir clarifies that Dominican history has systematically negated the mulatto; Mir's essay offers "a new way of understanding Dominican origins" ("Recordar para vivir" 29, my translation).

[11] "There is a Country in the World: A Poem, sad on more than one occasion" translated by Jonathan Cohen and published as part of a book entitled *Countersong to Walt Whitman & Other Poems* (Azul Editions, Washington, D.C., 1993).

However sparse, the inclusion of Dominican literature was very useful for those of us who were hungry, particularly because continuing to seriously study scholarship by and about Dominicans was not easy. For example, when Ramón decided to add the works of Mir in his dissertation, he met with resistance from most faculty. Flor too faced opposition that was very difficult to overcome when she declared that she wanted to write about Dominican literature: it is not a traditional topic; we don't have experts in that field who can guide you; why do you want to study your own people? (Yes, one professor asked exactly that question!) If she hadn't had her mentor's support and encouragement, she probably would not have completed the research.

"It was also very hard," Flor said, to write about Dominican matters "because you're almost self-taught, you know, because your advisers, as good-natured and willing as they may be, don't know much about these subjects and so they have little to add." Flor echoed the sentiment of many of us in this study who talked candidly about the exigency of having to teach ourselves about Dominican arts, culture, history, politics, and other aspects on the island and the diaspora so that we could proceed with our dissertations. Usually, graduate courses set the foundation for writing the dissertation, but there were no courses on Dominicans available to us, hence Ramón, Flor, and the three other participants who wrote our theses on Dominican topics had to undertake additional study on our own. Since none of us had attended school on the island long enough to have learned more than the fundamentals, and since there was a

---

There is/ a country in the world/ situated/ right in the sun's path./ A native of the night./ Situated/ in an improbable archipelago/ of sugar and alcohol./ Simply/ light,/ like a bat's wing/ leaning on the breeze./ Simply/ bright/ like the trace of a kiss on an elderly maiden,/ or daylight on the roof tiles./ Simply/ fruitful. Fluvial. And material. And yet/ simply torrid, abused and kicked/ like a young girl's hips./ Simply sad and oppressed./ Sincerely wild and uninhabited.

dearth of scholarship in English about us, we had to rely heavily on knowledge culled from parents, family, and sources on the island.

Other venues we used to learn included completing independent studies with faculty willing to learn along with us. (That way we could also earn credit for our coursework.) For instance, I sought the guidance of a Chicano professor who taught in the Spanish department. Like most Latino professors, he was overburdened by the demands of "minority" (not just Latino) students seeking mentoring from "minority" faculty.[12] He received no remuneration for taking on independent studies, or for guiding students. But he dedicated time to introducing me to the works of Chicana/os Gloria Anzaldúa, Richard Rodriguez, Sandra Cisneros, and Tino Villanueva, of Puerto Ricans Manuel Zeno-Gandía and Rosario Ferrer, and of Cuban Americans Gustavo Perez-Firmat and Oscar Hijuelos, among several others. Working with him led me to discover the poetry and prose of Dominican American Julia Alvarez, and that set the foundation for a substantial part of my dissertation and my subsequent scholarly investment in U.S. Latina/o literature and culture. Likewise, Flor sought an independent study with her mentor, the Puerto Rican professor, who introduced her to general ideas about the Spanish-speaking Caribbean.

There were no supportive professors for several other participants in this study. They had to research and teach themselves about their topics before they could begin thinking through the specifics of their dissertation. "A lot of extra work, for sure," Ramón remembered, "but at least I was researching a topic that meant everything to me

---

[12] That is one of the many difficulties "minority" faculty face in universities throughout the country. In "Retaining and Promoting Women and Minority Faculty Members: Problems and Possibilities" (a Discussion Paper published by the University of Wisconsin-Madison System Office of Equal Opportunity Programs and Policy Studies in 1990), researchers found that minority faculty receive too little help in addressing problems; they are often expected to carry disproportionately high teaching, advising, and service loads; they are undervalued for their research efforts; they are cut off from support services for themselves (such as mentoring, in and outside their departments); and they are frequently the victims of subtle but powerful ethnic, gender, or sexual harassment (10).

personally." Flor concurred: "it slowed me down a year, because I knew very little about Dominican literature, only what I had learned early in grade school. Definitely an impediment."

Ramón and Flor did find dissertation directors who were supportive and enthusiastic about their projects. Three participants had to "fight" to have their topics accepted, but with the exception of Flor (who focused on material that her grandmother could send from the island), the rest of us had to conduct truly original research because in the late 1980s and early 1990s there was an even worse dearth of scholarship in English by and about Dominicans.[13]

That is a major reason why those engaged professors made such a positive impact on our journey toward high literacy. Those few professors who provided information that allowed us to steer toward higher education, those who infused their courses with scholarship by and about Dominicans, those who supported our focusing on Dominican matters as we wrote dissertations—those professors provided a groundedness, an anchor, a source, and

---

[13] Until the CUNY Dominican Studies Institute was established, there was no one repository for research by and about Dominicans. That is a sad commentary for universities in New York especially, since most Dominicans live there, and since the city had a Dominican literary presence since the turn of the century. Many Dominican writers and intellectuals produced various texts in that city: for example, on or about 1914 a Dominican entrepreneur, Francisco J. Peynado, founded the cultural weekly *Las Novedades*. That same year, Manuel Florentino Cestero (1879-1926) published a book of poems, *El canto del cisne,* at the print shop of *Las Novedades*, and five years later he published a work of fiction entitled *El amor en Nueva York.* Other Dominican poets and fiction writers lived in New York at that time: José M. Bernard (1873-1954) published a volume of verse entitled *Renuevos* (1907) through a printing company called Imprenta Hispano-Americana; short story writer Fabio Fiallo (1866-1942) published *Cuentos frágiles* (1908); Andrés Requena (1908-1952) wrote a novel entitled *Cementerio sin cruces* (1951), which was published in Mexico under Editorial Veracruz; and Angel Rafael Lamarche (1899-1962) published *Los cuentos que Nueva York no sabe* (1949) through Talleres Gráficos La Carpeta in Mexico (Torres-Saillant and Hernández 112).

resource from which we drew to ease our journey and help us build positive attitudes about our ethnic identity and our place in academe.

Temporary Closure

I began this chapter by delineating our recollections of how certain professors understood our condition, and how they facilitated our journey toward high literacy and the professorate. One very strong theme in our stories is the claim that all (but two) of us encountered at least one professor who took an interest in us as individuals, who respected and validated our work and cultural backgrounds, provided the information that helped us maneuver academe, and who infused their courses with scholarship by and about Dominicans. Our stories highlight that we needed those mentors so that, at an essential level, we did not feel as isolated.

That kind of mentoring is crucial, literacy theorist Mike Rose maintains. In his book *Life on the Boundary*, he comments on his personal experiences and that of the many culturally marginalized students he encounters while teaching in the university:

> We live in America, with so many platitudes about motivation and self-reliance and individualism—and myths spun from them, like those of Horatio Alger—that we find it hard to accept the fact that they are serious nonsense. To live your early life on the streets of South L.A.—and to journey up through the top levels of the American educational system will call for support and guidance at many, many points along the way. You'll need people to guide you into conversations that seem foreign and threatening. You'll need models, lots of them, to show you how to get at what you don't know. You'll need people to help you center yourself in your own developing ideas. You'll need people to watch out for you. (47-48)

We in this study needed and fortuitously met those mentors, not a "lowering of standards," as some people might assume. We wanted and needed the academy to truly foster diverse cultural interaction, not just pay lip service to it. Our journey would have been more productive and less traumatic if, for example, there had been a larger pool of Latino faculty and students (not simply a few tokens); if there had been more majors and minors in Latino and Dominican studies; established symposia and publications that showcased our unique talents and contributions, and that considered our plight and interests as more than "marginal" issues; and if there had been more fellowships and postdoctoral opportunities, and even a national employment registry. It is imperative that we take note of these issues, because, sadly, the complex situation for Dominican Americans (and other Latinos) everywhere in the States right now has barely improved.

Again, there are no data specifically about Dominicans,[14] but the 1997-1998 American Council on Education's *Sixteenth Annual Status Report on Minorities in Higher Education* reports that the number of all Hispanics enrolled in higher education increased by 86.4 percent from 1986 to 1996, more so than the rate for whites and African Americans (Wilds 21). Despite that growth, in 1996 Hispanics represented only 8.7 percent of undergraduate students and 4.2 percent of graduate students. More seriously, Hispanics "had a slight decrease in their graduation rate" by one percent: women had a 48 percent graduation rate, men 42 percent (Wilds 26). There has been and continues to be a disparity between the enrollment and the number of degrees earned. In 1996 only 4.7 percent of those enrolled in a bachelor's program actually graduated, and only 3.3 percent of those seeking master's degrees (Wilds 31). That same year there was a 3.4 percent increase in the number of doctorates earned by Hispanics (Wilds 38). There were 335 doctorates in the social sciences (up 5.1 percent for the decade) and 251 in the humanities

---

[14] Research conducted in 1990 specifically on Dominicans affirmed that Dominicans living (predominantly) in New York City attained very low levels of formal education: of the twenty-five-year-old and above population, in 1990 Dominicans had the "highest proportion" of persons who had not completed high school, and the smallest proportion of those who had completed college; 52.3 percent had completed less than high school; only 8 percent completed college or more, compared to 29.9 percent of the overall population (Torres-Saillant and Hernández 72).

(up 4.6 percent for the decade) (Wilds 101). Men received slightly more of those conferred doctorates than women.

The Council also reports that Hispanics made headway as faculty in academe, as have all full-time faculty of color: the rate of employment increased by 6.9 percent from 1993 to 1995 (Wilds 41). But tenure rates for faculty of color did not change while the white rate increased slightly. Hispanic women achieved a 10 percent gain and men a 5.4, meaning that the number of women more than doubled; Hispanic men achieved 7.7 percent increase at the full professor level from 1993 to 1995, while the number of "female full professors declined by nearly 9 percent" (Wilds 44). Analogously, tenure rates remained "nearly steady": 66 percent of the men received tenure, as compared to 55 percent of the women (Wilds 44).[15]

Thus, it is vital that we acknowledge and understand these stories about the contributions our professors made to ease our acquisition of high literacy. These stories allow us to identify our needs, and how, in turn, we might service students today. Macedo's words about examining students' needs are particularly resonant at this juncture:

> By looking at students' cultural processes as forms of textual, social, and political analysis, educators will not only develop means to counter the dominant attempt to impose reproductive educa-

---

[15] In 1990 (before I officially began conducting this study) American Council on Education's *Ninth Annual Report* reiterated that although Hispanics/Latinos were the fastest-growing ethnic group in the nation, we were "grossly underrepresented" at the student and faculty level (16). At the graduate student level, Latino enrollment and completion appeared "to be increasing at a promising rate, but the rate of growth is built on a very small base and is not equal to the growth rate" of the Latino population (16). At the faculty level, even after affirmative action, Latinos continued to be grossly underrepresented as well. They existed in the trenches, hired as adjunct and lecturers in "marginal" departments such as Afro-American and Latino studies, and bilingual education, rather than in tenure-line positions. (Carter, Deborah J. and Reginald Wison. *1990 Ninth Annual Status Report on Minorities in Higher Education.* Washington, D.C.: American Council on Education, 1991.)

tional practices, but they will also equip themselves with the necessary tools to embrace a pedagogy of hope based on cultural production where specific groups of people produce, mediate, and confirm the mutual ideological elements that emerge from and affirm their cultural experiences. Only through experiences that are rooted in the interests of individual and collective self-determination can we create education for liberation. Cultural production, not reproduction, is the only means through which we can achieve a true cultural democracy. (151)

His words and our stories serve to remind us that there is grave danger in attributing the "success" of students like us represented in this study to simply individual motivation. Clearly, we needed professors to pay attention to our specific needs in order for us to complete our graduate programs. That is a clear indication that many barriers would be eliminated if our educational institutions endeavored to change policies so that students like us could receive honed attention.

Our stories can also function as a call to action for all of us to realize that if we are to have truly multicultural campuses it is not enough to accept students who are "different" in our campuses, or to provide monolithic programs meant to help them survive the academic experience. That is not enough. We must change our approach so that we create educational institutions that are pliable, not fixed in ideology meant to serve a privileged few in our society. We need to create an educational apparatus that acknowledges, validates, and serves all of those in our society who wish to acquire high literacy for whatever reason and to whatever aim. The results would surely be beneficial to all of us in that we would be educating our pluralistic society for a pluralistic world.

Antonio, Teresita, and their three children, Dulce María, Homerina, and Homero, about a year after living in New York, as we began the real work and struggle of getting an education and becoming Americans.

Antonio, Dulce María, and Teresita. Teachers' recognition and public acknowledgement (in the form of a diploma, especially) of succeeding in the educational system were truly valued and celebrated
by Antonio and Teresita.

Dulce María, Homero, and Homerina. We wanted to fit in, and so cultural markers were crucial: in our early years we discarded Los Tres Reyes and the Spanish pronunciation of our names. Dulce was called "Candy" for a while, Homero "Tony," and Homerina "Marina." As we went through school, matured, and (consequently, perhaps) learned about our Dominican heritage we reclaimed those aspects of our identity.

5

Dominican Cultural Markers

Last August, three friends and I rented a thirty-four-foot yacht for a long weekend cruise on the Chesapeake Bay. I had been sailing nineteen-foot Flying Scots confidently, alone most of the time, but this was my first time skippering such a large vessel, with a crew, over several nights. Early that sunny Friday morning we maneuvered out of the Annapolis marina. The main and the jib were hoisted; sheets were trimmed. Brisk winds, glistening waves, and my occasional deliberate heelings sailed us south toward Oxford, where we anchored for the night. After a long swim and dodging of tiny jellyfish, we set up the grill. The aroma of fresh salmon (and a giant Portobello mushroom for me, the vegetarian) promised palatable companionship to the fine champagne we sipped. We discussed a gamut of issues, and two played chess, while the stars shone and the boat swayed rhythmically. Once everyone had gone to bed, out on deck I wrote in my journal:

> Am I still daydreaming on my Bronx firescape? I can now afford the time and money to sail. Is this not elite? Have I "sold out"? Is this a marker of high literacy's transformation of me? A new so-

cioeconomic label? Can anyone see my internal markers?[1] April 28, 1965: Father is already in New York. The Dominican sun has not risen and we feel the tremor of massive tanks crossing the Ozama bridge, steps away from where my mother, siblings, and I sleep. They carry 23,000 Marines sent by President Lyndon B. Johnson to occupy my home, his guise being to protect U.S. interests, but really, neighbors murmur, it's to prevent Juan Bosch, considered too leftist, from regaining power and turning us into another Cuba. Tonight no level of literacy can describe what happens until September 3, 1965, when the civil war is "officially" ended. In therapy—maybe. Tonight I am sailing the Chesapeake, my home. And Tuesday I'll return to my family, friends, and students invigorated, with fresh ideas and new perspectives. "Apparent wind," I'll try to explain, "is not there naturally. Something has to make it, but you can use it just the same, to change your course, for instance, toward true wind. It's an exhilarating voyage when you take advantage of apparent wind to tack out of irons, or a blanket zone—positions that provide little hope of sailing."

Barely two months later, on a chilly windy morning, I stepped off the train on 138th in New York City. "Sammy," "Sosa," "Sammy Sosa," "66 home runs and counting" graffitied walls, windows, posters, sidewalks, banners—every inch of space between the station and City College announced his name. "A contract even larger than Mark McGwire's," I'd read in *Newsweek*, "an idol" in his San Pedro de Macorís, a town that produces more major leaguers per capita than any place on earth. "Young, born on November 12, 1968, but generous; he hasn't forgotten his roots," I'd heard over and over in various radio and television shows. I knew his story, although I don't follow baseball; I could not miss,

---

[1] Or, I should add, their consequences? For instance, my relentless awareness of massacres: July 1995, when Serbian death squads executed more than 7,000 Muslim people. One hundred days between spring and early summer 1994, when the ruling Hutus of Rwanda machete 800,000 Tutsis brothers, lovers, and grandmothers. East Timor, Haiti, Uganda, Algeria, Guatemala, El Salvador. . .

particularly in the Big Apple where Dominican Yorks[2] fueled the furor.

As a kid, his father long dead, Sammy worked as a limpiabotas, a shoeshine boy, in Parque Duarte so that he could help support his mother, Lucerisa Sosa, and three sisters, all of whom lived in a two-room house. But he loved baseball, played it even though all he had was an inside-out milk container that he used as a glove. Then Bill Chase, "el Americano" whom he learned to call "Papá," gave him his first ball. He was signed to play with the Phillies, but that contract was annulled because Sammy was too young. Then in 1986 at age 16 he signed with the Texas Rangers for $3,500. In 1989 he played his first major-league game; that's when he purchased a house for his mother. The White Sox bought him and traded him to the Chicago Cubs in March of 1992. In 1994 Sammy signed another deal; that's when he built a second story on his mother's house, and when he gave her a chauffeured Montero and a satellite dish. In 1996 he put up a shopping center in San Pedro de Macorís. He calls it Plaza 30-30 in honor of his biggest achievement at that point: hitting 30 homers and stealing 30 bases. He built a wishing well, too, with a statue of him in his Cubbies uniform: "fountain of the shoeshine

---

[2] "Dominican Yorks," yet another label that has been both imposed on and appropriated by Dominicans who live in New York, is polemical, partly because it highlights the tenuous demarcation between hating/resisting and loving/desiring American culture and commodities. Cultural critic Alan M. Klein explains that the term is "slightly derisive" and that it describes Dominicans who flaunt their new economic wealth. The term resonates of "conspicuous consumption and status differentiation among Dominicans," as well as of the hegemony of American politics, culture, ideology, and economy (which also props up the dominant class in the D.R.) (104). That label is a sort of banner that announces to the world "I'm becoming an American." It also exemplifies Klein's belief that as "Dominicans emulate and consume the culture of the colonizers, they sense they can distance themselves from the feeling of being colonized—it is a balm to them to be able to mimic their oppressors, even if somewhat ineffectively. Not all segments of Dominican society are equally enamored with American culture: its influence is more marked among those with some capacity for upward mobility—the upper and middle classes" (107).

boys," it reads. Reporters assure us that he, his wife Sonia, and their three kids, Keysha, Sammy Jr., and Michael, will enjoy the $42.4 million contract he has until the year 2001. Sammy Sosa, the Dominican Horatio Alger: a cultural marker to be proud of.

Cultural markers: they are dynamic (not fixed), uncertain, decentered, and (re)created symbols of our tradition, of our realities; they are conflicted, mediated, and interpreted signifying codes—frames of reference—that help us make meaning and that reveal our cultural groundedness. Cultural markers are also the fragmented ways of being and thinking that help us negotiate the difference between internally and externally defined identities—that is, between how we see or what we call ourselves and what others see, ascribe, and impose on us. Cultural markers are located at the fluid melding of mind, body, and sign where boundaries between fact and fiction, individual and collective, are blurred. That location is an intertextual and permeable territory that is continually made and remade, that is (re)constituted through the mutual play of discursive and corporeal coding. Cultural markers can be appropriated or assigned. Either way, the process, whether done collectively or individually, consciously or not, entails replicating and reproducing symbols and expressions that embody political agendas and reflect relations of power.

My aim in this chapter is to probe the cultural markers that surfaced repeatedly as I analyzed 1,500 pages of our transcribed interviews. Above all else, participants identified Dominican music as the most notable and active marker throughout our lives, and they talked less frequently but nonetheless passionately about baseball and foodways. I will examine these major signifiers and discuss how respondents believe they stamped our journey toward high literacy, the professorate, and the evolution of our ethnic and cultural identity. I begin with the least mentioned markers and continue with the most conspicuous.

1) Baseball and foodways: Pelota—béisbol—represents more than a pastime for Dominicans anywhere; it stands for (and reminds us of) public resistance to political, economic, and intellectual colonialism and at the same time for a melding of Dominican and Ameri-

can ways. Dominican foodways, what and how we ate as we grew up (and continue to eat today), is a more private kind of marker; it stands for a ritual, an affirmation, a nostalgic way to enact our ethnic identity.

2) Music: merengue and bachata, especially, were the "real Dominican" music we heard and danced at home while growing up; it is the marker that most of us in this study readily identified as part of our cultural legacy while in graduate school; it is the music that we continue to share with our own children and family.

Béisbol and Foodways

It is clear that participants in this study acknowledged that Dominicans everywhere are stamped by major signifiers: Roman Catholicism (Holy Week and the Crowning of Our Lady of Mercedes are momentous yearly events), cockfighting (which appeals almost exclusively to men of all colors and social strata), and certainly baseball, the American game Dominicans have made their own. Although many of the men played the game, none of the participants in this study are true aficionados of baseball, perhaps because all of our lives the lure of books and the life of the mind have kept us preoccupied.

But all of the participants talked about baseball's grip on our milieu on the island and in the States. And thus it is important that I discuss béisbol. In doing so we gain a deeper understanding of the relationship between the United States and the Dominican Republic, the space bridging both cultures that most of us inhabit, and the messages we internalized and that therefore have influenced the ways we've perceived ourselves, high literacy, and the professorate. Hence, I begin the first part of the chapter with further commentary on baseball, the Dominican national sport anywhere in the diaspora, but especially in the U.S., the country that claims the game among its own prominent cultural markers. I continue with a discussion about foodways, and I commence the second part of the chapter with an in-depth probing of Dominican merengue and bachata, the marker that all respondents identified as most significant.

Béisbol

César and Antonio talked about baseball as one of the few activities that served to bond them to other students while in college and graduate school, and that helped to make them feel as if they were part of American society while growing up. As a result, although Ramón (like the other male participants) did not have much time, energy, or interest in baseball at any point in his life, he made sure that he at least watched it on television, that he kept up with it so he could talk to other graduate students about it. And most of the women say that baseball was "always in the background, never in the forefront of" their lives. All of the participants say that "baseball was a constant presence"—"particularly" (María affirmed and echoed the sentiment of several others), as it is "present in the Dominican part of our ethnic identity." Consequently, I focus this discussion of baseball on the history and role it has played in society on the island, and on the ideological legacy that participants inherited.

Pelota—béisbol—on the island represents more than a pastime: it symbolizes the opportunity to escape abject poverty.[3] Baseball, brought from Cuba (where it had been introduced by American troops in the 1860s) to the D.R. in 1891 by the Aloma brothers, symbolizes other things too. Cultural critic Alan M. Klein maintains that béisbol "is the only area in which Dominicans come up against Americans and demonstrate superiority"(3). Pelota has thrived partly because it is revered as the game played by powerful Americans, but also as the game that Dominicans can win. It has always represented a form of opposition to colonialism. In 1914, Klein notes, the "entire country took notice when" Enrique Hernández ("El Indio Bravo") "pitched a no-hit, no-run game against a team of Americans from the U.S. Navy cruiser *Washing-*

---

[3] Bretón and Villegas explain further: the game "is simply the latest powerful foreign institution to have designs on the place proclaimed by Columbus as 'the fairest under the sun'" (80); "It is a story in which opportunity is held out like a lottery ticket that most impoverished Latin kids will never cash in" (35).

ton" (17). The United States had also taken notice of baseball's significance: in 1913 James Sullivan, the American minister to the D.R., sent this message to Secretary of State William Jennings Bryan:

> I deem it worthy of the Department's notice that the American national game of base-ball is being played and supported here with great enthusiasm. The remarkable effect of this outlet for the animal spirits of the young men, is that they are leaving the plazas where they were in the habit of congregating and talking revolution and are resorting to the ball fields where they become wildly partisan each for his favorite team. The importance of this new interest to the young men in a little country like the Dominican Republic should not be minimized. It satisfies a craving in the nature of the people for exciting conflict, and is a real substitute for the contest in the hill-sides with rifles, if it could be fostered and made important by a league of teams. . . . I trust that the Department will not believe that this suggestion is a trivial one, but will see that it well might be one factor in the salvation of the nation. (quoted in Klein 110)[4]

Baseball began to be more blatantly representative of Dominican resistance and national identity when the U.S. Marines invaded the country in 1916.[5] In 1921 the game was professionalized. In the 1930s Trujillo encouraged the playing of béisbol as a way to distract the masses, and as he did with merengue, as a way to create a marker for Dominican culture. In the 1940s sugar cane refin-

---

[4] Dispatch of American Minister to the Dominican Republic to Secretary of State Bryan, November 1, 1913, No. 13. Washington: National Archives, Department of State Records.

[5] Bretón and Villegas reiterate that the United States has invaded almost all Latin American nations producing baseball players. In fact, in the Dominican Republic "baseball symbolized the American occupation. Young Dominican men with no national identity to speak of after 1916 could do nothing as warships docked in their harbors and Marines stormed village after village. The only way they could measure up was by playing baseball. So they did" (82). Later, when the Marines disarmed the country, baseball became one of the few ways people found solace.

ery managers began to use baseball as a diversion for the field workers. In the 1950s pelota on the island began to be called "Béisbol romántico," because more attention was paid to the personalities of individual players and to their ability to bond with the fans. Klein asserts that "while no authors say so explicitly, the implication is that béisbol romántico is synonymous with Dominican cultural control"—that is, with Dominicans' attempt to extricate themselves from American influence and to be different and autonomous (30).

In the 1950s foreign players were allowed to join Dominican teams, and Dominican players finally began to sign with American teams. (For instance, Rudy Fuentes signed with the New York Giants and Manolete Cáceres with the Detroit Tigers.) Cross-influences increased; and Dominican players received more international exposure. By the 1960s Juan Marichal was established with the San Francisco Giants.[6] His name became widely known in Dominican homes on the island and in the States. He was the only Dominican with a public presence in mainstream American society). By 1989 sixty-five Dominicans were listed as roster players in the U.S., and 325 played in the minor leagues. For example,

---

[6] According to Dwyer, Juan Marichal (also know as "Manito") "set the standards of excellence that future Dominican players have sought to measure up to": between 1963 and 1969 he won "more games than any other pitcher in baseball" (90, 91). Marichal also personifies the journey out of poverty. He was born in Laguna Verde in 1938. His father died when Manito was three. At first he played for the Esso Company team, then in 1955 for a team called Las Flores that the Bermúdez Rum Company sponsored. He went on to play for the United Fruit Company, the Dominican air force, then professionally for the Escogido Leones, with whom he traveled all over the Caribbean and Latin America. In 1958 the San Francisco Giants signed him for $500. He arrived in the United States for the 1960 season. His career ended in 1975, but in 1983 he was voted into the Baseball Hall of Fame. Since he stopped playing Marichal has directed Latin American scouting for the Oakland Athletics. In 1994 he helped the Athletics negotiate the purchase of a complex right outside of La Victoria, a small town thirty-five miles outside Santo Domingo; it opened as Campo Juan Marichal in May of that year. Marichal's son, José Rijo, went on to pitch for the Cincinnati Reds.

fifty of the 170 players for the Oakland Athletics were Dominican (Klein 35, 37, 56). Currently there are approximately thirteen baseball academies in the Dominican Republic, and thousands of young impoverished hopefuls struggle to be the next Juan Marichal or Sammy Sosa. Klein writes that at Campo Las Palmas, one of the best-equipped academies, it is

> common for rookies never to have slept in a bed that has sheets. The dormitory is immaculate, and all Dodger rookies are taught to care for their beds as much as for their equipment. They also learn other basic skills: how to act in a group (in a weight room or television room, for example), how to keep a place clean. Those who cannot learn are released, but most sense that they are part of something special and are up to the challenge. (66)

Participants in this study, and my subsequent research, affirm that today, most boys and young men on the island see baseball as the way to escape illiteracy and poverty. Baseball's Dominican identity has become synonymous with economic success. Certainly, that trend has roots earlier in the century when sugar companies constructed barracks (called *batey*) and offered men jobs and the opportunity to play ball. Men (and women too) worked at least twelve hours a day, six days a week for twenty-five years in order to draw a pension. Other than the fact that automation has made those jobs scarce, today life on the *batey* has not changed much. Joyce describes one of those barracks:

> A few more houses have electricity, but not all of them yet. Running water is still a luxury item; many citizens carry drinking water by the pailful to their homes. The women balance the buckets on their heads. In various states of undress, or absolutely bone naked, the children hoist water in plastic containers back to their homes. Goats and pigs and dogs and horses walk around unattended or lie in the muddy, unpaved streets. (180)

Still, young men seek those jobs because they know they can play baseball, and because they can hold on to the hope that while playing they will be recruited by an American major-league team.

As poverty increases, baseball's myth as away out has intensified. Media in the United States and the Dominican Republic highlight the success of players like Sammy Sosa. Indeed, until the early 1990s the "most visible success achieved by Dominicans in North America" had been "attained on the playing fields of the 26 American major league baseball teams" (Dwyer 57).[7] In the 1980s there was Joaquín Andújar, pitcher for the St. Louis Cardinals, and Mario Soto pitcher for the Cincinnati Reds, George Bell left fielder for the Toronto Blue Jays, and Tony Fernandez shortstop for the Blue Jays. All of these men have one thing in common: baseball pulled them out of poverty. As Dwyer writes:

> Indeed, the entrenched poverty that is the lot of so many Dominicans does much to explain their spectacular success in baseball. For many young Dominican men, baseball represents their only real prospect for success. Many may never have known someone who went to college and achieved professional success, but most have heard of George Bell, Tony Fernandez, and Juan Marichal, of their athletic triumphs in los Estados Unidos . . . and of the wealth they have earned. The impoverished background of many Dominican baseball players helps explain everything from their batting style to the ferocity with which Dominicans react when they perceive that the prize that they have obtained through so much hard work—their athletic success—is in some way endangered. (104)

---

[7] What the media does *not* make visible is the huge number of players who are discarded and end up either back on the island or in New York, where many are forced to become petty laborers, thieves, and drug dealers. Bretón and Villegas dedicate an entire chapter in their book to these "discards": "they are out there and baseball knows it" (192). They write that those who don't make it in baseball

> can be found on countless street corners and alleyways of some of the most dangerous barrios in New York City. . . . [T]hey're baseball's rejects, those tossed aside in the search for that one star, those unlucky enough or unskilled enough to face the nightmare . . . of failure. They are the rule, while players who make it to the big leagues, the stars, the sudden millionaires, are the exceptions. (190).

Similarly, Gare Joyce writes that

> Wherever a *gringo* travels in the Dominican, he will be sur-
> rounded by young boys who, in chorus, beseech him for a *pelota*
> (ball) or *guante* (glove). A *pelota* is for those who think small;
> most think big and appeal for a *guante*. I have never been able to
> understand this: how can they expect someone travelling quite
> empty-handed to produce a dozen or so gloves on demand? I
> sought the foundation of this behaviour—perhaps there was a
> mythic *gringo* who went about the countryside planting gloves on
> the hands of needy kids; perhaps there was some sort of Johnny
> Appleseed with a bag of Rawlings instead of apple pips. An old-
> timer once told me that American servicemen always left baseball
> gloves behind when they shipped out, but the story did not have
> the ring of truth. (135)

The role of baseball in the construction of Dominican identity
has taken on a more complex meaning as the game on the island
has become more imbricated in American ways and politics. Today, it is difficult to differentiate Dominican from American aspects of the game. Nonetheless, Dominicans everywhere in the diaspora claim it as their national pastime. That is clearly evident
both on the island and in the States. Now, on any given day the almost sixteen thousand seats at Estadio Quisqueya in Santo Domingo (opened in 1955) are consistently filled to capacity. Similarly, Yankee Stadium in the Bronx is regularly packed with Dominican fans. For Dominicans, baseball is a major cultural marker,
a signifier of our collective and individual identity. Nonetheless,
participants in this study claimed that although baseball imprinted
our developing collective sense of self, it only loomed in the corners of our individual consciousness, not the forefront. We didn't
see the sport as a viable way to escape our condition. Our attrac-
tion to formal education was more powerful and consuming. On
the other hand, foodways, what and how we ate, was and continues
to be a clearly visible aspect of our lives, a clearly visible agent in
what impacted our evolving sense of self in and out of school.

Foodways

In just about every corner of Washington Heights in New York there is a woman selling her home-fried empanadas and pastelitos. On every corner there is also a bodega. Merengue and bachata boom out the doors. Every tropical product imaginable, usually displayed on the sidewalk, draws you in. Brown cassava, deep-purple eggplants, green plantains, large pumpkins, yellow bananas, succulent mangoes, oranges, soursop, huge avocados, lettuce, red ripe tomatoes, various kinds of rice and multicolored beans, creamy dulce de leche, guava paste, Goya products, Café Bustelo, and Café El Pico invite you in. Why does such a scene, food and eating, matter in a study on high literacy and ethnic identity?

The first answer is that along with baseball the participants in this ethnography identified Dominican food and eating as a salient issue—as an external marker of ethnic identity. Foodways has been and still is instrumental in our lives. And since food and eating are enmeshed in cultural practices, it is important to consider Dominican foodways and their role in our journey and evolving ethnic identity. As social theorist Sidney W. Mintz writes, eating is

> never a "purely biological" activity. . . . The foods eaten have histories associated with the pasts of those who eat them; the techniques employed to find, process, prepare, serve, and consume the foods are all culturally variable, with histories of their own. Nor is the food ever simply eaten; its consumption is always conditioned by mean-ing. These meanings are symbolic, and communicated symbolically; they also have histories. (7)

The second answer is that food is an external cultural marker that, like baseball and music, can be easily transported across internal and external geographies. It is a flexible signifier in that it allows us to perform symbolic group interaction, the metaphors that underlie group solidarity, and our ethnic identities in private and public ways. Food reflects and helps to construct collective (and individual) cultural and ethnic identity.[8] As cultural theorist Roger Abrahams notes, food is indeed one of the three "currencies of exchange of primary importance" in any society. He explains:

> [F]ood, sex, talk. Through the interaction of these three, we endow relationships with value and invest them with meaning through intercourse of several sorts. Each activity and each recurrent scene involves an etiquette, a repertoire of different foods and different ways of eating them, a decorum system that arises in the areas of talk and sex as well. As these scenes are learned, they invoke symbolic means, objects, and actions which are laminated with possible meanings to be achieved through interaction—meanings which carry the most profound, if everyday, cultural messages. Discerning with whom one may exchange sex, talk, or food is the central cultural lesson to be learned in growing up. I know of no culture that has not elaborated these access rules into symbolic as well as utilitarian processes, codes, and systems. (21)

Transcripts of our conversations reveal that participants and I talked quite a bit about sex, usually in terms of our parents' repression, or of our own battles with conflicting American and Dominican mores. And we chatted a great deal about religion and Dominican history and music. But Dominican food—the folklore and cultural history surrounding ingredients and their combinations—how to make certain dishes, what, how and when to eat—was perpetually present in our exchanges. We relished memories of cooking, eating, discussing, and learning about Dominican food. We also enacted those recollections, since almost all the interviews included either going to a restaurant, some of the participants cooking something for me, or me for them, or us cooking together. Each of our meetings involved sharing typically Dominican foods.

---

[8] To underline this point it is useful to remember what the word "parsley" has come to mean to both Dominicans and Haitians since the massacre of 1937 when Trujillo's troops distinguished Haitians who attempted to pass as Dominicans by asking them to pronounce the word "perejil" (parsley). If they could not say the word the way Dominicans do, thus revealing their so-called true national identity, they were killed.

Like in every culture, food and what we do with it "binds" individuals together. Cultural critics Keller Brown and Mussell stress that food helps to "define the limits of the group's outreach and identity," to "distinguish in-group from out-group," to "serve as a medium of inter-group communication, celebrate cultural cohesion, and provide a context for performance of group rituals" (5). Some of us in this study are very aware of the symbolism that Dominican food has had and continues to have in our lives. Whether it functions as a tool for us to bond with our mothers, or as the center of all our family gatherings, in various degrees of impact, Dominican food marks us as unique and different from other cultures. That may be because, as food theorist Elaine McIntosh writes,

> immigrants cling more tenaciously to eating habits than to clothing and language after their arrival in the United States. One reason for this behavior is that food confers identity, and this can be done privately in the home, free from possible censure by indigenous Americans. (156)

Most participants in this study affirmed to me that sometimes pridefully, sometimes shamefully, Dominican food has been and continues to be a remarkable and consistent element in how others shape and see our highly literate identities. When I conducted a first round of interviews in 1992, none of us knew of a Dominican restaurant, even in New York. Like other economic refugees who have experienced difficulty escaping poverty in the United States, Dominicans—still today—are not thought of as having a cuisine. Dominican food is not considered to be exotic and exciting and therefore worthy enough of being the sole focus in a restaurant. Moreover, most Dominicans do not have the capital to open their own restaurants, even if the food could draw a massive clientele like Chinese or Japanese food does.

Torres-Saillant and Hernández report that although Dominican food is delicious and as rich as any other, "it remains relegated to the boundaries of the community"; it is rare to find a "Dominican restaurant in any mainstream neighborhood, including those in New York's Greenwich Village which owe their reputation to a sumptuous display of ethnic diversity" (139). Torres-Saillant and Hernández explain:

> Dominican-owned cafeterias and restaurants combine the culinary resources of traditional American cuisine with the cooking styles, options, and preferences traceable to the Dominican Republic. Dominican food thus adds meaningfully to the diverse Hispanic kitchen in the United States. A close scrutiny of the eating habits of Dominicans in North America will most likely reveal that the community has widened the scope of its tastebuds to incorporate elements from other ethnic cuisines. The scrutiny will also most likely find that the diaspora has adopted styles and norms in the kitchen that were thought alien to Dominican cooking prior to migration. (139)

Dominican foodways have been as dynamic as our evolving (re)definition of ourselves. By 1995 when I was completing second rounds of interviews on the Upper West Side of New York City, there were many small restaurants featuring "mangú," "sancocho" and other typically Dominican dishes, though no one restaurant had yet been identified as a Dominican eatery the way Japanese and Mexican foods are marketed. Overwhelmingly, participants chose to conduct our interviews while we ate. We met in Caribbean restaurants, in Dominican cafeterias, or in their houses. Two participants cooked Dominican meals for me in their respective homes. Antonio prepared "moro" for us on the day I interviewed him in his home. We talked about the role of Dominican food. We asked: What do we learn about ourselves by examining Dominican foodways? What are the staples of Dominican cuisine? Can you remember what we learned from our parents, especially our mothers (since quite a few of our fathers still believe that cooking is "women's work")? What did they keep in our pantries, refrigerators, or growing in el patio? Why does examining our food matter to us? How is that linked to the process of becoming highly literate?

"I remember, as if it was a moment ago," I said to Antonio, "that throughout my childhood I sang 'Arroz con Leche'; that's surely one place where I learned to connect food, cooking, marriage, and what

everyone expected me to learn about being a woman. That song did
not teach me to value high literacy":

> Arroz con leche
> Me quiero casar con una viudita de la capital
> Que sepa cozer, que sepa tejer,
> que ponga la aguja en su mismo lugar
> Arroz con leche
> Me quiero casar con una viudita de la capital
> Con esta sí, con esta no
> Con esta viudita me casare yo[9]

Of course, in childhood to me that was just a song about my
favorite dessert, one that my mother cooked with extra measures of
raisins, cloves, and cinnamon just for me. But in talking with
Antonio I came to understand that songs like that taught me a great
deal about women, food, and Dominican gender roles. I had
internalized many messages. Further consideration, additional
conversations with other participants, and research have clarified
that, for instance, like Dominican people, Dominican foodways are
not a monolith. Although to-day the African flavor "reflected in the
use of more root vegetables and meats such as goat" is the most
apparent aspect of Dominican food, there are three clearly vivid
cultural and ethnic influences in what is now known as Dominican
cuisine: Taíno, Spaniard, and African (Bandon 100).

When Columbus arrived on the island, he really discovered
another *old* world, one that had been populated by diverse people
with distinct cultures (ancestors who had come from Asia via the
Bering Straits) some 20,000 to 28,000 years previously. They left
an imprint on the Taíno Indians he met. Taínos cultivated and enjoyed various native meats, vegetables, fruits, and fish. Much of
that food is still eaten today. For example, all of the participants in
this study, at some time in their lives, have eaten the following

---

[9] My rough translation follows: rice pudding, I want to marry a widow
from the city, who knows how to sew, who knows how to knit, who can
put the needle back in its place. Rice pudding, I want to marry a widow
from the city, this one yes, this one no, this young widow I shall marry.

staples of Dominican foods: beans, maize, and squash (Taínos' "alimentary trinity"), regular potatoes, sweet potatoes, guáyiga (a starchy tuber also called Zamia Debilis), and Cassava or manioc, which is made from yuca and is very popular. Other staples traced back to the Taínos include jaiba (freshwater crabs), shrimp and turtles, yaguazas (a type of wild duck), breads made from corn, and many fruits, among them guava (Myrtaceae family); caimito (Sapodilla, Sapotacease family); pineapple (Bromeliaciae family); guanábana (sugar-apple), anón and jagua (custard-apples, Annona family); jobo (hog-plum/cashew, Anacardiae family); mamey (mammee-apple/Mammea-Americana, Clusiaceae family); hicaco (cocoplum, Chrysobalanceae family); and caimoní (Roseaceae family) (McIntosh 64).

The Columbian Exchange, that swap of people, ideas, plants, animals, and diseases begun by Columbus in 1493, transformed both old worlds (the island and Spain/Europe). On his second voyage to Hispaniola Columbus brought 1,500 settlers, horses, dogs, pigs, cattle, chickens, sheep, goats, seeds, and cuttings. He brought sugar cane (which had been introduced to the Spaniards during the Moorish conquest in the eighth century) and planted it in Santo Domingo. And on his way back to Europe he took maize/corn and manioc/cassava. That produce then traveled with colonialism to Africa. In turn, colonialism and slavery brought the island rice, wheat, barley, oats, rye, coffee, eggplant, and mangoes (mango indifera), ñame (yam, Dioscorea family), guandul (green pigeon pea, the Leguminosae family), peppers, and watermelons.

Andalusian Spaniards who followed Columbus introduced varieties of beans, olive oil, flour, lentils, chick-peas, olives, nuts, carrots, turnips, radishes, lettuce, and wine for drinking and cooking (McIntosh 178). Bananas/guineas (musa acuminata), that most important of all fruit in Dominican diet, arrived via the Canary Islands in 1516 with Friar Tomas de Berlanga, a Catholic missionary priest who believed that bananas were the cheapest food that could be cultivated for the growing African slave population

(Mintz 39; McIntosh 67; Scott Jenkins 3).[10] Subsequently, an unbroken influx of immigrants from everywhere in the world has continued to change Dominican gastronomy, but the staples have always included rice, beans, plantains, garlic, onions, coriander, and oregano. All of those food items have been consistently present in our lives. All of them have been seen as markers of our "Dominicanness" in and outside of the island. To varying degrees of inclusion, all of that food traveled with us when we (or our parents) left the island.

Rereading the transcripts of our interviews emphasized for me how much respondents and I truly enjoyed talking about food. During our first interview in his home, Antonio told me stories about his parents' "patio" in the campo and all of the edible things in it. They didn't buy much food, because there were avocados, oranges, lemons, yams, yuca, plantains, coconuts, breadfruit, tamarind, guavas, oregano, sugarcane, coriander, onions, garlic, ginger, peanuts, molasses, peppers, and all sorts of other staples growing in the backyard. Milk and meat came fresh from the source. A chicken, for instance, was wrung dead and plucked by "abuela's" (grandmother's) own hands. A lechon (pig/pork) would have been fed all the right things to ready it for the Christmas roast. Flor's parents lived in "la capital," Santo Domingo, and their "patio" was not as big, so they could not grow as many of these cooking ingredients, but her mother bought them daily so as to get them fresh. When they migrated to the States her mother continued to shop on a daily basis. As adults, especially during graduate school when they were often stressed, both Antonio and Flor were particularly fond of remembering these aspects of their early life.

---

[10] Today, bananas are an important staple of the Dominican economy and the produce that is eaten and exported. Bananas have played a key role in the relationship between the Dominican Republic and the United States: the U.S. intervened in 1916 partly to protect its investment in the banana industry. By 1930 the United Fruit Company owned and managed vast acres of land for growing bananas. Scott Jenkins writes that before 1880 most people in the U.S. had never seen a banana, but today bananas have a secured place in the nation's culture and folklore and the Dominican Republic is still considered to be a "Banana Republic" (3).

By looking at our foodways, Antonio told me, we learn about ourselves. Like me, he was especially interested in discussing breakfasts, since they are most memorably the only times our families ate together, and hence when we heard our parents' admonishments about doing well in school. The typical Dominican breakfast is Mangú, green plantains boiled and then mashed with olive oil and garnished with sautéed onions, avocado, and one of the following—fried eggs with peppers, longaniza (salami), or fried white cheese—and usually presented with a cup of hot chocolate (or a tall glass of freshly squeezed orange juice or milk). Mofongo (mangú with pork rinds) is also popular.

When we lived in the Bronx breakfasts in my own family (like that of over half of us in this study) were not as elaborate as those eaten on the island, being that both my parents worked outside the house and had to leave early in the morning. My father insisted that the three of us children swallow the raw yolk of a fresh egg chased by a gulp of Manischewitz kosher wine. He believed that combination would help us grow into tall strapping Americans. I cringe even now. (The vegetarian in me also still winces at the memory of my mother making, and my father eating, mondongo, a seasoned heavy stew of pig entrails served with rice and root vegetable.)

As a child, and later as an adolescent, I considered those eating habits to be a source of shame. Like several other participants, I did not discuss those foodways with my American friends. But as an adult, while in graduate school, once I had matured, once I had been able to read about and to learn to appreciate my cultural heritage, I was proud to share those foodways with my non-Dominican friends.

Participants who spent their early years in the Dominican Republic talked in yearning ways about lunchtime as it is eaten on the island. That was when families gathered to eat the main meal of the day, when they talked and laughed and fought together. In the States, since most of our parents were out working and we did not return from school until after three, dinner became the prime meal. (In the D.R. dinner is light and may consist of pasta, sandwiches, fritters, steamed patties, sausages, salad, fruits or shakes.)

Most respondents say that while growing up in the States they ate TV dinners, hot dogs, a variety of fast foods, and other typically American meals, but it is the Dominican dinners that stand out in our memories as special and at the same time as mundane. Those are our sentiments now, though some of us do acknowledge that earlier in our lives we were not as candid, because that food marked us as "other." In the States our mothers cooked big dinners: meat, rice, beans, fritters, salad, dessert, and coffee. The main dish consisted of one or a combination of the following typical Dominican foods: *Moro*, a mixture of fluffed rice and beans with one or more legumes; *Locrio*, a blend of fluffed rice and beans with meat, sausages, fish, or seafood; *Sancocho*, a juicy soup of various meats, vegetables, tubers, seasonings, and fresh herbs (the richest version, Sancocho de siete carnes/seven meat soup, is usually cooked on festive occasions); and *Asopao*, a fusing of rice, poultry, beef, fish, or seafood into a thick soup.

Side dishes included fritters (made from plantains, yuca, sweet potatoes—anything that can be fried), casabe, and salad (usually lettuce, cucumbers, cooked and sliced carrots and chayote [squash], onions, radishes, tomatoes, beets, and avocado all seasoned with olive oil, vinegar, salt, and pepper). The most common desserts, plátanos al caldero (baked ripe plantains in a cinnamon-wine sauce), raspadura de leche (milk candy wrapped in royal palm bark), and arroz con leche (milk and rice custard), were also abundant for snacks at any time. Coffee was present at all meals and in between, even for the children. After school we usually had a milk shake, like "Morir Soñando" (dying dreaming), a mixture of (sometimes freshly squeezed) orange juice, milk, tons of sugar, and ice. Or, if the local bodega in the States had any, we drank Mabí (also called bejuco Indio), a fermented juice made from the bark of colubrina reclinata, a liana.

During our first interview at his house, Antonio and I reminisced and compared notes on what we ate when we were children, and what we now cook as adults. He remembers and enjoys "recreating Christmas eve dinners" when peanuts, hazelnuts, almonds, dates, raisins, dried figs, breadfruit, and spiked ponche de huevo (eggnog), fill the table way after everything else has been eaten and everyone is exhausted but still dancing. In graduate school I occasionally made moro for friends who'd never heard of it; that usually occasioned positive discussions about the Dominican Republic, and therefore it provided instances of affirmation and validation for me. But of all the Dominican foods I was exposed to, it is the habichuelas con dulce (sweet red beans) that stand out in my memory as the most important Dominican food—something that I cook now in my own multicultural kitchen.

I remember that my mother made habichuelas con dulce during Lent, the traditional time every other Dominican household on the island and in the States also ate it. As I helped my mother cook, she explained that beans are high in protein, and that Dominicans usually made the dish during Holy Week partly to supplement their diet during a time when (as Catholics) they were not allowed to eat meat.

My mother and I made habichuelas con dulce together for the last time about a month before she died. By then she knew that I was proficient at it, but she insisted on guiding me through the process. "Make enough for about 12 small bowl servings," she said, because everyone likes habichuelas con dulce, "and don't forget to line up all the ingredients" (which I can do as if on auto-pilot):

3 cups of dry red beans
8 cups of water
4 cups of milk
1 cup evaporated sweetened condensed milk (undiluted)
3 cups sugar
1 teaspoon of salt
3 small cinnamon sticks
10 whole cloves
½ teaspoon of nutmeg
4 cups cubed sweet potatoes
1 cup of coconut milk
1 cup seedless raisins
5 or less tablespoons of margarine
casabe bread

I soaked the beans overnight. In midmorning I placed them in a large saucepan with 8 cups of water, covered it, and let it go to full boil then to simmer (adding water when needed) for an hour and a half (or until the beans were very tender). Next, I puréed the beans with a fork or in a blender, put then back in the saucepan and added the milk, sweetened condensed milk, sugar, salt, cinnamon, cloves, and nutmeg. I brought the whole thing to a brisk boil again and stirred it for ten or fifteen minutes until all the ingredients were thickly blended. Then I reduced the heat, added the sweet potatoes and cooked it uncovered for about 20 minutes. At that point I added raisins and butter (and only sometimes, because I don't like it, coconut milk). I let it simmer, stirring occasionally, for about 30 minutes, then let the pot cool for about 15 minutes. My mother and I usually served the habichuelas hot, though cold is delicious too, with crumbled pieces of casabe on top.

"Hay sí claro, I love habichuelas con dulce," María said to me on the phone as we planned our next interview. "But what I really like to cook, and to eat, is frituritas de berenjena con sofrito de ají, cebolla y tomate [eggplant fritters seasoned with garlic, onion, and tomatoes]; let's make it together when you visit." It was the fourth time we'd talked on the phone. Our follow-up interview would be the second we met. Since I'd be traveling sixteen hours to her home, María wanted to make our session festive. We had discussed cultural and ethnic identity and Dominican influences in detail, food being a major marker. I offered to bring enough ingredients for six to eight fritters:

½ chicken bouillon cube dissolved in 2 tablespoons of hot water
2 tablespoons grated parmesan cheese or vegetable oil
1 large eggplant
1 ½ cups all-purpose flour
¾ cup water, room temperature
2 teaspoons salt
2 garlic cloves, crushed
1 medium white onion, chopped
½ tablespoon of olive oil
1 medium tomato, seeded
1 medium green pepper, chopped

When I arrived at her house we immediately cut the eggplant in lengthwise slices, sprinkled them with salt, and put them aside for an hour. In the meantime, we conducted the interview, occasionally stepping out of the scholarly mode to mix the flour with water and make a smooth batter. An hour and half later, we patted the eggplant dry, dipped each piece into the batter, and browned both sides in vegetable oil. We put them in a warming tray to keep them crisp while we sautéed the garlic, onion, tomato, and pepper in olive oil, and then added the chicken bouillon and let the whole thing cook for 3 minutes. Finally, we poured the mixture over the fritters, topped it with parmesan cheese and sat down to eat and talk. What a way to do ethnography! And what a difference (from when we were younger) in attitude about Dominican foodways.

So many of us in this study talked about the frequent times in our childhood when we argued bitterly with our parents because they insisted on feeding us rice, beans, and other typically Dominican foods. We wanted to eat White Castle and McDonald's hamburgers; we wanted all those American fast food products advertised on television: Wendy's, home-delivered pizza, TV dinners.

As we were growing up there was much focus on food and nutrition in the States. President Johnson's War on Poverty had been launched by the passage of the Economic Opportunity Act of 1964. In 1972 Congress passed legislation authorizing the Special Supplemental Food Program for Women, Infants and Children (WIC). In 1974 the Food Stamps became a nationwide program. Media coverage of food and health issues became standard. In the 1980s the widespread emphasis on fitness and weight control exacerbated our resistance to eating Dominican foods. We began to characterize it as only "greasy," "fatty" and as the main reason why our bodies (particularly the women's) would not conform to standard American sizes.

In graduate school, as we learned and gained a clearer understanding of our cultural heritage, Haydee, Flor, César, and Antonio affirmed, we "reclaimed" Dominican foodways. We realized that consuming the culturally familiar food (then and now) provides us with a sense of belonging and with an opportunity to maintain Dominican ethnic group boundaries and collective identity. Like

our self-identity, today our kitchens and dining rooms reflect a melange of influences. Acknowledging and openly "celebrating" Dominican foodways, is, as Antonio explained, "one way we express
Dominican ethnic continuity and integrity, one way that we articulate our hybrid identity."

Merengue and Bachata

The role of merengue and bachata music in our lives is certainly a
significantly recurrent theme easily identifiable as I analyzed our
transcribed interviews. Dominican music is *the* signifier of our collective and individual identity, most participants claimed. Haydee,
for instance, believes that we have "el merengue en la sangre, definitely in our blood; our hips are preprogrammed." That's what she
said when we discussed the sorts of things she noted as Dominican
markers while attending graduate school. And during our third interview, conducted (in a storefront restaurant in Washington Heights)
while Juan Luis Guerra's "Guavaberry" played over the loudspeaker,
she said competing with the volume, "I loooove that merengue because it is about the regional customs of Cocolos."[11] She went on
to explain excitedly: "it's about black Dominicans like me who are
descendants of Anglophone Caribbean people who arrived in the
19th century; that's why the lyrics are in Spanish and English."
Guerra's song boomed over the speakers and some patrons stood
up to dance in the narrow aisles meant just for walking:

---

[11] Cocolos, a derogatory label for blacks, are descendents of the thousands who left other Caribbean islands such as St. Kitts, Nevis, and An-
guilla looking for a better life in the Dominican Republic. Haitians, who
are often called Cocolos, are still rejected and believed to be uncultured
and foreign. In fact, Duany reports, between "June and September 1991,
the Balaguer government sent back more than 50,000 Haitians to their
country of origin. However, many deportees were Dominican nationals
or were born in the Dominican Republic. This fact reveals the predomi-
nant view of Haitians [and all Cocolos] as inassimilable elements into
Dominican culture. From this perspective, Haitian [and anyone of black]
origin becomes a tarnish on one's past that cannot be erased in one or
two generations ("Ethnicity, Identity, and Music" 71).

I like to live in the streets
of San Pedro de Macorís
I like to sing my song
in the middle of Malecón
and drinking my guavaberry
watching the sun go down . . .
Quiero vivir junto a tí . . .
quiero bailar mi canción . . .
bebiendo guavaberry
al ritmo de un tambor . . .
I wanna hear the song
of cocolo beating beating the drums
drinking my guavaberry . . .
woman that's all I need
in San Pedro de Macorís

Haydee clarified why she likes that particular song and why she feels such an affinity with merengue and bachata in general:

That song celebrates our traditional drumming and Christmas Eve drink. It's about the myth that Dominicans are a deracialized nation, a myth that we carry into the diaspora, especially to places like the U.S. and Spain, where racism is so different from ours. All merengues are about ourselves, our identity, about some aspect of Dominican history and culture on the island and the diaspora. I don't know to what degree the music shaped our sense of self or how it reflects who we are. You know . . . I'm not sure where one aspect begins and the other ends. I always play merengue and bachata. It's my music. I want to show it off to everybody, 'cause it's so catchy and it tells so much about who we are. It reveals—in sounds—*who* we are.

I smiled and without thinking I said to Haydee, "but merengue is not really indigenous to the D.R. Why do you consider it such a profound part of our identity, especially since during our lifetime it has been deeply influenced by U.S. culture?" Haydee responded: "Neither is baseball! That's the point! Merengue may not be native but we Dominicans have surely made it our own; it's just like us, infused with Americanisms, multicultural—*not* a monolith—and that's precisely why it is the quintessential icon for our culture." I added, "bachata is autochthonous, and its development parallels our emigrating experiences since the 60s; perhaps that's a more accurate signifier." "Maybe," Haydee maintained, "but it seems to me that bachata is only about love the way men see it. Merengue is about everything. I think that both kinds of music reflect *and* help construct who we think we are."

My ensuing research on merengue and bachata confirms that Haydee was right on target. As Puerto Rican anthropologist Jorge Duany notes, we have to remember that all popular music "articulates the dominant themes and concerns of a national culture" ("Ethnicity, Identity, and Music" 65). Ethnomusicologist Paul Austerlitz reminds us that merengue is syncretic and that it "has endured as a symbol of Dominican identity for its very success in articulating the contradictory forces at play in Dominican life" (*Merengue* 8). Pacini Hernández affirms that merengue's long and rich history reflects "the country's attempts to come to grips with race, class, and cultural authenticity, issues which have been significant features of the country's evolving national identity" ("The Merengue" 167). And bachata, which emerged in 1961, Pacini Hernández states, is a mirror of "profound changes in Dominican society," particularly about sexuality and gender relationships (*Cantando* 351). Examining each form of music can reveal multilayered aspects of how and why our diasporic identities evolve (d).

In 1978 there was a conference titled "Encounter with the Merengue" in Santo Domingo. Its major aim was to clarify where merengue originated—which was the same as asking, Pacini Hernández contends, "Where did we Dominicans come from, and who are we?" Answering that question "forced cultural observers of all socio-political persuasions to acknowledge—or reject—the country's African heritage"; that conference also helped to point out that "merengue serves as a window onto the social changes transforming Dominican society since the 19th century" ("The Merengue" 171).

Various scholars admonish that we may never find out where merengue really originated, but that there is no doubt that it has thrived vigorously in the Dominican Republic, and that it is the best-known cultural export. Torres-Saillant and Hernández add that the "most salient cultural presence of Dominicans in the United States has occurred in the realm of popular music with the increasing acceptance of merengue, the best-known Dominican dance music, in Latino entertainment circles during the 1980s and 1990s" (133). Surely, participants in my study insist, listening to and dancing merengue and bachata are noteworthy ways we learned about our history, our condition, and who we are (becoming).

Scholarship and popular folklore date the emergence of merengue to the Haitian occupation between 1822-1844, and show it to be "a product of syncretic creolization" in that it fuses originally disparate African (probably southwest Nigeria) and European contredanse (Manuel 98). The word *merengue* is presumably derivative of the French *méringue*. Austerlitz writes that the first song was composed in 1844 (during the battle of Talanquera in the War of Independence) as a sort of ditty about a wounded Dominican soldier who deserted. The side-to-side movement of the dance is supposed to simulate how one of the soldier's feet dragged behind the other. That first merengue is titled "Thomas fled with the flag":

Toma' juyó con la bandera,
Toma' juyó de la Talanquera,
Si fuera yo, yo no juyera,
Toma' juyó con la bandera.[12]

Nascent versions of Dominican merengues were played with stringed instruments, the tambora (a drum played sideways with one hand and a stick), one or more percussion instruments, and a güiro (a horizontally serrated dried hollowed calabash that is scraped with a gancho or púa [a piece of wood with hard wire inserted at the end]). In the 1870s, when German immigrants brought the accordion with them, it was added to the assortment of instru-

---

[12] Austerlitz's translation: Thomas fled with the flag/ Thomas fled from Talanquera/ If it had been I, I wouldn't have fled, / Thomas fled with the flag.

ments, and shortly after so was the saxophone. Since then, trombones, trumpets, congas, keyboards, electric bass guitar, and güiras (a metallic güiro) have been added.

In the mid-1800s, when merengue began to be danced, written, and talked about, elite Dominicans elided it because of its African influence, its sexually suggestive frenetic hip movement, and because it is a couple's dance (rather than a group's). It was considered vulgar and uncivilized, a dance/music of the poor (campesinos, former slaves, and sugarcane workers) that was performed in cockfighting rings (galleras) and in brothels. But among the poor, merengue developed in two major types: típico, which is played by small rural conjuntos, and merengue de orquesta, which is played by large urban ensembles. All merengues are composed of three parts: the introductory paseo (an instrumental section that allows dancers time to find partners and get on the floor); main cuerpo or merengue proper; and the jaleo (a sort of call and response that allows musicians to play as long as the dancers want to continue). Juan Bautista Alfonseca (1810-65) was one of the earliest known Dominican composers of merengue.

During the first U.S. invasion in 1916 merengue gained more widespread acceptance across social classes, because it began to represent vernacular culture as threatened by foreign domination. "La Protesta," written by Ñico Lora, is one of the first examples of merengue being used as a national and cultural symbol (Manuel 101).

En el año diez y seis
Llegan los americanos,
Pisoteando con sus botas,
El suelo dominicano.
Francisco Henríquez Carvajal,
Defendiendo la bandera,
Dijo, "¡No pueden mandar
Los yanquis en nuestra tierra!"
El americano, como se entromete [repite];
Los haremos ir, dandole machetes [repite].
Los haremos ir, con fuerza y valor [repite];
El americano, por abusador [repite].

En tierra de Duarte, no pueden mandar [repite];
Los americanos, dijo Carvajal.[13]

During that first invasion, another type of merengue developed: merengue estilo yanqui (Yankee-style merengue), also known as Pambiche (said to be a phonetic reproduction of the words Palm Beach), is danced very fast and very close almost like grinding.[14] In the early 1920s all types of Dominican merengues began to appear in elite dancing clubs, and consequently (as wealthy Dominicans traveled) in New York. Groups such as Trio Borinquen (also called Trio Quisqueya) performed in New York and earned contracts with Columbia Records. On the island merengue gained momentum as a communicative tool between leaders and the masses. For example, "Horacio Salió," a popular merengue in the 1930s (composed by Isidro Flores or Ñico Lora) celebrated the departure of President Horacio Vásquez and the ascendancy of Trujillo.

Horacio salió
y ahora entra Trujillo.
Tenemos esperanza
en nuestro caudillo.

---

[13] Manuel's translation: The Americans came/ in 1916/ Trampling Dominican soil/ With their boots./ Defending the flag,/ Francisco Henríquez y Carvajal/ Proclaimed that "Yankees/ Cannot rule our land!"/ We'll attack them with machetes, we'll make/ them leave [repeat];/ The Americans, the intruders [repeat]./ With power and courage, we'll make them/ leave [repeat];/ The Americans, the abusers [repeat]./ Carvajal said that Americans/ Cannot rule the land of Duarte.

[14] Austerlitz writes that the merengue is named pambiche because during the occupation many American Marines attempted to dance by combining the one-step and fox-trot. Dominicans imitated their movements or (another version of the story says) they tried to accommodate the Americans' inability (to dance like the natives) by inventing merengue estilo yanqui. That new style was initiated with a song about a fabric called Palm-Beach. And so the folklore is that the name indicates that "as the Palm Beach fabric is neither cashmere nor drill, pambiche is neither merengue nor fox-trot" (41).

Todo cambiará,
en marcha caliente.
Pues ahora Trujillo
es el Presidente.
Se acabó la bulla, se acabó.
Se acaban los guapos, se acabó.
Ni "colú" ni "bolo," se acabó.
Eso de partidos, se acabó.[15]

As he did with baseball, Trujillo recognized the power of merengue as a political tool that could help him control the overwhelmingly illiterate population. He made deliberate efforts to raise merengue out of the campo and brothels and into the ballrooms of high society. He renamed the leading band, Lira del Yaque, Orquesta Generalísimo Trujillo, and he commanded its leader, Luis Alberti, to drop the accordion and to compose lyrics that would exalt Trujillo and his regime. The band went on the road with Trujillo whenever he campaigned. By 1936 merengue had become a mouthpiece for Trujillo's political propaganda. Spurred by the increasing Puerto Rican, Cuban, and other Latino immigrant population in New York, by the 1950s singers like Angel Victoria (who led an ensemble called Conjunto Típico Quisqueyano) were recording many popular numbers for Ansonia Records. By May 30, 1961, when Trujillo was killed, merengue was an established Dominican cultural marker. With Trujillo dead and his family exiled, masses of Dominicans migrated out of the rural areas, into Santo Domingo, and then out of the country (mostly to the United States). Of course, they brought along their favorite and easily transported music.

Like most participants in this study, merengue kings of the 1960s and early 1970s straddled the two islands—the D.R. and

---

[15] Austerlitz's translation: Horacio is gone,/ And now Trujillo is in./ We have faith/ In our caudillo./ All will change,/ With fiery motion,/ Because now Trujillo/ Is the President./ No more noise, it's over./ No more bullies, it's over./ No colú, no bolo, it's over./ No more political parties, it's over. ("Colú" and "bolo" are cockfighting terms that also refer to political parties.)

Manhattan: Johnny Pacheco was born in New York, Primitivo Santos lived there, and Joseíto Mateo visited often. They were instrumental in bringing the music, in 1967, to Madison Square Garden on 34th Street. Cross influences accelerated. Johnny Ventura, for instance, refashioned merengue performances into a "combo show." He narrowed the orchestra, added the bass drum and spicy lyrics, incorporated the contemporaneous beats of salsa and disco, and, inspired by soul singer James Brown's revue, had his band members dress in flashy costumes and do snazzy dance steps (Manuel 106).

In the 1970s merengue continued to thrive as massive numbers of Dominicans dispersed through the United States and Europe—Madrid, Rome, and Amsterdam, for instance. Many began to face even greater risks by leaving the island illegally, especially by small boats that attempted to cross the turbulent Mona Passage leading to Puerto Rico. Still today numerous boats capsize in the shark-infested waters.[16] Thousands have perished and merengueros have taken it upon themselves to sing about it. Bandleader Wilfrido Vargas warned would-be emigrants in one song:

> Puerto Rico queda cerca, pero móntate en avión.
> Y si consigues la visa, no hay problemas en inmigración;
> pero no te vayas en yola, no te llenes de ilusiones,
> porque en el Canal de la Mona, te comen los tiburones.[17]

---

[16] Such horrific stories take on various shapes. For example, on September 4, 1980, only twelve of the thirty-four men who attempted to flee in the ballast tank of the Regina Express survived. All thirty-four wanted a better life. So they mortgaged their houses, sold their lands, borrowed, did anything to raise the $2,800 for the illegal voyage that would transport them to Miami in the freighter's airtight container. Among the dead were Félix Tavarez, a carpenter who'd been out of work for five years; Rafael Flores, a farmer who had sold his farm, cows, and his house—his two daughters were left with nothing—and Alfredo Cáceres, a lottery ticket vendor who had tried once before to leave the island (Dwyer 47).

[17] My translation: Puerto Rico may be close, but take a plane. If you get a visa there won't be problems with immigration. Don't go in a boat; don't fill up with illusions, because in the Mona Passage sharks will eat you.

In the 1980s, when most of the participants in this study were in graduate school, merengue continued to reflect and to influence Dominicans' sense of themselves and their worlds. The historically male-centered combos and orchestras began to include women vocalists who then took the lead and began to sing about women's perspectives. New female-centered combos formed. One group, Milly, Jocelyn y Los Vecinos, began performing in New York. They sing predominantly about the hardships women face because of patriarchy and emigration.

In the mid- and late-1980s merengue took its widest turn to date: Juan Luis Guerra (who studied at the Dominican National Conservatory and Boston's Berklee College of Music) appeared on the scene and put merengue firmly on the global map. Many of the respondents in this study said that his lyrics mirror and help to construct Dominicans' evolving diasporic identity. "Visa para un sueño" is a prime example:

Eran las cinco en la mañana.
Un seminarista, un obrero,
Con mil papeles de solvencia,
Que no les dan pa'ser sinceros.
Eran las siete en la mañana.
Uno por uno en el matadero,
Pues cada uno tiene su precio,
Buscando visa para un sueño.
El sol quemándoles las entrañas,
Un formulario de consuelo,
Con una foto dos por cuatro,
Que se derrite en el silencio.
Eran las nueve en la mañana,
Santo Domingo, ocho de enero.
Con la paciencia que se acaba,
Pues no hay visa para un sueño.
Buscando visa de cemento y cal,
¿Y en el asfalto, quién me va a encontrar?
Buscando visa, la razón de ser,
Buscando visa para no volver.
¡La necesidad, que rabia me dá!
¿Golpe de poder, que más puedo hacer?

Para naufragar, carne de la mar,
La razón de ser; para no volver.[18]

"Visa" is typical of Guerra's songs: reenvisioned rhythms and
harmonies coupled with and "mediated by," as Duany writes,
"carefully crafted verses" and "a complex series of poetic transformations" ("Ethnicity, Identity, and Music" 76). Like so many of
his others, this song comments on the current dire psychic and
economic situation of most Dominicans on the island. It describes
what it is like trying to get a visa, trying to flee the island in a legal
way: applicants stand like starving docile animals on long lines and
provide myriad documentation to prove that they are financially
solvent and thus do not need to look for sustenance elsewhere—(a
huge lie, a selling of the soul, the lyrics suggest, since insolvency
is the main reasons Dominicans want to leave). In the background
we hear the sound of an INS helicopter reminding us that the day
may be wasted, that reception in the States is not warm and wel-
coming, and that the hope for economic mobility is tenuous at best.
The process of getting a visa is degrading, depleting, and often fu-
tile, and so we the listeners are prompted to think of the thousands
who attempt to leave the island by falsifying documents or by
boarding yolas (tiny boats) that carry them across the Mona Passage to Puerto Rico.

A preponderance of Guerra's lyrics are infused with that kind of
commentary, social consciousness, and sympathy for the dispos-

---

[18] Manuel's translation: "Visa for a Dream": It was five o'clock in the
morning./ With a thousand documents proving economic solvency./
Which do not allow them to be honest./ It was seven o'clock in the morning./ Lined up at the slaughterhouse,/ Everyone has his price,/ Seeking a
visa for a dream./ Everyone has his price,/ Seeking a visa for a dream./
The sun burning their entrails,/ With only application forms to console
them,/ And a two-by-four-inch photo,/ Which melts away in silence./ It
was nine o'clock in the morning./ Santo Domingo, the eight of January./
With patience almost at an end,/ There are no visas for a dream./ Seeking
a visa of cement and limestone./ Who will I meet in the concrete jungle?/
Seeking a visa, a reason to be./ Seeking a visa, never to return./ Necessity, I am infuriated!/ A forceful blow, what else can I do?/ I'll be ship-
wrecked, food for the sea./ Never to return, a reason to be.

sessed, María, Ramón, and Haydee claimed. His merengues and bachatas chronicle the daily lives of common Dominicans on the island and the diaspora. At the same time, they deliberately critique the power structures and in doing so merengue and bachata continue to function as a powerful vehicle for social protest and raising of political consciousness—and for both reflecting and helping to create Dominicans' collective and individual sense of themselves.

Most participants in this study said that even if they had not been aware of the influence while they were young, today they realize that merengue and bachata were very influential in teaching us about our Dominican selves. It influenced how we conceived and appropriated cultural markers. "I like our music," Haydee said to me during a follow-up phone interview,

> not just because I enjoy dancing it, but because I can claim it as part of my heritage, as part of who I am today. It's something Dominican that most Americans have at least heard of and don't usually align with poverty or immigration. Yeah, they sometimes think of our music—and by extension *me*—as "exotic," something they remember from their holiday in the Caribbean, which of course means that they turn me into an object, some sort of tourist attraction they can use while on vacation and then discard as "too spicy for everyday consumption." But also my music is something that I don't have to apologize for, or defend constantly the way I do with phenotypes.

Younger participants in this study talked more about bachata, logically, I gather, because it's a music that grew up along with us since the 1960s. It's also music that tends to romanticize campesino life, something that is captivating particularly to those of us who grew up in the States and did not visit the island often if at all. If merengue is music for the feet and hips, ethnomusicologist Peter Manuel explains, bachata is a guitar-based music for the soul. "The battered Dominican peasant soul, driven by poverty" from rural Cibao to urban slums and often on to Puerto Rico and Upper Manhattan. Bachata originated in the sector of society that Dominicans compare to concón, the burnt rice at the bottom of the pan (Manuel

113). That is precisely why the music is known as bachata, a word that defines a clamorous lower-class fiesta. In the beginning, bachata belonged to the uneducated socially marginalized campesinos and urban poor. Today, given Guerra's global popularity, bachata belongs to every social strata, but the songs still usually express the frustrations and bitterness of unemployed devalued men. Pacini Hernández writes that initially bachata lyrics reflected the "changing social environment" and often refer explicitly to what was "happening in the bar context: drinking, easily obtained sex, male camaraderie" ("*Cantando*" 353). Today the lyrics also mirror other socioeconomic and gender issues.

All of us in this study have been aware of bachata for a long time; some of us are aficionados; a couple of us (Haydee, for example) dance it regularly. Since bachata grew up along with us, and since like other forms of popular music it has didactic as well as recreational functions, it is particularly interesting to use it as a lens through which we can view the dialectic between how the music shapes and reflects our ethnic and cultural identity.

The first bachata songs were slow, plaintive, and romantic, like boleros. In the 1970s the songs began to comment on relationships between men and women. Pacini Hernández explains that while in "early bachata a man might indeed complain that a woman has left him," as the form developed the man usually went on to "vilify her and to condemn all women"; in contemporary bachata men "are not merely talking to each other; they are teaching each other as well ("*Cantando*" 354). That makes a lot of sense given that overwhelmingly popular bachata songs are composed by men, men who need "to express the complex relationship between rural expectations and urban constraints"; in turn, Pacini Hernández affirms, those who listen to bachata "learn what to expect from life in the city—especially in terms of the relationships between men and women" ("*Cantando*" 356). The following song, "Aquí la mujer se daña" by Manuel Chalas, is an illustration of that sort of reflective/didactic symbiosis:

Voy a hablar de la mujer
Que viene a la capital
A los tres días se pone

Que no se puede anguantar
Y se tira a caminar
A la calle sin compaña
Y hasta con otro te engaña
Quizás con tu propio amigo
Y por eso es que te digo
Que aquí la mujer se daña[19]

This very popular song that most of us heard either on the island or in the States expresses men's hostile anger at losing control over women 's behavior. "Let me tell you," the singer says, "that women change when they migrate to the city. In the city they learn to be autonomous," which of course is equated with them behaving as men, particularly when it has to do with sex. What messages did these songs deliver to us about who we should be? Ramón said that in retrospect he understands that those lyrics taught him to want to create clear demarcations between men and women's ways of being, and to believe that liberated Dominican women in the States (or anywhere) could be considered "bad" and certainly not worth marrying. And if they were autonomous in seeking high literacy then they were to be questioned. Even though formal education is a "loftier" goal and therefore not as "bad as moving to the city and acting like a man."

Like several of the other female participants in this study, María explained that in growing along with the women's movement in the States as an adolescent she was reactive to the themes she

---

[19] Pacini Hernández's translation:

I'm going to tell you about women
Who come to the capital
After three days she gets
So you can't put up with her
And she starts to walk
In the streets alone
And she even deceives you
Perhaps with your own friend
And that's why I'm telling you
That women here go bad

heard in bachata (and in its counterpart, American Blues). She resisted the messages about men being disillusioned because women "betray" them just by becoming autonomous. One song, she said, "really ticked [her] off": "No te amargues for ella" by Confesor González explicitly claims that men should not feel blue about women's behavior, since none are to be believed, and none are as worthy as men.

> Ya me desengañe
> De toditas las mujeres . . .
> Ya no creo en ningunas las mujeres
> Porque cada día ellas se ponen peor
> Ellas se vuelven mariposas en los jardines
> Y van cogiendo el sabor de cada flor . . .
> No te amargues por ella
> Que un hombre vale más que una mujer"[20]

But María also noted that she now enjoys listening to other bachatas because they push her to react; they "inspire and challenge" her to fulfill her "intellectual and other kinds of potential." "Besides," she said to me, "bachata is changing; women are influencing the music." Contemporary bachateras are composing songs that comment on the demise of traditional forms of marriage, consensual arrangements, and the new and often conflictive interactions between men and women (particularly as emigration and feminism affect them). A good example, Pacini Hernández also notes in "Cantando," is "La sufrida" by Mélinda Rodríguez:

> ya no me importa
> que me digan que soy mala

---

[20] Pacini Hernández calls that kind of bachata "música de amargue." I found a translation of "No te amargues por ella" in her article entitled "Cantando": I've lost my illusions/ About all women . . . / I don't believe in any woman anymore/ Because every day they get worse/ They become butterflies in the garden/ And they flutter from flower to flower. . ./ Don't get bitter over her/ Because a man's worth more than a woman.

en esta vida
yo me siento feliz
en la otra vida
que es la que llaman la buena
yo sufrí mucho
y por eso la cambíe...
yo soy mala
y seguiré siendo mala
porque es mucho
que sufrí por ser buena
es mejor ser mala
y parecer buena
que ser buena
y que me culpen de mala.[21]

Music is a cultural expression that encapsulates collective values and in turn helps to shape individuals' worldviews. Merengue and bachata are the main signifiers of Dominican authenticism and nationhood, of identity in and outside the island. It is one of the constants in the construction of identity, one of the strands that travel across race, socioeconomic class, geographies, and generations. Austerlitz affirms that the music has "remained central not only to national identity as outside influences inundated the Republic in the late twentieth century, but also to the transnational identity that developed as many Dominicans sought work abroad" (*Merengue* 11). For those of us in this study, Dominican music (on its own and as it has been influenced by American music) has indeed been a visible marker that has both reflected and helped to shape our sense of ourselves.

---

[21] Pacini Hernández's translation: I don't care anymore/ If they tell me I'm bad/ In this life/ I feel happy/ In another life/ The one they call good/ I suffered a lot/ And that's why I changed it . . . / I'm bad/ And I'll keep being bad/ Because I suffered/ Too much for being good/ Its better to be bad/ And seem good/ Than to be good/ Than to be good/ And be blamed for being bad (364).

Temporary Closure

My aim in this chapter has been to probe the Dominican cultural markers that surfaced repeatedly as I analyzed our transcribed interviews: baseball, foodways, and music (merengue and bachata). I have attempted to describe how respondents believe these major signifiers stamped the evolution of our ethnic and cultural identity and thus our journey toward high literacy and the professorate. Baseball and foodways have stood for (and have reminded us of) public resistance to political, economic, and intellectual colonialism, and for the melding of Dominican and American ways we embody. Dominican foodways, what and how we eat, have functioned as a more private kind of marker—private in the sense that we've generally share it with our family, friends, and Dominican communities (since there is still no general acceptance of Dominican cuisine). Foodways have been a ritual, an affirmation, and a nostalgic way for us to enact our Dominican ethnic identity. On the other hand, music (merengue and bachata) is the signifier that most of us in this study readily identified privately and publicly as part of our cultural legacy. It is the music that we continue to share with our families and members of our non-Dominican communities, particularly because it is widely recognized on its own and as part of the salsa music phenomenon.

These markers travel with us across private and public concerns, geography, socioeconomic status, time, and cultures. They are the major strands that helped us stay anchored in an identity as we navigated our ways through academe. At times, those two signifiers served as bridges to other "ethnics" or "people of color" with whom we shared stories of marginalization. At other times, they functioned to link us to people outside our milieu. In either case, these markers work as enactments, as displays of our evolving sense of self, especially in the public sphere.

All of these markers have taught us history and have allowed us to reveal the importance of Dominican traditions and practices, and how/why we create enduring values and commitments as individuals and members of various communities. They have been more or less "safe" symbols of our identity, and have, hence, provided us with places and occasions to express Dominican cultural behaviors and to feel affirmed. By the same token, as these markers have come into contact with American multicultural society (and thus have taken on a variety of new meanings), they have given us opportunities to reconfigure and recontextualize (and therefore to create new understandings) about our identities. As they are easily transported across borders, these markers have become sites for carving, negotiating, and asserting our identity-in-the-making and for creating new social patterns—in other words, for performing what we adopt and reject from ways of being in the United States and the Dominican Republic (and whatever other places and circumstances have helped us constitute our sense of self).

Teresita and Antonio Ferreyra in the Dominican Republic, 1950s, when they began to dream about having a family, emigrating, and making a life where their children could have all of the education they could not acquire on the island.

MAY 1966

Antonio, who had left the Dominican Republic in 1964, is reunited with his wife, Teresita, and their three children, Dulce María, Homerina, and Homero at Kennedy Airport in New York.

6

Ruminating . . . A Measure of Closure

My father was not there when it happened, but he says that
everybody on the island knows how the dictator was killed on May
30, 1961. Generalissimo Rafael Leónidas Trujillo Molina (who by
then owned over 60 percent of the country's land and wealth) was
in the back seat of a light blue Chevrolet Bel Air sedan heading out
of Ciudad Trujillo. As the car sped past the grounds of the Fair of
Peace and Fraternity of the Free World, a black Chevrolet began to
follow. Shortly after, Trujillo's chauffeur pressed on the brakes as
gunfire shattered the rear window. A bodyguard attempted to
protect Trujillo, but one of the assassins rushed out of the black car
and fired his gun directly at El Jefe. Five bullets pierced his body.
Trujillo staggered out, turned, fell to his knees, and then collapsed
dead on his face.

Henceforth, life in the Dominican Republic and the United
States was dramatically changed forever. For one thing, Trujillo's
assassination prompted two massive waves of migration out of the
island and into the States. The majority of those fleeing were
educationally underprepared. Forty years later, the one million
Dominicans who live in the States still have great difficulty
acquiring literacy—particularly beyond high school. That reality
can be minimally explained by Dominicans' resistance to becom-

ing fully integrated participants in United States society. There are
reasons for that resistance, though: most arrive with the belief that
life in the States is temporary, that as soon as they become
financially stable, and as soon as their children finish school, they
will return home to the island.

Emotional holding back is one significant impediment that
participants in this study had to overcome in order to acquire high
literacy. Carmen described the dilemma during our first interview:

> Dominicans are not political refugees like Cuban immigrants who
> cannot return to the island. I know that in my family we always
> discussed whether or not we were going to go back. We
> understood that we'd come on a transitory basis, always longing to
> return, to go back once we'd had enough money to build a little
> house and to live without starving—to go back to our *real* home.
> Who's going to think of settling down and making meaning and
> building a culture out of the mixture if you're always thinking
> you're going to go back to the Dominican Republic?

Moreover, most Dominicans live a marginal existence in the
States. An overwhelming part of the one million population sur-
vives on the fringes, in precarious and inequitable conditions. Despite the potential opportunities, there is relentless psychological
warfare, racism, poverty, unsafe housing, inadequate schools and
health care. "Who wants to live like that for ever; no wonder we
dream about going home; no wonder we refuse to settle down; no
wonder more of us don't succeed educationally," Carmen explained:

> Besides, even if the American educational situation was more re-
> ceptive to Dominicans, the way it is to Cuban immigrants, we are
> simply consumed by the process of surviving. That is all we have
> time and energy for—survival. Many of us believe that we should
> take advantage of whatever bits we can get in the States, save a
> few dollars and return to the island where life is hard but familiar
> and welcoming. Back home at least you have trees and sunshine
> and you can sit and talk with your neighbors. Almost all of us are
> unwilling immigrants. We were forced to abandon the island. For-
> eign investment—a lot of it from the United States—in the indus-

trial sector increased unemployment and therefore forced migration from the campo and then out of Santo Domingo. So really, we Dominicans are exiles and like exiles we hold on to (a sometimes utopian view of) our country. We find it difficult to integrate fully.

That transient mentality reinforces myths about both the United States being the "land of unlimited opportunities" and the island being "Eden." Several participants in this study told me that a transient mentality "mystified" our existence. Our baffled understanding was further compounded by the fact that in migrating we were transformed into the "Other," the "minority," at times the "spic." We were rejected, segregated culturally, religiously, economically, and in endless other ways. Consequently, our need to (re)create Dominicanness was reified. All participants in this study described that condition recurrently, though we also affirmed that it is only one in the convoluted set of factors that prevent Dominicans in the States from acquiring high literacy. Ironically, that very same need to (re)define Dominican identity is also one of the strongest impetus for and consequences of becoming and being highly literate.

Unlike the majority of Dominican immigrants, I not only graduated from high school, I completed a doctorate. When I finished I wondered how it all became possible. I wanted to know how those few other Dominicans from my generation had done it. Back then, in the early 1990s, ethnographer Barbara Myerhoff's words kept echoing in my mind. In the last film she made, *In Her Own Time*, she said: "You study what is happening to others by understanding what is going on in yourself." That is one reason I have written this book. I wanted to understand how I and other Dominicans like myself (those who either migrated or were born in the States and completed most of their formal education in American schools) surpassed numerous impediments and managed to finish doctoral programs, and then to become university professors in the humanities and social sciences—those same disciplines that reify our notions about the definition and role of literacy. I wanted to dissect that process in the hope that my respondents, the readers of this book, and I would gain deeper self-awareness, and perhaps a version of Freire's conscientizaçao. I also hoped to contribute specifically to the making of Latino-Dominican cultural studies and literacy studies.

I define *high literacy* as the enactment of dynamic skills that extend beyond encoding and decoding the printed word, and which include the ability to comprehend and manipulate symbols (the words and concepts) in two or more culturally prescribed ways. My aim in this book has been to examine the practices of everyday life, to echo Michel de Certeau's words, that allowed those of us in this study to become highly literate. By extension, I have intended to describe an aspect of the ongoing negotiation between cultures in the States and in the Dominican Republic. In other words, I have examined what Cuban American cultural critic Gustavo Pérez-Firmat calls the dynamic "cohabitation" of cultures and languages—particularly as it pertains to the acquisition and use of high literacy. I rooted this study in the "Third Generation," as Harvey J. Graff calls it, of scholarship on literacy. That is, I follow along, and attempt to push, the boundaries of precepts current studies address. For instance, what is the relationship between literacy and social progress? How does literacy affect individual development? Does literacy transform or facilitate self-awareness and thereby cultural identification? Does it equalize groups and classes? Or is literacy only an *enabling* component, a small part of the gamut of factors impacting the evolution of immigrants such as the Dominicans in this study? With those general questions in mind, I proceeded to ask more pointed questions of myself and the participants in my study.

Having analyzed all of the data I gathered in pursuit of answers, my findings reveal, above all else, that for this group of Dominican Americans the attainment, use, and implications of acquiring and being highly literate cannot be seen as a simple dichotomy: for us high literacy is not constraining or liberating; it is not just an instrument of conformity or an instrument of creativity. For this group of Dominican Americans (and quite possibly for most immigrants and other marginalized people in the United States, as evidenced by the work of Gloria Anzaldúa, bell hooks, Trinh T. Minh-ha, and Theresa Hak Kyung Cha, for example) becoming highly literate is—in more ways than one—like holding a double-edged sword in the palm of your hand. At the very least, high literacy functions as the instrument that restrains and frees—that is, high literacy shapes us into seemingly conventional Americans and yet also spurs our imagination to resist total consumption into the American way. We gain innumerable compensations, but we also pay an immense emotional price in the process of becoming highly literate. That price is the forced forging that is inherent in the process, the deracination we experience.

Given those fundamental revelations, in this chapter I want to first summarize my findings, to unpack the consequences of becoming and being highly literate, and to discuss the ways we use (are using) it. Finally, I will discuss the repercussions of this study for those of us who teach literacy (for instance, composition) in higher education.

Summary of Findings

Almost all of the participants in this study explain that we were "compelled" to become highly literate by a need to disprove erroneous stereotypes and assumptions about us being "those Dominican immigrants who are incapable of functioning at an intellectual (and successful) level." We claim to have had a zealous yearning for validation, especially from mainstream American society. That is what pushed us to strive. All participants maintain that becoming highly literate prompted a more personally meaningful and satisfying awareness of our individual selves and our selves in relation to specific communities and mainstream America—in other words, that it fashioned a new understanding of our singular and collective identity(ies). I can clarify this point further by analyzing class and gender.

Middle and higher socioeconomic respondents (men particularly) say that seeking high literacy seemed to be the logical next step, something that families anticipated. It was "the thing to do next." Our parents' modeling of literate behavior taught us to simply expect that we would also complete graduate education, though not necessarily a doctorate (especially for the women). More than anyone else in this study, the participants with more stable economic means assert that our secondary motivation for seeking high literacy was to disprove erroneous stereotypes about Dominican immigrants.

Lower socioeconomic participants profess that we were pressed to acquire high literacy by an urgent need to escape poverty: the hardships we (and our parents) experienced in emigrating, and in living on the margins of United States society, prepared us for overcoming impediments; it made us stronger, defiant, determined, and resilient. Lower-class participants say that acquiring high literacy was *the* viable means for escaping poverty, the vehicle to improve our lives, an investment that consequently provides financial stability, upward mobility, and thereby a measure of power, status, and prestige.[1] As María explained, that is "the thing to do in Amer-

---

[1] It is fascinating to note that the attitude has remained the same in over twenty years. In 1974 Hendricks wrote:

It is part of the role of a proper Dominican to send his children to school. . . . The mere act of coming to New York enhances the individual's status in the eyes of those within his social field. Therefore, it is not unexpected that New York immigrants, especially those whose presence is more than temporary, regardless of their long-term commitment, place strong emphasis on school attendance for their children who are too young to work. Education is prized almost universally for its instrumental value. . . but the components of this instrumental value vary from individual to individual. For most, schooling is seen as a means for learning English and hence, greater control of their destiny. . . employment range and resulting economic opportunities are greatly expanded for those who can use English effectively. However, for some this positive valuation can be withdrawn whenever it is perceived that school attendance no longer has such a functional value. When a teenager reaches a level of language competence whereby he can obtain a "good" job or, in rare cases, where a "good" job is found which is not dependent upon language, parental support for school attendance is often withheld. This is especially the case where no ideological commitment to remaining in New York has been made. . . . For other parents the formal education of their children represents public and private validation of the geographical move

ica." It is the enactment of the Horatio Alger myth: you come to America (or you are born impoverished in America), you work hard (principally at becoming highly literate, in our case), and consequently you "make it out" of dire circumstances.

Although being poor functioned as a significant impetus for acquiring high literacy, it was also the source of much frustration. Many of the respondents, such as Ramón, explain that financial struggles depleted us. In graduate school we were consistently physically and emotionally exhausted, always rushing to complete assignments on time, and always feeling that we could have done a better job if we had had more time. Ramón's family could not afford a bigger apartment, therefore he did not have his own space to read and write. He studied while riding the subways. Ramón often felt discouraged and fractured because he could not participate fully in either the factory or school environments. It took him twelve years to complete the Ph.D., and he could have done it in half the time, enjoyed it more, and been more productive if he had had the economic means to concentrate solely on studying.

Gender also served as a noteworthy motivator. A few of the male respondents claim that it was "natural" for them to pursue high literacy, since, despite their parents' disapproval, they considered it the vehicle that would allow them to carry out their traditional male responsibilities. These male respondents believe high literacy prepares them for better and more prestigious jobs, which therefore allow them to perform their roles as breadwinners. One male, Homero, echoed the sentiment of several other participants, including some females. He believes that it is more difficult for men to pursue graduate studies, because they have to fulfill too many roles; "women only have to be students," but men have to fight against long-held stereotypes about what constitutes "real" men's work." Women have "an easier time," he said, partly because as young girls they are restricted to the home, where often their only diversion is reading and writing. Thus, from childhood they are geared ("maybe predisposed") to engage in literate activi-

---

from the campo to New York, as well as the social transition from campesino to—at least—proletarian New Yorker. (132).

ties. As young adults females are generally not pushed to find jobs or to provide financial support; therefore they can dedicate more time and energy to school matters. Additionally, Homero said, males are frequently dissuaded (sometimes reviled) from engaging in literate behavior, since reading and writing are not considered to be "work" and hence not masculine endeavors. Notably, Homero and other participants did not acknowledge that women fulfill various demanding roles (homemakers, students, mothers, "good" wives and more), or that women have to expend a great deal of energy resisting the social expectations that render them subservient.

On the other hand, most female participants reiterate that becoming and being highly literate was and continues to be an act of affirmation and defiance. The accomplishment is proof of our ability to explode patriarchal boundaries. It validates our rebellion against traditional beliefs regarding women. As Marina and others attest, in acquiring high literacy women gain a public voice personally and professionally; we are consequently fuller participants in public life and other opportunities that have been historically reserved for men only.

Most of the women still express surprise at having made it that far. We continue to be incredulous. Only two of the male participants expressed that kind of amazement. The rest of the men are pleased to have "made it," particularly those from impoverished backgrounds, but having attained high literacy seems "more natural, the logical thing," for them. Most of the women perceive our achievement as "happenstance," even those from wealthy and educated families who expected us to complete college. Today we are "astonished" to have doctorates.

Some of the women say they pursued high literacy naively—in other words, that we really did not understand the degree of difficulty. That "turned out to be a good thing," Haydee says, because that allowed us to approach the process with less apprehension and fewer preconceived notions. Most of us, though, believe that we absolutely knew what we were involved in, and that seeking the highest level of formal education was a deliberate effort to escape from all of the patriarchal restrictions imposed on us. We wanted to "re-make" ourselves. A few women, Carla, for instance, explain that our determination stems from the immigrating experience, because in moving to the United States we began to feel "less restricted socially" as women and more eager to experiment and push boundaries.

Both males and females in this study wonder how our accomplishment would be different if we hadn't had to combat stereotypes and subordination. In the process of becoming highly literate we endured many unnecessary indignities that often inhibited our progress (and that scarred our psyches). For instance, like several other participants, early in his graduate career Ramón curtailed his participation in classes because others made him feel inferior: his worldview was not appreciated, a few professors assumed that Dominican mulattos have limited mental capacities, and many people commented on the thickness of his accent. Even now that he is a "successful" tenured professor, like other participants, he acknowledges that he is constantly aware of and consistently battling feelings of inadequacy. And Haydee "gave up" the study of psychology because a professor told her Hispanics are not good at it. Still today while awaiting her tenure verdict she wonders if she should return to school to train in the discipline she really loves.

To varying degrees, all of us in this study used other people's resistance to our ethnicity and race (as well as gender and class) as a driving force to achieve. It can be said, as Audrey Lord encouraged African Americans to do, that this group of Dominicans learned "to stand alone, unpopular and sometimes reviled. . . in order to define and seek a world in which" we could prosper; we took our "*differences* and made them strengths" (99, my emphasis). We used rejection and prejudice (and the resulting loneliness and pain) to delve into ourselves, to (re)define and (re)shape self-perceptions. We experienced a forced forging that many of us realize is the "inescapable" consequence of being educated in the United States, of being bicultural. The process was painful because it entailed appropriating mainstream American ways of thinking, which implicitly and explicitly devalued Dominican culture (and thus the core of our being). For us (re)definition was a charged and torturous journey. At the same time, the process of attaining high literacy was reaffirming, because it provided the language to understand and name what was happening.

Participants maintain that the metacognitve skills we learned, the "thinking about the thinking," continues to provide comfort and a measure of control. In that way, completing doctorates for us was like usurping "the master's tools" so that we could "dismantle the master's house" (Lorde 99); that is, we used (are using) formal education to "improve" our socioeconomic and intellectual circumstance, and then to work actively to eradicate oppressive power structures. Now, we *use* high literacy, in part, as a tool to battle denigrating stereotypes, to (re)compose our identities and (re)frame our experiences.

In one way or another, all participants in this study say that acquiring high literacy "recreated" our self-identity/ies: the process gave us a sanctioned social status, and to varying degrees, "transformed" us into "successful" members of United States and Dominican societies. People in both places look to us for answers and solutions. Some treated us as if in becoming highly literate we increased our human value. We gained respect and appreciation. Hence (some more slowly than others, some not at all), we began to see ourselves as "certified" and assured that we are productive and engaged individuals. That affirmed sense of self has helped us to be more confident in our ability to negotiate complex subjects, and to give greater credence to our own ideas and culturally mixed sensibilities. It also "empowered" us to "use" high literacy in personally and professionally deliberately rewarding ways.

My findings clearly reveal that becoming (and being) highly literate is "transforming"—but not just in the obvious ways (such as improved socioeconomic status).[2] The process is empowering in that it prompted us to "think deliberately" about our condition. That is the "crucial" consequence, as Marina says: "you are in-

---

[2] Of course, all the participants in this study are employed in colleges and universities in the United States. Had I included other highly literate Dominicans in this study (e.g. those who are unemployed, or those who have achieved the same significant level of success and social position through means other than high literacy) the results would surely be different.

duced to think consciously and methodically about who you are and what your place is in both societies and in the world." "Maybe thinking about myself is a luxury, a sort of narcissistic (dis)ease," Haydee commented; "maybe it is an Anglo habit that's transmitted to us through formal education," but whatever the root reason, she and others insist, becoming and being highly literate "names, enables, and organizes our thinking."

Consequences of Becoming Highly Literate

Thinking about ourselves, most of us note, is empowering because, at the very least, it prompts us to *use* high literacy to analyze our condition and to recognize and battle injustice. We use high literacy as a weapon. For example, like many others in this study, Flor explains that she uses high literacy to "excavate a new consciousness," one that allows and demands that she extend herself beyond her boundaries and imagine new possibilities. She uses high literacy to "prove that Dominican immigrants are worthy, able, and willing to participate in an activity traditionally denied to women and 'marginal' people in the United States."[3]

Sandra asserts that she uses literacy in general (and high literacy in particular) as "a vehicle for obtaining information and finding solutions." She believes that regardless of the situation, "from fixing the plumbing to dealing with emotional problems," reading, writing, "knowing how to make meanings within the specific context of a culture, especially in the United States, makes all the difference in the universe." Becoming and being highly literate, Sandra and others reiterate, "can get you through, can guide you through, any problem, anything." Having that "tool," Sandra contends, makes her "empowered" and "successful" (which in turn

---

[3] That kind of use can be likened to theorists Langer and Scribner's definitions of literacy as being a "state of mind" or "state of grace." Enacting high literacy in that way, most participants maintain, provides intellectual, aesthetic, and spiritual meaning, significance, and pleasure. In that sense, becoming/being highly literate indeed transformed us into successful individuals.

marks her "as a valuable person and woman" and makes her feel "satisfied"). Of course, the term "successful" has to be unpacked. [4]

Having an academic job, getting tenure, being able to provide for your family's economic needs, to have leisure time—those are signs of "success," Homero and others say, "at least according to the standards of societies in the States and the D.R." But then he adds, as other respondents often did, that there are more "personal" criteria that define the word: he is "not really successful," because he "would have liked to be an academic in the D.R.," but that is impossible if he is to sustain the same standard of living. Other participants say they are not successful because they still must confront demeaning stereotypes and prejudices about Dominicans. Carla, for one, feels ambivalent:

> Do I feel successful inside? You know, somebody once told me that unless you internalize good feelings about yourself, you could be on top of the world and you would be incapable of feeling successful. I think there's a side of me that won't let me be satisfied. I don't know if it's personality; I don't know if it was the immigration and the loss and the feeling so marginal for so long—even when I accepted my ethnicity. Maybe it's part of being a minority.

Carla wonders if perhaps those "buttons" (those feelings of being marginal, of being unsuccessful and dissatisfied) should "ever be turned off." Those feelings and self-perceptions "make a lot of noise" in her head; that "deafening" noise pushed her toward high

---

[4] In 1974 Hendricks wrote about the "success" of Dominicans as it pertains to the formal education of children:

> The criterion for success from the parental viewpoint is still drawn from their own Dominican experience, not from dominant American attitudes toward education. . . . for the majority, support for school attendance is rapidly withdrawn after the child reaches employable age, or, in the case of girls, is eligible for marriage. Nevertheless, parents almost invariably include the importance of the opportunity for schooling for their children when they recite reasons for migrating to New York, though this ranks below economic reasons. (133)

literacy, and still prompts her to be "productive, to think constantly," and to "use" high literacy "to help others."

Marina feels similarly. She believes that the "dissatisfaction" ("maybe inferiority complex") that has tormented her since arriving in the United States is the same motivator that has always driven her to accomplish, what has pushed her to do "something better." Feeling "unsuccessful, which is not necessarily the same as feeling like a failure," she says, is not "healthy," but since she could not get rid of the anguish, she used it to her benefit. At some point, "you have to come to terms with" your "success," she emphasizes, but that is particularly difficult to do when mainstream American ethos continues to brand Dominicans as the Other, even after completing the highest level of formal education available.

Nevertheless, Haydee and others clarify, the reality is that in both societies people with Ph.D.s are thought to be endowed with special qualities: intelligence and wisdom, for example. In the States, ethnic minorities (like the Dominicans in this study) are furthered labeled as being "extra special." The common attitude is that these few minorities made it through higher education, therefore they must be more than intelligent; they must also have immeasurable strength, perseverance, and conviction. Clearly, they must be tokens and anomalies. In one sense that is accurate, but in another it is still a way of marginalizing Dominicans. Both attitudes "eat away at our ability to live peacefully," Haydee, María, and other respondents say.

Nonetheless, Haydee and the others feel better equipped and more empowered to live, not just survive, in both societies, even if that means having paid a high price for that feeling. Empowerment costs; it comes at a price. Attaining high literacy is a very painful process. Still today many of us battle feeling alienated from family and academe. We live on the borders of both worlds, and we constantly strive to reconcile them. No matter the gains, being marked as Other (whether it suggests inferiority or superiority) is a burden. High literacy itself is a load, for the women especially, since in many circumstances it marks us as "unfeminine thieves," as Carmen says. Hence, many of us live with a sense of collusion—and sometimes guilt—for having wrested what we are told is not rightly ours.

Feeling Distant from the Family

For lower socioeconomic participants (those with a history of minimal formal education in their family, especially), more so than for the others, psychological (and often physical) separation from relatives is one of the most salient consequences of becoming highly literate. That distance becomes apparent as soon as we begin attending school in the U.S. Then it widens as we continue through graduate school. As children, participants claim, we compare our family and home community's values with those of mainstream America. There is always a pull (despite class status) between Dominican and American values, particularly for the women who are more eager to adopt the United States' more liberal attitudes.

The separation is a complex phenomenon. Male participants explain that although their families express appreciation for their being intellectuals, they also frequently repudiate them for not having "real" men's professions such as medical doctors or attorneys. Likewise, although on one hand women are admired for having acquired high literacy, they are also shunned. Often parents feel disappointed if their daughters have not married and given birth to several children, if they have not fulfilled their traditional role.

Marina, for example, had an active input in deciding where she, her husband, and their daughter would live. He is also a professor, but he has no tenure-line job. Therefore, he followed her. His salary is less than hers. He has taken major responsibility for maintaining their home and caring for their daughter. He cooks and he cleans willingly. It is unlikely that a Dominican man could have been so accommodating, Marina concludes. Her family thinks it is odd and often comments that she is reneging on her role. The difference in their attitudes often leads to tension and distance. Many of the female participants explain that family members "frustrate" them by treating them as if they are "lesser men," as if they have "infiltrated men's domain," or "stolen" men's rightful place.

Sandra, Carmen, María, and almost all the women in this study talk about "feeling like impostors and intruders," as if they disillusion people when they realize that "Dr. So and So" is not a man. And Haydee says that unlike her mother she has an "audible public voice" that disturbs both the men and the women in her family: men behave as if she's "out of line"; women warn that "it's not good" for females to be so assertive, since that behavior makes it "difficult to find a man to marry." The consequence for both men and women is that they feel "isolated" and "distant" from the very people they love.

Ties to the Dominican Republic

Becoming (and being) highly literate results in "outcomes" other than "emotional feelings" we have about our identity and condition. One of those consequences is an increased desire to learn more about our cultural heritage by retaining some ties to the island. To participants who were born in the States or who emigrated before age ten and who did not return often while growing up, the island generally represents tourism, pleasure, and adventure. Those who spent most of their childhood on the island consider it their "true home," or as Antonio says, "the cradle." Others conceive of the D.R. in very sentimental ways as a mythical place where an idyllic life "could have been."

Sandra returns to the D.R. as a tourist. It is fascinating, she says, that of all her family, she has the closest tie with Santo Domingo. She started visiting every year when she graduated from college; her family has not returned since they emigrated. When she visits she goes "as a nobody." Only her relatives know she is a success, a professor and accomplished administrator, and she prefers it that way. She likes to "walk the streets and visit people and just mingle like a regular Dominican woman." That keeps her grounded in reality and renews her commitment to use her doctorate to "make a difference for Dominicans everywhere."

Carla visits the island because she is "attached," not as much as Homero since her home and immediate family are in the States, but because she believes that is the place where her roots are found. It is difficult for her to visit, though, because she cannot escape being confronted with masses of people "working toward just getting enough for the day."

> That's what I mean that you feel privileged and pampered in being someone whose job is to think and care about words. That need is staring you in the face and somehow it's fanciful to be sitting there reading or writing. In a way, that isn't going to help anybody. I find it very hard, very, very disjunctive.

But she visits anyway: it is the "treasured" place of her beginnings, her heritage.

María visits for similar reasons. She first went after college, a journey she undertook trying to "find" herself. Although she was born and raised in New York, she felt excluded in the States: "I'm not white and Anglo and I don't really fit, gosh; you wouldn't believe that since New York is totally 'ethnic.'" She felt like an outsider in the private high school she attended, and like an intruder at the mostly white college where she teaches. When she arrived on the island she realized that she did not fit there either. She was an "alien." She says: "People would look at me as a stranger, la gringa. I have a totally different frame of mind, a totally different way of thinking." María says she is more "liberal, free, and open" than women on the island, even if they are almost as highly educated, or if they're of higher socioeconomic status; "they're not as open":

> I would blurt out what I was feeling and thinking and they were all very controlled. I was constantly shocking them. I wasn't really trying to shock them. This is just who I am. I was just being myself. I think it was surprising, and sometimes offensive (which was disturbing to me, since I didn't know how to deal with it), that all of my actions are so bold and direct.

Haydee returns at least two times a year: "I want to go back and teach there," she says. Part of her wants to go and stay permanently, but she hesitates:

You see, it's interesting. I have a feeling that if I stay there I am going to become stupid. I will be less exposed to what I have been exposed to here in the States. I will stop growing. To me Santo Domingo is cut off from what is really happening in education and the arts. I would die spiritually, or at least become, you know, de-fallecería. I don't want that to happen. It frightens me.

She returns, although increasingly each trip has become a "test to see how much Dominicanness" she has lost. Haydee struggles with wanting to retain what she knows as a Dominican cultural heritage, and that is the main reason she goes back. At the same time, she does not want to give up the "intellectual freedom and sustenance" she finds in the States. She "would love to go back and stay" but only if she could find "a way of keeping in touch" with academe in the U.S. Ultimately, she is sure she would not stay. She does not want to "die intellectually." Hence, for the present, Haydee chooses to daydream about living on the island.

Carmen visits about once a year "but with a distant attitude." That's where she goes to rest, to recuperate after a long teaching semester. She goes with the understanding that she has changed and that Dominicans on the island "play by a different set of rules." Each trip is painful. It hurts her to see that "women in Santo Domingo still don't have any status," but it also keeps her "honest" and "thankful" for what she has in the States. "I would never live there," she says, "I would be very frustrated and angry as a woman."

It took Carmen a long time to accept women's condition on the island and to face the fact that, despite the inequities, part of their system does work for many people. "Look at the family structure and the destruction of it in the States," she asserts; "at least in the Dominican Republic most of the families—or a large percentage—are still intact." There is a sense of family and unity, "despite all the problems y la bagamundía de los hombres." She believes that the struggle with her identity is not as "intense" on the island: "Everybody has an identity and you're accepted, hasta esos que son hijos de la calle." Dominicans in the States do not have that, she says. That is one major reason she continues to visit, and because she genuinely admires "the good things in that country that need to be held on to." Her visits keep her honest and in touch with who she could have been and is "grateful" she is not.

Like several other participants, Homero thinks of the Dominican Republic as his true "home." He has attempted to find employment there, but university jobs are not available. And those few fortunate ones who are appointed as professors must supplement the extremely low salaries by maintaining at least two other jobs. Academics have left in droves (generally for the United States, Mexico, and Spain). Homero realizes that it'd be impossible for him to work there and also preserve his standard of living:

> I'd like to live in the Dominican Republic. That would be my cherished desire. But I know that it's not possible for me to do my scholarly work and live there unless I have an alternative source of income and the connections to use libraries outside of the island.

He says that it is "mighty ironic that it's easier to do research on the Dominican Republic here in the States." The college where he teaches provides him with an office, a computer, funding for conferences, research grants, a stocked library, a fax machine, and access to a telephone he uses to keep in touch with colleagues all over the world. He teaches three days out of the week and the other two he focuses on his own writing: "It would be impossible for me to do that in the Dominican Republic." Nonetheless, he misses the D.R. and returns every summer to visit and "reinvigorate" himself.

Antonio willingly fantasizes about the island, Gurabo in particular, where he spent his youth. His imaginary (and sometimes real) trips are "always a return to paradise." He knows that he would "never be able to live there, never: I would be suffocated by it." But he enjoys thinking of the island as "a paradise." In his imagination it is "a safe place" where he rests, "an idyllic haven" for respite.

Participants affirm that maintaining ties with the island is often a consequence of having renewed, as a result of becoming highly literate, an interest in all things Dominican. Returning to the island, even if only sporadically, helps us to resee ourselves and to reframe the appreciation of Dominican culture and heritage that we gained in becoming highly literate.

Struggling with Language

Being hyperconscious of our struggle with language is yet another "consequence" of becoming highly literate. No matter how
long participants have been in the States, or the experiences we
have had with English and Spanish, all of us struggle with issues of
language.[5] My findings indicate that only one thing is clear: despite doctoral training in English, Spanish is a salient presence and
marker of our identities.

Participants who arrived in the States after age fourteen use
Spanish as the dominant language in private. With the exception of
respondents who teach Spanish, Italian, or French language and
literature, the rest of us consider English to be our dominant language in private and public. That is, we write and publish and are
evaluated as "successful" academics in English, but our lives are
infused with Spanish. The struggle for most of us lies in having to
resist other people's beliefs about Spanish, namely that mainstream
society in the United States does not think highly of it. Using
Spanish in public can often be a way to experience shame and deri-
sion. Nonetheless, despite the struggle, participants persist in using
both languages.

Homero, who believes that he is "part of the Hispanic world in
the United States, but not part of the Anglo world view," explains
that he uses Spanish in almost all situations, but that he writes in
English because it is "another window to knowledge," and because
he has to publish in a language that his colleagues can read; he
needs to get tenure. But, when he does get tenure he intends to
write in Spanish: "I'll have somebody else translate what I write."
He prefers to write in Spanish because he is "better" at it. "I have
more vocabulary resources," he says. Similarly, Marina says that
she writes in English because she has to, but that she feels more
"secure" when she writes in Spanish:

---

[5] As Stavans elucidates, all Latinos are hybrids, and the fact that we
speak Spanish and English helps to remind us that we cannot escape colonialism (154).

When I say things in English I have to think it five times. In English I always have doubts. Spelling is not much of a problem for me. For me it's construction of sentences, syntax. Also, I like to play with language and I can't do it in English. The titles of my chapters are creative and poetic. I like to use turns of phrases and themes, and I have trouble doing it in English. I also don't do it because others label my "play" as inadequacy.

Antonio says that he prefers to write in Spanish, but that he publishes in both: "Somebody calls me and says, 'I want you to present a paper and it has to be in English.' Or somebody is editing a collection of articles and asks 'would you be willing to cooperate?' So I use both languages." On the other hand, Marina has deliberately tried to "write in both English and Spanish, and more than that," she says:

I publish in the U.S., Europe, the Dominican Republic, and Latin America. I think that's the only way to establish yourself professionally. If you are an academic in the United States there is no other way, not if you want a readership. I write in Spanish to meet my personal needs, but the cold reality is that to make it professionally in the United States, to get that ticket to success, you have to write in English.

Carla agrees. She says that her colleague who publishes in Spanish "goes through a lot of headaches" because as she writes she is also "trying to figure out who is going to translate it." Flor too says that she writes in both languages. That's how she ensured getting tenure and how she maintains scholarly connections in both worlds. "In the United States," Flor explains, "Spanish represents Otherness, your colonial experience. Therefore it is very difficult to have my colleagues validate it." But she uses it anyway, since it is an integral part of her essence, since it helps to mark her as the woman she wants to be.

These participants say that becoming highly literate has "heightened, problematized, and politicized" our awareness of how language marks us. Although several respondents are also fluent in

French and Italian, Spanish and English are the languages that "cause" us "heartaches." They are the languages that mark our identities as the Other. Consequently, many of us have deliberately chosen to retain our accents. Only one participant revealed that she had speech therapy to "erase the thickness" with which she pronounced English. Facing our heightened awareness of the role of language in the formation of our (re)definition, is one consequence that half of the respondents attribute to having acquired high literacy. The result is that we "make informed decisions" and along with "feeling more validated and empowered" we also "choose more freely."

Using High Literacy

To *use*, as defined by several of the respondents, means to be aware of the immense power inherent in reading, writing, thinking, and manipulating symbols and ideas in a formally trained (and hence socially sanctioned) manner; it means to conceive of high literacy as "a tool," a means to an end. Of course, the most obvious use of high literacy for this group of Dominican academics involves teaching, but participants also affirm that we "deliberately use" high literacy outside academe for two other major purposes: "to help improve the lives" of our families and other Dominicans in the diaspora, and to "figure out what labels" we should appropriate—that is, to wrestle with (re)defining ourselves.

Teaching

Most of us in this study think of our profession, teaching and producing scholarship, as undeniably linked to a "desire" to develop all matters concerning Dominicans wherever they are in the diaspora. Some participants are very active in that endeavor, but to varying degrees almost all of us have that desire. "We teach all the time," and we learn as well, about Dominicans, Flor maintains. She gives one example of how her teaching extends beyond the regular classroom: she attended a conference where a well-known Puerto Rican critic was speaking:

he picked Manuel del Cabral, Luis Palés Matos, and Nicolás Guillén as representatives of the Negrismo movement in the Caribbean, the poetry that came out in the forties.[6] And he starts to quote Manuel del Cabral. I didn't know how to react. Here was Manuel del Cabral comparing Haitians to four-legged animals. I felt shame at that moment, because we Dominicans have much to explain to the rest of the Caribbean. But most of all I wanted to take the opportunity to comment further on that history, so that we just don't end up demonizing Dominicans.

Like several other participants, Flor has also made it her responsibility to bring literature and scholarship written by Dominicans, especially women, to the United States. She explains that there are few women writing on the island, partly because they cannot afford to just write (unless they are independently wealthy), but that those who manage to write and publish must be read outside of the island. Flor translates and critiques those women's works; she helps to create a presence for them.[7]

We teach "all the time," formally and informally, in and out of the classroom. Antonio explains why: "You acquire knowledge, you finish the highest level of formal education, so that—I be-

---

[6] Manuel del Cabral, Nicolás Guillén (born in Cuba, 1902), and Luis Palés Matos (born in Puerto Rico, 1898-1959) interpreted the reality of blacks in the Spanish Caribbean and thereby prompted racial and cultural "self-discovery." Manuel del Cabral (born in Santo Domingo, 1907) is best known as a poet, although he writes prose (*Chinchina busca el tiempo* [1945] and *30 Parábolas* [1956], for example). His *Trópico negro* (1942) typifies the Afrocentric Caribbean poetry of the 1940s.

[7] Those women include Carmen Natalia Martinez ("Oda heroica a las Miraba") and Jeanette Miller ("Formulas Para Combatir el Miedo"), who wrote short stories in the 1950s and 1970s, respectively. For further information see "Women Writers of the Spanish-Speaking Caribbean" in *Caribbean Women Writers: Essays From the First International Conference*, edited by Selwyn R. Cudjoe. Wellesley, Mass.: Calaloux Publications, 1990, 339-345.

lieve—you can pass it on like a baton; you have to share what you know, not keep like a trophy." Haydee explains too:

> I want to touch others, the hearts and minds of all students, not just Dominicans, because those are the people who grow up and become tourists on our island, or who invest in it or who exploit it; I want to show them who we really are.

Dilia resounds Haydee's sentiment. But she focuses on a target audience; she has taken it upon herself to teach her colleagues about Dominicans, since, she contends, "they often treat us unfairly because they lack information about us." Dilia also volunteers as a tutor in a literacy program in a Dominican neighborhood. She says:

> Those of us who have been successful in education *have* to be active. We have to educate young Dominicans so they can take our place. We have to educate them so we can empower our community, so that we can grow and get out of the ghetto.

Ramón is also involved with the Dominican community. He helps to organize major events, participates in local politics, and translates documents for neighbors. "In the community," he says, "I am a model. I am the person who writes the press release and who does things that have to do with articulating ideas." Similarly, Carmen is "fully committed" to helping Dominicans "who are entangled in the vicious cycles of disempowerment, poverty, and hopelessness." She says:

> I translate letters, attend meetings with illiterate people, speak to every bloody doctor because a member in the family is sick and doesn't know the language. I'm the one who goes to the unemployment line with my mother, the one who demands that she be treated with respect, the one who makes sure I fight for their rights. Yeah, sure, I know I'm doing all that. I want to be a model for them and everybody else.

You have to "model," Carla believes. Her students are predominantly non-Latinos; she rarely encounters a Dominican in her classroom. "And here I am," she says, "a Dominican immigrant teaching them English, writing, literature, Chaucer, Milton, Shakespeare. It blows my mind." In effect, Carla affirms, she also teaches before she speaks. Her presence, what and whom she represents, offers a lesson. She is very much aware of that and tries to use her persona as an example. Like Dilia and most of the participants, Carla is passionate about her aim:

> Dominicans have to be represented in higher education. It is important that we show them *how* we gained success, how we worked for it, how we made it happen despite everything that is against us in the American educational system. We must do that; it is the responsibility we inherit simply by being in the professorate.

Improving Dominicans' Lives

Sandra uses high literacy to "improve" herself: "whenever I have a personal problem I read things that will help me work it out." María writes sonnets "because it's very fulfilling and I learn about myself." Carla explains that she uses writing as "a way to think and integrate" ideas about who she is and how she functions. Antonio echoes her and goes on to clarify that having the "time and opportunity" to use high literacy to analyze his identity is indeed a "privilege" that he does not take lightly, and that he recognizes as a "powerful weapon":

> Ask somebody what he can do: I know how to make shoes. Okay. What can you do? I know how to make tables. Okay. What can *I*, Antonio, do? I can think. My gosh. I can help you to make the shoes. I can help you to make the table. I can help you to make this and that. I mean, a dentist is somebody who earns perhaps three times more money than me, but the dentist is somebody who knows the teeth. I know the human mind, the human condition.

Many of the participants understand how "privileged" we are, and those, especially, use literacy "to improve the lives" of family members and others." Almost all of us, particularly those of us from low socioeconomic backgrounds, use high literacy to help our families negotiate American society. Like Carmen, many of us are consistently consulted about every aspect of living in the States; our families know that becoming highly literate is synonymous with becoming intimate with American ways. For example, Dilia takes informative pamphlets to her siblings and says, "listen, I think you can do this. This is perfect for you. Let me help you fill out the application." Consequently, two of them are attending college; one graduates in a year. She did the same thing with her spouse:

> My husband is also Dominican. When he came here he wanted to go to college, but then the financial situation was so bad that he could not. He was an honor student, but he had to go to work. Then when we got married I encouraged him to go back. He didn't know how to proceed, how to apply, what to do. I guided him through the system and he finished college with honors.

Many respondents explain that one of the most important personal uses of their high literacy skills entails improving the lives of their children. That means that as professional parents we are able to sustain a higher socioeconomic status, and thereby lead less hectic, less threatened lives than our parents. It also means that we model how to acquire and then use high literacy. Sandra says that she has consciously invested all that she gained by becoming and being highly literate in her daughter:

> I don't drive a Mercedes Benz. I put my money into educating my kid. She's in this very exclusive upper-class environment. It's very expensive. She knows people from all over the world. During Desert Storm she was able to discuss what was going on firsthand. One of her classmates is the future prince of Saudi Arabia.

Sandra's own literate sense of herself allowed her to teach her daughter to be secure in her hybrid identity, and to be at ease with people from any socioeconomic level, any race and any circumstance. Invariably, her daughter spends summer vacations in the

D.R., so that she can learn about her heritage. Similarly, María uses high literacy to help her children, her young son especially:

> Instead of beginning to say words at one, he started at two. And he didn't start saying sentences until he was almost four. At that point I was already in my Ph.D. program. I became aware of whole language, literacy, and language development. I saw that my son was behind and I became involved in using whole language to help him improve and develop his language skills.

Later, María wrote a paper on her experience for a class she was taking. "It was exciting," she says, "because what I studied I also applied directly to help my own son." Now the boy is in second grade and reading at a fifth grade level. "His writing is excellent," María exclaims, "and he's great at spelling because we've been reading a lot and talking about books, and his vocabulary is very advanced." Through her modeling her son learned to love reading too. María is very proud that she has been able to give her son something she "truly doubts" she could have provided if she had not been highly literate herself.

(Re)Defining Our Identity(ies)

My findings reveal that the most salient deliberate "use" of high literacy entails (re)defining our identities: we write, read, discuss, analyze; we knowingly use all of the ways of being a highly literate person in order to figure out who we have been, who we are, and who we want to be. Through studying, researching, reading, and writing (often in our many journals), we sift through the endless labels, and we appropriate, "in an informed manner," those we deem suitable.

Antonio has concluded that he is no longer bothered by what society wants to call him. He will "never be a full American or a full Dominican." And there is no such thing, he contends, because, as history illustrates, both places have always been infused with "all sorts of people and influences." There is "no pure anything anywhere." Antonio maintains that in becoming highly literate he learned that his identity is defined more by his childhood memories, not his physical appearance, culture, nationality, or whatever other people label him. He says that he is very proud of having been born in the Dominican Republic, and of living in the United States, but that he has never had "this problem of I-want-to-be-identified-with-one-or-the-other." He feels allegiance to one place, Gurabo in the D.R., where he spent his childhood. That is where his memories are rooted, where he imagines his grandfather and grandmother gardening or "nourishing the níspero tree," where, when he is stressed, he envisions green meadows, mango trees and the "fence sloping up toward" the house.

Other respondents say that becoming highly literate has allowed them to acknowledge and articulate that they are bothered by what society labels them. Carla, who is white, explains that the process of becoming highly literate heightened her awareness of her skin color. In the D.R. "money matters more; in the U.S. you're always black first," she says.[8] In the same way, Sandra agrees that becoming and being highly literate helped her to understand that the color of her skin has always been the most prominent part of her identity anywhere she has lived. When she was younger she resisted being called black. Even her family taunted her and called her "negra," black:

> I grew up in an environment where the discussion about people of color was always very negative. My mother es blanca [is white] and my father is black. My family never forgave her for marrying him. Their attitude was that *we* the children had the responsibility of making up for her mistake. I was always rejected and reminded of my skin color.

---

[8] That concept is becoming more widely accepted. In his book Klein writes:

> Dominicans are given to racial hair splitting: in their social scheme a person can disdain those who are darker and be disdained in turn by those who are are lighter. Dominicans are incredulous that in the United States one is either black or white (lighter-skinned Dominicans are afraid to believe this—it means they would lose their advantage in the United States—and darker-skinned Dominicans can barely conceal their glee). (82)

Before beginning graduate studies she insisted on being labeled
Hispanic or Dominican, but as she learned about and analyzed the
history of race relations on the island and in the States, she began
to feel empowered to label herself black. She is the only one in her
family who identifies as black. The rest see themselves as colorless
or Dominicans who are indio, but "they don't spend a lot of time
thinking about it." Their "unexamined beliefs," Sandra affirms, are
"proof" that the process of becoming highly literate "certainly
raised" her awareness. She says that the more she learns the more
her identity has become "fluid." Today she labels herself Latina
(not Hispanic, because that's a term fabricated by the United
States), of African background (which is very hard for people in
this country to accept), from Santo Domingo."

César, who is white, used to be bothered when others refuse to
believe he is Dominican. He says mainstream people in the States
do not want to accept that a "minority can look like" them. It used
to bother him that they consistently assume he is not Dominican.
But in the process of becoming highly literate he learned to unpack
the history of that phenomenon, and consequently today César is
comfortable labeling himself "a proud American born son of Dominican parents." And when people comment that he does not
"look" Dominican, he seizes the opportunity to explain that Dominicans are not a monolith. César agrees that the ease he gained
in becoming a professional, the sanctioned status he acquired,
makes it "easier" for him to challenge general beliefs. He also recognizes that culturally and linguistically he is more American than
Dominican, and that he has "a legal as well as emotional right" to
call himself American.

Marina considers herself "white only in the Dominican context." She acknowledges that "not being black" has made it easier
to exist in both Dominican and United States societies, but that in
the States she is not a "white woman." She still struggles with how
others label her. She feels judged every time she walks into a classroom, where students "see" her as Hispanic, a term she does not
like because it resonates of discrimination. Becoming highly literate taught her that she did not want to expend energy on refusing
that label, that instead she wanted to "figure out" how to proceed

in such situations. Ninety percent of her students are white, many of them from lower middle class, who "come from their segregated ethnic neighborhoods where discrimination against Hispanics is high." So, she asks herself, "what do I do in that kind of context?" Marina says she does not have a good solution yet, but that she deals with the situation every semester.

She also realizes that she does not want to be "mad" when others view her negatively, because it won't help her to grow: "It's not going to help the students. It's not going to help Hispanics in general. It's not going to help anybody." After much consideration, now her strategy is "to walk in the classroom like the most confident white male," but being simultaneously aware "that the white male will gain respect in two seconds," and that it will take months before students accord her the same attitude. Marina learned that Hispanics intensify the problem by being angry and bitter about discrimination. She believes that that attitude does not help anybody: "you cannot be a good teacher by hating" students who "hate you." Some people might say that is a conservative approach, she says, but she does not think so.

She understands that if she was "a white male—or even a white female—it would be much easier," but she chooses not to waste her energy with frustration and hatred. The best thing she can do is to show students—not necessarily with words—that she knows what they think of her. "You have to walk in the classroom like a normal human being with all the concerns that" any person has, but at the same time with solid confidence and "deep awareness," not arrogance. "They can think whatever they want to think about me and probably they do, starting with my accent," she says, but her aim is to demonstrate to her students that she commands the material, that she is capable, and "not the devil" or "an alien." "I'm different from them in many ways," she wants to say to them, "I even have an accent, fine, but I can teach you something and I can learn something from you." That confidence, she claims, is the result of learning about and understanding why racism and prejudice exist both on the island and in the States.

Marina says she is not too bothered by her students and society's attitudes, because in becoming highly literate she constructed her ethnic identity. She knows who she is. She identifies herself as "a Dominican living in" the States: "I am not even a citizen. I carry a Dominican passport and I plan to keep it as long as I can." She deems herself Dominican because she was born and raised in the Dominican Republic. Marina contends that in becoming highly literate she realized that even though she calls herself a Dominican living in the States, she is no longer "fully anything." She realized that she lives "in two worlds." She is "not one hundred percent" of either culture. It's an "advantageous situation," she has concluded, because being part of two worlds allows her to be an insider and outsider in each, so that she can always provide the contrasting view.

Dilia also calls herself "a Dominican living in the States," because she "read Dominican history and the writings of los padres de la patria, Duarte, Sanchez y Mella." She "knows" that history and culture, and once her parents emigrated in her early teens, in the States they lived among other Dominicans, continued to eat the same foods, to listen to the same music, to teach her to be "proud" of their heritage. They "did everything to pass on" Dominicanness to her.

Homero also thinks of himself as a Dominican living in the States. "I don't have any problems with identity," he says, "I know I'm a Dominican." To him that means that he is not "part of the thought in the United States," part of the American way of looking at things. Like a few other respondents, Homero explains that he chose his identity after much thinking. He chose the label he has appropriated once he identified the conditions that mark him as a Dominican, once he examined the evidence, "as a scholar does." Homero enumerates the characteristics of those conditions: being born and pretty much raised on the island; experiencing primary education there; having parents who feel vehemently about maintaining Dominican culture (e.g., speaking Spanish and celebrating Dominican holidays and traditions); living in a predominantly Dominican neighborhood.

Similarly, Haydee explains that high literacy has prompted and allowed her to examine why she "feels" Dominican: she emigrated in her late teens when she was formed; therefore, she says, "everything I brought with me was Dominican." Haydee grants that her feelings may be based on idealized memories of what it means to be Dominican, that she needs "to go back and find out for sure," and that, of course, the "everything Dominican" is itself a mélange of influences. She likes having a specific identity; that makes her feel "whole" in American society where she is "continually torn apart."

My analysis of these Dominican American academics' stories reveals that prior to experiencing the acquisition of high literacy our decisions about our identity(ies) and the labels we adopt were based on gut reactions to mainstream Americans' treatment of us and other Dominicans. After, those decisions became the result of purposeful and informed considerations. For instance, Flor and Haydee emigrated when they were teenagers, Carmen at twenty-one. They all used to label themselves Dominican, but in becoming highly literate they began to unpack the complexities of that label. Each reasoned their choices. Haydee thinks of herself as a Dominican living in the States; she calls herself Dominican. She wonders if she should, admits perhaps she should not, because she has intentionally discarded many "typically Dominican precepts": "I have changed many things, many of the values my country has about women, for example. I reject them now."

Flor calls herself Dominican while in the U.S. and American when traveling:

> You see, the reason I hesitate to say I am American [while in the U.S.] is because I don't like to consider myself a second-class citizen anywhere. If I say Dominican at least I am a full citizen somewhere.

She realizes that that rationalizing is problematic, partly because she has been in the United States most of her life; she is married to a man born in the U.S.; her sons were born in the U.S. "The future of my blood is in this country," she exclaims, but she calls herself Dominican so that Americans will not challenge her and deny her an undivided identity. "Am I denying my Americanness? My experience in the United States? In a way, yes," she affirms, but it is less traumatic to do so. And when she visits the D.R., Flor calls herself "American" for the same reason, so that she does not have to feel fractured. It is not quite the same trade-off, though: in the States when she labels herself Dominican, however whole she feels, it is not valuable enough; it is a stigmatizing classification. But when she calls herself American while visiting the island (and most other countries), she is appreciated and admired.

I go through the same rationalizing process. While traveling abroad I call myself American (which, after all, is correct, since the Dominican Republic is also geographically America), but at home in the States I name myself Latina or Dominican American.[9] That choice makes it easier for me and those who ask about my ethnic heritage or nationality. I want to make it easier because since age ten I have continuously explained who I am, and it is tiring, particularly when people seem surprised that I don't fit their idea of what a Dominican woman looks like, or what profession she should have.

Carmen believes she is a hyphenated woman, a Dominican American. She has also "intellectualized" how she chooses to be named:

> I've lived in this country for a long time, but I consider myself a Dominican American, and I'm trying to find out what that means as I move deeper and deeper into my life: what it means in terms of my relationships with people and what it means in the classroom, what it means when I sit in front of the computer—all those things.

---

[9] Again, the label "Dominican Americans" is problematic. It is redundant, since the Dominican Republic *is* America, being that the name refers to the entire Western Hemisphere. As Torres-Saillant and Hernández write, when

> in 1507 the German cartographer Martin Waldseemüller proposed to name "the new world" America, in honor of Amerigo Vespucci, he had in mind specifically the Caribbean and South America, the only lands that had up to then been viewed by Europeans. Dominicans come from a region called America. To call them Dominican Americans, then, is repetitious. (xxi)

Other participants also said that becoming highly literate pushed them to analyze and choose an ethnic label. Laura "fights" to be recognized as an American. That does not mean she wants to diminish her Dominican heritage, but she finds it unwieldy and "somewhat dishonest" to use a hyphenated label:

> I had been telling people when they asked me, "I'm originally from the Dominican Republic." And that word, "originally," I used in my vocabulary until about five or six years ago when after becoming politicized I realized that I'm definitely—that I see the Dominican Republic as a reference to the past. I live here now in the United States. I never call myself Dominican American.

Although Laura hesitates, as if in fear, as if questioning the right to say that she is indeed an American, she explains that she has thought about the issue quite a bit, and that now she feels comfortable labeling herself American. If she lived in New York or Philadelphia where there are Dominican communities, she might consider calling herself Dominican American. But on the West Coast there are so few Dominicans that inevitably she has to explain where the island is and that it is not the same place as Dominica. By calling herself American she bypasses the "trouble of having to explain." She believes that she has more in common with Americans than with Dominicans. Dominicans in the States are predominantly low socioeconomic and she cannot relate to them. Self-identity, she learned in becoming highly literate, is a matter of socioeconomic status, not nationality or culture.

Flor, on the other hand, believes that the matter is more complex: "I see gender as a very definitive kind of thing. I relate better to women—of high or low economic status, educated and uneducated—than to highly educated men." But when faced with highly literate Dominican and non-Dominican women, Flor says, "I have more in common with the Dominicans."

"Look," Ramón reiterates, the answer is "not to identify yourself in ethnic or cultural terms." Those "distinctions," Haydee adds, "place you in unnecessary boundaries, in divisions that should not exist." It is more productive, Ramón claims, to identify yourself "as an educator who serves a particular community."

Similarly, Antonio considers himself "a professor, a poet who writes in Spanish, and a human being" who enjoys teaching and "helping others to grow." Likewise, María has thought about and read a great deal about the formation of identity, and she has decided to label herself "a woman" first and foremost:

> I don't usually say Dominican. I have so many cultures integrated into who I am: for example, I'm a native New Yorker; I am an activist for civil rights and education. I'm very much into the gay movement—definitely a lesbian, a mother, but above all, I'm a woman.

A few respondents acknowledge that at some point in their lives they "hated" having to find a label for themselves. It made them feel inferior and therefore ashamed. Non "ethnic" people didn't seem to be burdened with that task. One participant who did not want me to reveal these particular ideas, even though she knew I'd be using a pseudonym, talked candidly about "internalizing damaging ideas" about her identity, and only coming "to terms" with who she is after reading the work of Chicana feminists while in graduate school.[10] "It's true," she says, "the light bulb went on after I read Cherríe Moraga's confession about her identity":

> It is frightening to acknowledge that I have internalized a racism and classism, where the object of oppression is not only someone *outside* my skin, but the someone *inside* my skin. In fact, to a large degree, the real battle with such oppression, for all of us, begins under the skin. (*Loving* 54)

It took "tremendous energy" for this participant to realize that for a long long time she disdained herself, because she had absorbed "endless derogatory messages" about Hispanics. She believed herself to be substandard and unworthy. It took becoming highly liter-

---

[10] She shared her favorite passage with me during our second interview: "I have so internalized the borderland conflict that sometimes I feel like one cancels out the other and we are zero, nothing, no one. A veces no soy nada, ni nadie" (*Borderlands* 63).

ate and much introspection for her to recognize that everyone has an ancestry, for her to understand the power structures, the historical and psychological forces that subordinated her heritage, and which in turn shaped and determined her anguish and coming to consciousness.

Whatever label we choose, participants affirm, having to do so is invariably painful, labor intensive, and intense. Moreover, questioning our identity(ies) does not end once we choose, not just because we continue to grow and change, but because social circumstances are fluid. Our identities are not fixed; they shift as contexts change. Our views of ourselves are always already uncertain, never fully knowable. None of us has final answers; none of us feels totally comfortable. We are conscious of having to engage and (re)configure our sense of ourselves. That task is sometimes daunting; it keeps us in a straddling position, a condition that can be beneficial but is always consuming. It demands engagement in ever-increasing critical analyses and dialogue as they are situated in our personal and professional lives, our biographies, conflicts, and questions we and others pose.

Implications for Teachers

Identity is a narrative. We all live storied lives. Concrete experiences do not necessarily determine our sense of identity. The stories we tell others and ourselves shape who we have been, who we are in the present, and who we wish to be in the future. Stories are the means by which we construct our identity(ies). That is one significant reason why it is crucial that we look at highly literate Dominicans; the process can help to reveal how and why we are who we are becoming, and how in turn we can help other Dominicans achieve greater success in higher education. That is why it is imperative that we stretch our educational system, that we reenvision it, force it open to change, greater tolerance and inclusiveness. It is crucial that we acknowledge that our educational system today is not serving more of us as it should. Macedo's words seem fitting here; he writes:

What we have in the United States is not a system to encourage
independent thought and critical thinking. Our colonial literacy
model is designed to domesticate in order to enable the "manufac-
ture of consent." The Trilateral Commission members could not
have been more accurate when they referred to schools as "institutions responsible for the indoctrination of the young." I see no real
difference between the more or less liberal Trilateral Commission
position on schooling and Adolf Hitler's fascist call against independent thought and critical thinking. As Hitler noted, "What good
fortune for those in power that people do not think." (36)

My research, conducting this study, has affirmed for me that institutions of higher learning in the United States must stop
reproducing the dominant ideology. They must end the privileging
of myths about the supremacy of Western heritage, and the
devaluing of the Other. That is why cultural narratives such as the
one (re)presented in this book are important; they help to elucidate
the realities of those who exist on the margins of our society, even
if it is a privileged highly literate margin. We must continually ask
about our values, expectations, our distinct history and worldviews. In doing so, and in coming to consciousness about our identities and our place in American society, we might very well make
changes.

Examining these Dominicans' narratives affirms that all of us
must be reflective, confrontational, and willing to problematize the
social and political contexts of our educational practices, to probe
our experiences, how they are constructed and how individual
teachers reproduce them. Without this kind of deliberation the
much-needed work will not be accomplished. If this book is a form
of activism in any way, I want it to be as follows: I want these stories to help teachers and Dominicans to be more discerning, so that
in analyzing our circumstances we can be vigilant, and we can
safeguard the gains we have made.

For Dominicans and for all teachers, these stories can illustrate
the importance of seeking self-knowledge and thus self-actualization. Indeed, in teaching and working to step out of the margins
of our society, it is imperative that we examine what we think and
feel about ourselves. Without self-knowledge we cannot address

those aspects that block our teaching, or that impede us from being more effective. It is imperative that as teachers and human beings we scrutinize our conscious and unconscious ways of being. It is the surest way we can make powerful choices.

Works Cited

Abrahams, Roger. "Equal Opportunity Eating: A Structural Excursus on Things of the Mouth." In *Ethnic and Regional Foodways in the United States: The Performance of Group Identity*, edited by Linda Keller Brown and Kay Mussell, 19-36. Knoxville: University of Tennessee Press, 1984.

Abu-Lughod, Lila. "Writing Against Culture." In *Recapturing Anthropology*, edited by Richard Fox, 137-162. Santa Fe, N. Mex.: School of American Research Press.

———. *Writing Women's Worlds: Bedouin Stories*. Berkeley: University of California Press, 1993.

Alcántara, Almánizar José. "Black Images in Dominican Literature." *New West Indian Guide* 61 (1987): 3-4; 161-73.

Alfau Durán, Vetilio. "La biblioteca dominicana." *¡Ahora!* 272 (Jan. 27, 1969): 36-39.

Alvarez, Julia. "An American Childhood in the Dominican Republic." *The American Scholar* 56 (winter 1987): 71-85.

———. *Homecoming*. Reprint, New York: Plume, 1996.

———. *How the Garcia Girls Lost Their Accents*. 1991. Reprint, New York: Plume, Penguin Books, 1992.

———. *In the Name of Salomé*. Chapel Hill, N.C.: Algonquin Books, 2000.

———. *In the Time of the Butterflies*. Chapel Hill, N.C.: Algonquin Books, 1996.

————. *Something to Declare*. Chapel Hill, N.C.: Algonquin Books, 1998.

————. *The Other Side/El Otro Lado*. New York: Plume, 1995.

————. *Yo!* Chapel Hill, N.C.: Algonquin Books, 1997.

Anzaldúa, Gloria. *Borderlands/La Frontera: The New Mestiza*. San Francisco: Spinters/Aunt Lute Book Company, 1987.

Austerlitz, Paul. *Merengue: Dominican Music and Dominican Identity*. Philadelphia: Temple University Press, 1996.

————. "Local and International Trends in Dominican Merengue." *World of Music* 35, no.2 (1993): 270-89.

Balaguer, Joaquín. *La isla al revés: Haití y el destino dominicano*. Santo Domingo: Fundación Antonio Caro, 1983.

Bandon, Alexandra. *Dominican Americans*. Footsteps to America Series. Parsippany, N.J.: New Discovery Books, 1995.

Bankay, Anne María. "Contemporary Women Poets of the Dominican Republic: Perspectives on Race and Other Social Issues." *Afro-Hispanic Review* 12, no. 1 (spring 1993): 34-41.

Behar, Ruth. *The Presence of the Past in a Spanish Village: Santa María del Monte*. 1986. Reprint, Princeton, N.J.: Princeton University Press, 1991.

————. *The Vulnerable Observer: Anthropology that Breaks Your Heart*. Boston: Beacon Press, 1996.

Behar, Ruth, and Deborah A. Gordon, eds. *Women Writing Culture*. Berkeley: University of California Press, 1995.

Berger, John. *Ways of Seeing*. New York: Penguin, 1972.

Bretón, Marcos, and José Luis Villegas. *Away Games: The Life and Times of a Latin Baseball Player*. New York: Simon and Schuster, 1999.

Cartagena Portalatín, Aída. *Yania tierra: A Documentary Poem*. Washington, D.C.: Azul Editions, 1995.

Clifford, James. "On Collecting Art and Culture." In *The Predicament of Culture*, 215-251. Cambridge, Mass.: Harvard University Press, 1988.

Cocco de Filippis, Daisy. "Entre dominicanos: Una lectura de 'Las cuatro niñas.'" *Bulletin Centro de Estudios Puertorriqueños* (winter 1989-1990): 91-95.

————. *Sin otro profeta que su canto: Antología de poesía escrita por dominicanas.* Santo Domingo, Dominican Republic: Biblioteca Taller No. 263, 1988.

————. *Tertuliando/Hanging Out: Dominicanas & Amiga(o)s /Dominican Women and Friends.* New York: Ediciones Alcance, 1997.

Contreras, A. Reynaldo. "The Odyssey of a Chicano Academic." In *The Leaning Ivory Tower: Latino Professors in American Universities,* edited by Raymond V. Padilla and Rudolfo Chávez Chávez, 111-129. New York: SUNY Press, 1995.

Coopersmith, Jacob Maurice. "Music and Musicians of the Dominican Republic: A Survey." *Musical Quarterly* 31, no. 1 (1945): 71-78; no. 2:212-226.

Christian, Karen. *Show and Tell: Identity as Performance in U.S. Latina/o Fiction.* Albuquerque: University of New Mexico Press, 1997.

Davis, Martha Ellen. "Music and Black Ethnicity in the Dominican Republic." In *Music and Black Ethnicity in the Caribbean and South America,* edited by Gerard Béhague, 119-156. New Brunswick, N.J.: Transaction, 1994.

de Carías, María. *Dominican Cookbook.* Colombia: Pilón, 1993.

De Certeau, Michel. *The Practice of Everyday Life.* Berkeley: University of California Press, 1984.

de Moya, E. Antonio, and Rafael García. "AIDS and the Enigma of Bisexuality in the Dominican Republic." In *Bisexualities and AIDS: International Perspectives,* edited by Peter Aggleton, 121-135. Bristol, Pa.: Taylor & Francis, 1996.

del Castillo, Jose, and Martin F. Murphy. "Migration, National Identity and Cultural Policy in the Dominican Republic." *The Journal of Ethnic Studies* 15 (fall 1987): 49-69.

Diaz, Junot. *Drown.* New York: Riverhead Books, 1996.

Duany, Jorge, ed. *Los dominicanos en Puerto Rico: Migración en la semiperiferia.* San Juan, Puerto Rico: Ediciones Huracán, 1990.

————. "Ethnicity, Identity, and Music: An Anthropological Analysis of the Dominican Merengue." In *Music and Black Ethnicity in the Caribbean and South America,* edited by Gerard Béhague, 65-90. New Brunswick, N.J.: Transaction, 1994.

Duarte, Isis. "Household Workers in the Dominican Republic: A Question for the Feminist Movement." In *Muchachas No More: Household Workers in Latin America and the Caribbean,* edited by Elsa M. Chaney et al. Philadelphia, Pa.: Temple University Press, 1989.

————. *The Impact of Structural Adjustment on Women in the Free Zones of the Dominican Republic.* Santo Domingo, D.R.: The Institute for the Study of Population Development, 1994.

Dwyer, Christopher. *The Dominican Americans.* New York: Chelsea House Publishers, 1991.

Ellsworth, Nancy J. et al., eds. *Literacy: A Redefinition.* Hillsdale, N.J.: Lawrence Erlbaum Associates, Publishers, 1994.

Escala, Miguel José. "The New Policy on Higher Education of the Government of the Dominican Republic: Some Descriptive and Evaluative Aspects." ERIC, 1985. ED267-675.

Espaillat, Rhina. *Lapsing to Grace: Poems and Drawings.* East Lansing, Mich.: Bennet & Kitchel, 1992.

————. *Where Horizons Go.* Kirksville, Mo.: New Odyssey Press, 1998.

Espinal, Rosario. "Between Authoritarianism and Crisis-Prone Democracy: The Dominican Republic After Trujillo." In *Politics and Society in the Caribbean,* edited by C. Clarke, 145-165. London: Macmillan, 1991.

————. "The 1990 Elections in the Dominican Republic." *Electoral Studies* 10, no. 2 (1991): 139-144.

Ferdman, Bernardo M. "Literacy and Cultural Identity." *Harvard Educational Review.* 60, no. 2 (May 1990): 181-204.

Fernández, Carmen Lara. *Historia del Feminismo en la República Dominicana*. Ciudad Trujillo, Dominican Republic: Imp. Arte y Cine, 1946.

Finlay, Barbara. *The Women of Azua: Work and Family in the Dominican Republic*. Westport, Conn.: Praeger/Greenwood, 1990.

Fischkin, Barbara. *Muddy Cup: A Dominican Family Comes of Age in a New America*. New York: Scribner, 1997.

Foster, Barbara. "Libraries in the Shadow of History: The Dominican Republic." *International Library Review* 19, no. 2 (April 1987): 105-111.

Fox, Geoffrey. *Hispanic Nation: Culture, Politics, and the Construction of Identity*. Tucson, Ariz.: The University of Arizona Press, 1996.

Freiband, Susan et al. "Las Bibliotecas y la Bibliotecología del Caribe Español: Un Estudio Comparativo Cuba, República Dominicana y Puerto Rico." *Perspectiva*, Año VI, núm.1, segundo semestre (1995-1996): 15-21.

Freire, Paulo. *Pedagogy of the Oppressed*. Trans. Myra Bergman Ramos. New York: Continuum, 1988.

Galván, Manuel de Jesús. *Enriquillo: leyenda histórica dominicana*. 1882, Reprint, New York: Las Américas, 1989.

Garris, Ivelisse, et al. "AIDS Heterosexual Predominance in the Dominican Republic." *Journal of Acquired Immune Deficiency Syndromes*. 4, no. 12 (1991): 1173-1178.

Geertz, Clifford. *Works and Lives: The Anthropologist as Author* Stanford, Calif.: Stanford University Press, 1989.

Georges, Eugenia. *The Making of a Transnational Community: Migration, Development and Cultural Change in the Dominican Republic*. New York: Columbia University Press, 1992.

Gimbernard, Jacinto. *Historia de Santo Domingo*. 5th ed. Santo Domingo, Dominican Republic: La Editora Cultural Dominicana, 1974.

Goody, Jack, ed. *Literacy in Traditional Societies*. New York: Cambridge University Press, 1968.

Goris-Rosario, Anneris. "Rites for a Rising Nationalism: Religious Meaning and Dominican Community Identity in New York City." In *Old Masks, New Faces: Religion and Latino Identities*, edited by Anthony M. Stevens-Arroyo and Gilbert R. Cadena, 117-141. PARAL Studies Series. Vol. 2. New York: Bilner Center for Western Hemisphere Studies, 1995.

Graff, Harvey J. "The Legacies of Literacy." In *Perspectives on Literacy*, edited by Eugene Kintgen et al., 83-91. Carbondale, Ill.: Southern Illinois University Press, 1988.

———. *The Literacy Myth: Cultural Integration and Social Structure in the Nineteenth Century*. 1979. Reprint, London: Transaction Publishers, 1991.

Grasmuck, Sherri, and Patricia Pessar. *Between Two Islands: Dominican International Migration*. Berkeley: University of California Press, 1991.

Heath, Shirley Brice. *Ways with Words: Language, Life, and Work in Communities and Classrooms*. New York: Cambridge University Press, 1983.

Hendricks, Glenn. *The Dominican Diaspora: From the Dominican Republic to New York City Villagers*. New York: Teachers College Press, 1974.

Hernandez, Ramona, et al. *Dominican New Yorkers: A Socio Economic Profile*. New York: City University of New York, 1990.

Hirsch, E. D., Jr. *Cultural Literacy: What Every American Needs to Know*. Boston, Mass.: Houghton Mifflin Company, 1987.

Hoetink, Harry. "Los americanos de Samaná." *Eme Eme: Estudios Dominicanos* 2, no. 10 (1974): 3-26.

———. *The Dominican People, 1850-1900: Notes for a Historical Sociology*. Baltimore: Johns Hopkins University Press, 1982.

hooks, bell. *Remembered Rapture: The Writer at Work*. New York: Henry Holt and Company, 1999.

———. *Talking Back: Thinking Feminist/Thinking Black*. Boston, Mass.: South End Press, 1989.

———. *Teaching to Transgress: Education as the Practice of Freedom*. New York: Routledge, 1994.

Johnson, C. *Nutritional Adequacy in the Dominican Republic*. Medford, Mass.: Tufts University Press, 1988.

Jordan, Howard. "Dominicans in New York: Getting a Slice of the Apple." *NACLA: Report on the Americas* 30, vol. 5 (March/April 1997): 37-42.

Joyce, Gare. *The Only Ticket Off the Island*. Toronto, Canada: Lester & Orpen Dennys Limited, 1990.

Kaestle, Carl F. et al., eds. *Literacy in the United States: Readers and Reading Since 1880*. New Haven, Conn.: Yale University Press, 1991.

Keller Brown, Linda, and Kay Mussell, eds. *Ethnic and Regional Foodways in the United States: The Performance of Group Identity*. Knoxville: University of Tennessee Press, 1984.

Kintgen, Eugene R., Barry M. Kroll and Mike Rose, eds. *Perspectives on Literacy*. Carbondale, Ill.: Southern Illinois University Press, 1988.

Klein, Alan M. *Sugar Ball: the American Game, the Dominican Dream*. New Haven, Conn.: Yale University Press, 1991.

Langer, Judith, ed. *Language, Literacy, and Culture: Issues of Society and Schooling*. Norwood, N.J.: Ablex Publishing Corporation, 1987.

Leavitt, Roy, and Mary E. Lutz. *Three New Immigrant Groups in New York City: Dominicans, Haitians, and Cambodians*. New York: Community Council of Greater New York, 1988.

Levine, Kenneth. *The Social Context of Literacy*. London: Routledge and Kegan Paul, 1986.

Lorde, Audre. "The Master's Tools Will Never Dismantle the Master's House." In *Sister Outsider: Essays and Speeches*, 110-113. Trumansburg, N.Y.: Crossing Press, 1984.

Luis, William. *Dance Between Two Cultures: Latino Caribbean Literature Written in the United States*. Nashville, Tenn.: Vanderbilt University Press, 1997.

Macedo, Donaldo. *Literacies of Power: What Americans Are Not Allowed to Know*. San Francisco, Calif.: Westview Press, 1994.

Manuel, Peter. *Caribbean Currents: Caribbean Music from Rumba to Reggae*. Philadelphia: Temple University Press, 1995.

McIntosh, Elaine N. *American Food Habits in Historical Perspective*. Westport, Conn.: Praeger Publishers, 1995.

McCracken, Ellen. *New Latina Narrative: The Feminine Space of Postmodern Ethnicity*. Tucson: University of Arizona Press, 1999.

Miller, John P. *Education and the Soul: Toward a Spiritual Curriculum*. New York: SUNY Press, 2000.

Mintz, Sidney W. *Tasting Food, Tasting Freedom*. Boston, Mass.: Beacon Press, 1996.

Mir, Pedro. *Hay un pais en el mundo y otros poemas*. Santo Domingo: Taller, 1991.

Monroe, James. "The Monroe Doctrine." In *The Evolution of Our Latin American Policy: A Documentary Record*, edited by James W. Gantenbein, 323-325. New York: Columbia University Press, 1950.

Moraga, Cherríe. *Loving in the War Years: Lo que nunca pasó por sus labios*. Boston, Mass.: South End Press, 1983.

Moraga, Cherríe, and Gloria Anzaldúa, eds. *This Bridge Called My Back: Writings by Radical Women of Color*. Watertown, Mass.: Persephone Press, 1981.

Mortensen, Peter and Gesa E. Kirsch, eds. *Ethics and Representation in Qualitative Studies of Literacy*. Urbana, Ill.: NCTE, 1996.

Mota, Vivian M. "Politics and Feminism in the Dominican Republic, 1931-45, 1966-74." In *Sex and Class in Latin America,* edited by June Nash and Helen Safa, 265-278. New York: Praeger, 1976.

Moya Pons, Frank. *Manual de historia dominicana*. 7th ed. Santiago, Dominican Republic: Universidad Católica Madre y Maestra, 1983.

———. *The Dominican Republic: A National History.* New York: Hispaniola Books Corporation, 1995.

———. "Dominican National Identity: A Historical Perspective." *Punto 7 Review* 3, no. 1 (fall 1996): 14-25.

Myerhoff, Barbara. *In Her Own Time: The Final Fieldwork of Barbara Myerhoff.* Lynne Littman, director. Santa Monica, Calif.: Direct Cinema Limited, 1984.

Narayan, Kirin. "How Native Is a 'Native' Anthropologist?" *American Anthropologist* 95, no. 3 (1993): 671-686.

Nelson, Candace, and Marta Tienda. "The Structuring of Hispanic Ethnicity: Historical and Contemporary Perspectives." *Ethnic and Racial Studies* 8, no. 1 (January 1985): 49-74.

Nueba yol. Angel Muñiz, director. Cigua Films and Miravista Films (Kit Parker Films), 1995.

Ogbu, John U. "Literacy and Schooling in Subordinate Cultures: The Case of Black Americans." In *Perspectives on Literacy,* edited by Eugene Kintgen et al., 227-242. Carbondale, Ill.: Southern Illinois University Press, 1988.

Pacini Hernandez, Deborah. *Bachata: A Social History of a Dominican Popular Music.* Philadelphia: Temple University Press, 1995.

———. "*Cantando la cama vacía*: love, sexuality and gender relationships in Dominican *bachata.*" *Popular Music* 9, no. 3 (October 1990): 351-367.

———. "La lucha sonora: Dominican Popular Music in the Post-Trujillo era." *Latin American Music Review* 12, no. 2 (1991): 106-121.

———. "The Merengue: Race, Class, Tradition and Identity." In *Americas: An Anthology,* edited by Mark B. Rosenburg, A. Douglas Kincaid, Kathleen Logan, 167-172. New York: Oxford University Press, 1992.

———. "Social Identity and Class in *Bachata,* an Emerging Dominican Popular Music." *Latin American Music Review* 10, no. 1 (spring/summer 1989): 69-91.

Peguero, Valentina, and Danilo de los Santos. *Visión General de la historia dominicana*. Santiago, Dominican Republic: Universidad Católica Madre y Maestra, 1979.

———. "Japanese Settlement in the Dominican Republic: An Intercultural Exchange." In *Caribbean Asians, Chinese, Indian and Japanese Experiences in Trinidad and the Dominican Republic*, edited by Roger Sanjeck, 96-109. New York: Queens College, 1990.

Pérez, Loida Maritza. *Geographies of Home*. New York: Viking, 1999.

Pérez-Firmat, Gustavo. *Life on the Hyphen: The Cuban-American Way*. Austin, Texas: University of Texas Press, 1994.

Pessar, Patricia. *A Visa for a Dream: Dominicans in the United States*. Boston, Mass.: Allyn and Bacon, 1995.

———. "The Linkage Between the Household and Workplace of Dominican Women in the U.S." *International Migration Review* 18:4 (winter 1984): 1188-1211.

———. "The Role of Gender in Dominican Settlement in the United States." In *Women and Change*, edited by June Nash and Helen Safa. Mass.: Bergin & Garvey, 1985.

———. "Social Relations Within the Family in the Dominican Republic and the U.S.: Continuity and Change." *Hispanics in NY: Religious, Cultural and Social Experiences*. Educational Office of Pastoral Research. New York: Archdioceses of New York, 1982.

Robinett, Emma Jane, and Daisy Cocco de Filippis, eds. *Poems of Exile and Other Concerns: A Bilingual Selection of the Poetry Written by Dominicans in the United States*. New York: Alcance, 1988.

Rodríguez, Richard. *Hunger of Memory: The Education of Richard Rodriguez, an Autobiography*. Boston, Mass.: D. R. Godine, 1982.

Roorda, Eric Paul. *The Dictator Next Door: The Good Neighbor Policy and the Trujillo Regime in the Dominican Republic, 1930-1945*. Durham, N.C.: Duke University Press, 1998.

Rosaldo, Renato. "Grief and a Headhunter's Rage: On the Cultural Force of Emotions." In *Culture and Truth: The Remaking of Social Analysis*. Boston, Mass.: Beacon Press, 1989.

Rose, Mike. *Lives on the Boundary: The Struggles and Achievements of America's Underprepared*. New York: Macmillan, 1989.

Ruck, Rob. *The Tropic of Baseball: Baseball in the Dominican Republic*. New York: Carroll & Graf Publishers/Richard Gallen, 1991.

Said, Edward. *Out of Place: A Memoir*. New York: Alfred A. Knopf, 1999.

Sandoval Sánchez, Alberto. "La identidad especular del allá y del acá: nuestra propia imagen puertorriqueña en cuestión." *Bulletin Centro de Estudio Puertorriqueños* IV, no. 2 (spring 1992): 28-43.

Sardello, Robert. *Facing the World with Soul*. New York: Lindisfarne Press, 1992.

Scott Jenkins, Virginia. *Bananas: An American History*. Washington, D.C.: Smithsonian Institution Press, 2000.

Scribner, Sylvia. "Literacy in Three Metaphors." In *Perspectives on Literacy*, edited by Eugene Kintgen et al., 71-81. Carbondale, Ill.: Southern Illinois University Press, 1988.

Scribner, Sylvia, and Michael Cole. *The Psychology of Literacy*. Cambridge, Mass.: Harvard University Press, 1981.

Sellew, Kathleen Troxell. *Dominican Republic: A Study of the Educational System of the Dominican Republic and a Guide to the Academic Placement of Students in Education at Institutions of the United States*. Washington, D.C.: American Association of Collegiate Registrars and Admissions Officers, 1987.

Sommers, Laurie Kay. "Inventing Latinismo: The Creation of 'Hispanic' Panethnicity in the United States." *Journal of American Folklore* 104, no. 411 (winter 1991): 32-53.

Spalding, Hobart. "Dominican Migration to New York City: Permanent Residents or Temporary Visitors." *Migration Review* (May 1989): 47-69.

Stacey, Judith. "Can There Be a Feminist Ethnography?" In *Women's Words: The Feminist Practice of Oral History*, edited by Sherna B. Gluck and Daphne Patai, 111-119. New York: Routledge, 1991. 111-119.

Stavans, Ilan. *The Hispanic Condition: Reflections on Culture and Identity in America*. New York: Harper Perennial, 1995.

Stern, Stephen, and John Allan Cicala, eds. *Creative Ethnicity: Symbols and Strategies of Contemporary Ethnic Life*. Logan, Utah: Utah State University Press, 1991.

Street, Brian. *Cultural Meanings of Literacy*. Geneva, Switzerland: UNESCO. International Bureau of Education, 1990.

———. *Literacy in Theory and Practice*. New York: Cambridge University Press, 1984.

Szwed, John F. "The Ethnography of Literacy." In *Perspectives on Literacy*, edited by Eugene Kintgen et al., 303-311. Carbondale, Ill.: Southern Illinois University Press, 1988.

Tancer, Shoshana B. "La Quisqueyana: The Dominican Woman, 1940-1970." In *Female and Male in Latin America: Essays*, edited by Ann Pescatello, 209-220. Pittsburgh, Pa.: University of Pittsburgh Press, 1973.

Torres-Saillant, Silvio. "Diaspora and national identity: Dominican migration in the postmodern society." *Migration World Magazine* 25, no.3 (March-April 1997).

———. "The Tribulations of Blackness: Stages in Dominican Racial Identity." *Latin American Perspectives* #100 25, no. 3 (May 1998): 126-146.

Torres-Saillant, Silvio, and Ramona Hernádez. *The Dominican Americans*. Westport, Conn.: Greenwood Press, 1998.

Trinh, Minh-ha T. *When the Moon Waxes Red: Representation, Gender and Cultural Politics*. New York: Routledge, 1991.

Trueba, Enrique T. *Latinos Unidos: Ethnic Solidarity in Linguistic, Social, and Cultural Diversity*. New York: Rowman & Littlefield Publishers, 1998.

Tyler, Stephen. "Post-modern Ethnography: From Document of the Occult to Occult Document." In *Writing Culture*, edited by James Clifford and George Marcus, 122-140. Berkeley: University of California Press, 1986.

UNESCO. *Statistical Yearbook 1990. United Nations Educational, Scientific and Cultural Organization (UNESCO)*. Paris, 1991.

Venezky, Richard L. "Definitions of Literacy." In *Toward Defining Literacy*, edited by Daniel A. Wagner and Barrie S. Ciliberti. Newark, Del.: International Reading Association, 1990.

Visweswaran, Kamala. *Fictions of Feminist Ethnography*. Minneapolis: University of Minnesota Press, 1994.

Wagner, Daniel A., and Barrie S. Ciliberti, eds. *Toward Defining Literacy*. Newark, Del.: International Reading Association, 1990.

Whiteford, Linda M. "Children's Health as Accumulated Capital: Structural Adjustment in the Dominican Republic and Cuba." *Small Wars: The Cultural Politics of Childhood*, edited by Nancy Scheper-Hughes and Carolyn Sargent, 186-201. Berkeley, Calif.: University of California Press, 1998.

Wilds, Deborah J., and Reginald Wilson. *Minorities in Higher Education: Sixteenth Annual Status Report*. Washington, D.C.: American Council on Education, 1997-1998.

Wilkie, James, Enrique C. Ochoa, and David E. Lorey, Eds. *Statistical Abstract of Latin America*. Vol. 28. Los Angeles, Calif.: UCLA Latin America Center Publication, 1990.

Williams, Eric. "Racism in the Caribbean." In *Americas: An Anthology*, edited by Mark B. Rosenberg, Douglas Kincaid, and Kathleen Logan, 157-159. New York: Oxford University Press, 1992.

Wolf, Margery. *A Thrice Told Tale: Feminism, Postmodernism & Ethnographic Responsibility*. Stanford, Calif.: Stanford University Press, 1992.

Wucker, Michele. *Why the Cocks Fight: Dominicans, Haitians, and the Struggle ffor Hispaniola*. New York: Hill and Wang, 1999.

Index

About the Author

Dulce María Gray holds a Ph.D. in Literacy Studies. During the last fifteen years she has been teaching composition, cultural studies, and contemporary Latina/o literature and culture at universities on the East Coast, and in the Midwest and mid-Atlantic regions. Her current research project focuses on the relationship between traveling and constructing a diasporic self-identity. She and her husband live in Northern California.